Ballads and songs of Peterloo

Manchester University Press

Ballads and songs of Peterloo

Alison Morgan

Manchester University Press

Copyright © Alison Morgan 2018

The right of Alison Morgan to be identified as the author of this work has been asserted by her in accordance with the Copyright, Designs and Patents Act 1988.

Published by Manchester University Press
Altrincham Street, Manchester M1 7JA, UK
www.manchesteruniversitypress.co.uk

British Library Cataloguing-in-Publication Data is available

ISBN 978 1 7849 9312 2 hardback
ISBN 978 1 5261 4429 4 paperback

First published by Manchester University Press in hardback 2018

This edition first published 2019

The publisher has no responsibility for the persistence or accuracy of URLs for any external or third-party internet websites referred to in this book, and does not guarantee that any content on such websites is, or will remain, accurate or appropriate.

Typeset by Servis Filmsetting Ltd, Stockport, Cheshire

Contents

List of illustrations	*page* vi
Preface	vii
Acknowledgements	ix
Introduction	1
1 'Rise Britons, rise now from your slumber': the revolutionary call to arms	40
2 'Ye English warriors': radical nationalism and the true patriot	65
3 'Base brat of reform': the victimisation of mother and child	93
4 'Your memorials shall survive the grave': elegy and remembrance	118
5 'Those true sons of Mars': chivalry, cowardice and the power of satire	150
6 'Freeman stand, or freeman die': liberty and slavery	194
Appendix	217
Select bibliography	232
Index of poem titles	234
Index	236

List of illustrations

1. To Henry Hunt, Esq. as chairman of the meeting assembled on St. Peter's Field, Manchester on the 16th of August, 1819. Anon. © The Trustees of the British Museum.   *page* 1
2. Map of St Peter's Field. Courtesy of Manchester Central Library.   6
3. Announcement of 16th August Meeting. Courtesy of Manchester Central Library.   7
4. Plaque commemorating the Peterloo Massacre, Manchester. Replacing an earlier plaque that spoke only of the 'dispersal by the military'. Photo by Tim Green. CC-BY 2.0.   9
5. Peterloo banner. Courtesy of Rochdale Arts and Heritage Service.   21
6. *Massacre at St Peter's or 'Britons strike home'!!!* Cruikshank. © The Trustees of the British Museum.   94
7. *The Belle Alliance, or The Female Reformers of Blackburn.* Cruikshank. © The Trustees of the British Museum.   96
8. *Reform Among Females.* J.L. Marks. © The Trustees of the British Museum.   97
9. *A Representation of the Manchester Reform Meeting Dispersed by the Civil and Military Power. August 16, 1819.* John Slack. © The Trustees of the British Museum.   98
10. *Manchester Heroes.* Cruikshank. © The Trustees of the British Museum.   99
11. Ceramic jug. Courtesy of Manchester Art Gallery.   100
12. *Liberty Suspended! – With the Bulwark of the Constitution.* Cruikshank. © The Trustees of the British Museum.   197

Preface

The main criterion I have used for the selection of these poems and songs is their publication date. All of the poems and songs selected were written and published in radical newspapers and journals or as broadsides in the few months following the massacre. Although dating broadsides is more problematic, I have endeavoured only to include those which appear, to my satisfaction, to have been written within six months or so of Peterloo. Quite simply, I have included all of the texts I have found, making no decisions regarding their 'literary value'.[1] Of the seventy or so poems included in the anthology, almost half were published in radical periodicals, ranging from the moderate *Examiner*, with only two Peterloo poems, to the ultra-radical *Medusa* with twelve. The most prolific publisher of Peterloo verse is the *Manchester Observer*, with a few of its poems later re-published in other journals. It is unfortunate that I have not been able to track down some December issues of the *Manchester Observer*, as I am sure that they would have yielded yet more poems and songs.

Whilst most of the poems make explicit reference to Peterloo, there are a few which do not. I have included them here, as I feel that any contemporaneous reader would not have missed the allusions to the event, which was one of the most significant in the years following the Napoleonic Wars. Readers will also note that most of the poems and songs are anonymous or have initials appended to them, which, for the most part, have proven impossible to trace. The poems are printed using the original spellings and punctuation and, on occasion, due to the illegibility of the original, words are unavoidably omitted. All italics are as in the original texts. Although I have endeavoured to provide notes to support the reading of the texts, I intend them to stand alone, read singly or *en masse*, but, nevertheless, conveying as much of the original publication as I could in order not to dilute the authenticity.

I have decided to group the poems according to theme, rather than chronologically or by publication because I want the reader to note the similarity between so many of the poems, from the repeated images of brutalised women to numerous exhortations to rise and avenge the slaughter. Grouped in this manner, one cannot avoid the voices echoing down the centuries, speaking to us of the horrors of the time in texts that can no longer be ignored.

I long debated the inclusion of the most famous Peterloo poem, Shelley's *Masque of Anarchy*. Having studied and written about Shelley's Peterloo poems for several years, I am greatly aware of their cultural significance.[2] It was through my study of Shelley that I discovered these hidden poems and songs. My decision not to include *Masque of Anarchy* in the main body of the anthology is two-fold: firstly, despite being written only weeks after the massacre, *Masque* was not published until 1832, therefore its contribution to the cultural response to the massacre can only be viewed in hindsight. Secondly, I did not want Shelley's undoubtedly magnificent poem to overshadow the ones included in the anthology. Languishing in archives or little-read journals, the poems and songs I have included deserve to be read in their own right as opposed to footnotes to *Masque*. By placing *Masque* in the appendix, I acknowledge its continuing significance to the representation of Peterloo to those of us interested in commemorating this seminal event in English history. Hopefully, readers will appreciate it anew by reading it alongside the ballads and broadsides of the time and noting the remarkable similarities in style, theme and tone.

When I started collecting these poems, I amassed about twenty. Despite uncovering another fifty, I am sure that yet more remain hidden in archives. It is remarkable that such an event as Peterloo would result in such poetic outpourings. 'An Humble Address' was written two days after the massacre and published in the *Manchester Observer* three days later.[3] The poems and songs which tumbled onto the pages of newspapers, journals and printed as broadsides in the ensuing weeks and months convey the range of emotions felt by a downtrodden people: rage, grief, righteousness and vengeance. Through poetry and song, they sought and continue to seek to commemorate and condemn, arouse and avenge, their power undimmed. It is to be hoped that with the bicentenary of the massacre and in years to come, the voices of these anonymous balladeers will once again be heard on the streets of Manchester and beyond.

Acknowledgements

The idea for this book came from research I undertook as part of my doctoral thesis on Percy Bysshe Shelley and Peterloo. I am particularly grateful to Professor Sharon Ruston for her faith in me at that time and encouragement to pursue my idea for this book. I also owe a debt of gratitude to Professor Brian Maidment for sharing his personal collection of Peterloo poems with me, which became the foundation of this collection. Dr Robert Poole has provided some welcome answers to a few of my unanswered queries and has generously shared his research with me. Staff at the Working-Class Movement Library, Manchester Central Library and Chetham's Library have been most helpful, as have curators at Rochdale Arts and Heritage Service and Manchester Art Gallery who have graciously allowed me to reproduce images of their Peterloo artefacts. My friend and colleague at the University of Warwick, Paul Taylor-McCartney, has encouraged me along the way and, through the granting of scholarly leave, enabled me to take time out of my day job to conduct research.

My greatest debt of gratitude is to my family: my parents, Trevor and Dawn, and children, Dan and Frankie, for their love and support and also a special thanks to Frankie for her help as an unofficial research assistant on various trips to Manchester. Finally, to my husband, Pete, who not only uncomplainingly tolerates my working at weekends and on holidays but also tirelessly champions my work to musicians from far and wide with a view to getting these songs heard once again.

Notes

1 The only exceptions are two poems, the length of which precluded them from being included. They are: T. Brown, *The Field of Peterloo* (London: 1819); *Who Killed Cock Robin* (London: 1819).

2 A. Morgan, 'Shelley and Peterloo: Radical, Nationalist and Balladeer', PhD Thesis, University of Salford, 2012.
3 Chapter 5, number 16.

Introduction

Peterloo

The hustings remained, with a few broken and hewed flag staves erect, and a torn and gashed banner or two dropping; whilst over the whole field, were strewn caps, bonnets, hats, shawls, and shoes, and other parts of male and female dress; trampled, torn and bloody. The yeomanry had

1 To Henry Hunt, Esq. as chairman of the meeting assembled on St. Peter's Field, Manchester on the 16th of August, 1819. Anon.

dismounted, – some were easing their horses' girths, other adjusting their accoutrements; and some were wiping their sabres. Several mounds of human beings still remained where they had fallen, crushed down and smothered. Some of these were still groaning, – others with staring eyes, were gasping for breath, and others would never breathe more. All was silent save those low sounds, and the occasional snorting and pawing of steeds.[1]

This was the scene described by the poet and radical, Samuel Bamford, at St Peter's Field in Manchester at 2.00pm on 16 August 1819, barely twenty minutes after Henry Hunt had stood on the hustings to address a peaceful crowd on a hot summer's day.[2] These twenty minutes resulted in one of the most significant events in modern British history, in which an estimated 18 people were killed and more than 650 injured by the combined efforts of the Manchester and Salford Yeomanry Cavalry (MYC) and the Fifteenth Hussars.[3] Samuel Bamford's harrowing eye-witness account of what he saw that day remains a powerful testimony to the sanctioned brutality of a repressive regime intent on destroying those who sought greater political freedom. The crowd was campaigning for the three pillars of the reform movement: universal male suffrage, annual elections and a secret ballot.[4] Entitled 'Peter Loo' only five days later on 21 August in the *Manchester Observer*, this event quickly entered into the public consciousness, creating furore on all sides of the political spectrum and generating a panoply of letters, newspaper articles, cartoons and poetry.[5]

England in 1819 under the government of Lord Liverpool was, according to Robert Reid, 'the most repressive regime in modern British history' which had come 'closer in spirit to that of the early years of the Third Reich than at any other time in history'. Such a startling comparison serves to illustrate the ruthlessness of an unpopular government, supported by an even more unpopular monarchy in a time of unprecedented change. England was undergoing a seismic shift both economically and socially. A prolonged period at war, combined with the agrarian and industrial revolutions, were resulting in an anonymous, industrialised state where the demands of factory life created an urban poor: disaffected and disenfranchised. Manchester epitomised this fundamental change of life for the labouring classes, acting, as Reid outlines, 'as a template for the world in both its growth on technological foundations, and in the manifestation of the brutal social and cultural consequences which accompanied that unparalleled growth'.[6] Its excellent transport links, damp climate and local coal mines created the ideal centre for the burgeoning cotton industry. Named 'Cottonpolis', Manchester witnessed the rapid growth of industry and people, from a population of approximately 22,500 in 1773 to 84,000 in 1801 and 250,000 in 1841.[7] This unprecedented increase led to the development of slums: cheap, high density housing, rapidly and carelessly built to house the urban workforce. And yet, despite this wholesale change in the town, in 1819 Manchester did not have a single MP and did not become self-governing until the mid-nineteenth century.

Granted a charter in 1301, the Moseley family held the rights from 1596 until 1846, when it was bought out by the Manchester Corporation, finally gaining city status in 1853. Governed by a Court Leet and headed by a boroughreeve to ensure parliamentary law was adhered to, church leaders and magistrates were key figures in maintaining law and order. On a visit in 1837, the reformer, Richard Cobden, noted that the inhabitants were 'living under the feudal system'.[8] Despite this 'leisurely regime', as described by Frank O'Gorman, Stuart Hylton notes some good examples of public services, such as hospitals, the asylum and public baths, all built at the end of the eighteenth century.[9]

Accompanying the difficulties posed by a country moving swiftly from an agrarian economy to an industrial one, Britain had experienced high unemployment, economic recession and poor harvests since the end of the Napoleonic Wars in 1815. The price of wheat was artificially high due to the imposition of the Corn Laws in 1815 and, as a consequence, people were starving. Lord Liverpool's policy in all matters was that of *laissez-faire*, all matters with the exception of political unrest, the fear of which resulted in 25,000 troops being stationed in manufacturing towns prior to the end of the Napoleonic Wars. The government's attitude to political agitation was established at the beginning of the administration. When the Luddites attacked machines in the north and midlands during 1812, seventeen of them were executed in York the following January. Lord Sidmouth, the Home Secretary, believed that such a draconian response would curb the violent aspirations of other would-be insurgents.[10]

The Pentridge Uprising of June 1817 is perhaps even more revealing about the lengths to which the Liverpool administration would go to curb what it regarded as insurrection. Fearing a resurgence of Luddite violence, retribution was fierce. This small, badly organised, embryonic rebellion of about one hundred men in a small Derbyshire village aiming to attack Nottingham was led by the former Luddite, Jeremiah Brandreth. The rebels were quickly arrested and tried. Brandreth and two of his accomplices were executed and a further twenty-three transported. Whilst the Pentridge Uprising has been largely forgotten, E.P. Thompson argues that its import lies in the fact that it was a wholly working-class attempt at insurrection, exploited by the government as an opportunity to destroy the reform movement, using its leaders as examples and setting out a stark warning to the rest of the country: 'The Government wanted blood – not a holocaust, but enough to make an example.'[11]

Within this climate of fear and oppression, intensified by the suspension of Habeas Corpus from February 1817 until January 1818, the radical movement was somewhat stymied. The more extreme, ultra-radical movement under the leadership of Arthur Thistlewood and 'Dr' James Watson was regarded suspiciously by middle-class reformers, who, under the leadership of the MP Sir Francis Burdett, were rather quiet during this period. The radical journalist, William Cobbett, thought it wise to travel to the United States in March 1817 where he remained safely until the end of 1819. Burdett returned to his country estate in order to avoid the authorities, leaving the stalwart Major Cartwright and the self-styled 'Champion of Liberty', Henry Hunt, to lead the radical movement.[12] Many historians often cite Hunt's arrogance and vanity as disadvantages to his aspirations for leadership, whereas John Belchem defends him, describing him as one of the true radicals of the nineteenth century.[13] Indeed Hunt's flamboyance won him many supporters and afforded a celebrity lifestyle which he appeared to enjoy; nevertheless it must not be forgotten that he was imprisoned for two and a half years for his role at Peterloo. Unlike his fellow radicals, Cobbett and Bamford, Hunt never abandoned his quest for reform; however, the lack of unified leadership, whether middle-class or labouring-class, was instrumental in the failure of the reform movement to capitalise on the terrible events of 1819.

Whilst the radical movement in London lacked direction and leadership after 1815, the situation in Manchester worsened. Poor harvests and the reduction in demand for cotton had resulted in wage cuts. When their wages fell from thirty shillings to fifteen shillings a week, the spinners went on strike, but the masters refused to concede.[14] The weavers' plight was even worse; their earnings were as low as four shillings and sixpence a week.[15]

Despite the appalling conditions for the labouring classes in Manchester and Lancashire in the aftermath of Waterloo, conditions were undoubtedly as bad in other industrial cities throughout England. The probable reason for Peterloo, the 'biggest ever demonstration ever seen in England up until then' is the strength and size of the radical movement in the north-west.[16] Dating back to the early eighteenth century, both labouring-class and middle-class radicalism were closely linked with dissenting religions, whilst the loyalists, comprising traders and manufacturers, were Anglican.[17] Katrina Navickas notes that, born out of a strong regional Protestantism, Orange Lodges were established in Lancashire from 1802 with membership including magistrates and the clergy. These middle-class Protestants, together, perhaps surprisingly, with many Jacobites, formed numerous loyalist clubs, the most notable being the Church and King Club founded in the 1790s.[18] At the same time, Hampden Clubs, friendly societies and patriotic unions sprang up across the region where radical leadership was more organised than the disparate movement in London. The inclusion of women is also key. Anna Clark notes that thirty-seven female reform societies were established in Stockport alone between 1794 and 1823. Spurred on by the tradition of female preachers in Lancashire and their large presence in the cotton mills, women became radicalised and played a significant role within the Manchester reform movement, resulting in Manchester becoming, according to Paul Mason, 'the most seditious part of the country'.[19]

Civic unrest in Manchester dates back to the mid-eighteenth century when food riots, including the 'Shude Hill fight' took place. Following four years of bad harvests, which resulted in food price increases, food riots again took place in 1812. By 1816 disaffection among working people began to spread. Under the leadership of the charismatic eighteen-year-old James Bagguley, between 40,000 and 60,000 people assembled at St Peter's Field on 10 March 1817, with the aim of marching to London to present a petition to the Prince Regent, alerting him to the awful conditions in Lancashire.[20] Unfortunately for the Blanketeers, as they were known, government spies had infiltrated them, and the authorities were well prepared: the Riot Act was read, the leaders arrested and the marchers attacked by the cavalry, leaving one person dead.[21] It was a foreshadowing of events two years later.

On 16 August 1819, during the summer wakes holiday season, 'half of Manchester', around 60,000 men, women and children gathered together at St Peter's Field, 'this being the traditional home of Lancashire grievances', having marched from many outlying districts of Manchester, wearing their best clothes, singing songs and carrying banners, to hear the famous Henry 'Orator' Hunt speak on the need for reform.[22] The meeting had twice been postponed whilst the leaders sought advice from lawyers in order to establish its legality. To ensure the meeting was legal, the initial aim of selecting an MP had been altered to: 'consider the propriety of adopting the most LEGAL and EFFECTUAL means of obtaining a REFORM in the Commons House of Parliament'.[23] The organisers called for order and sobriety whilst Hunt specifically told them to come 'armed with NO OTHER WEAPON but that of a self-approving conscience'.[24] The authorities, fearful of

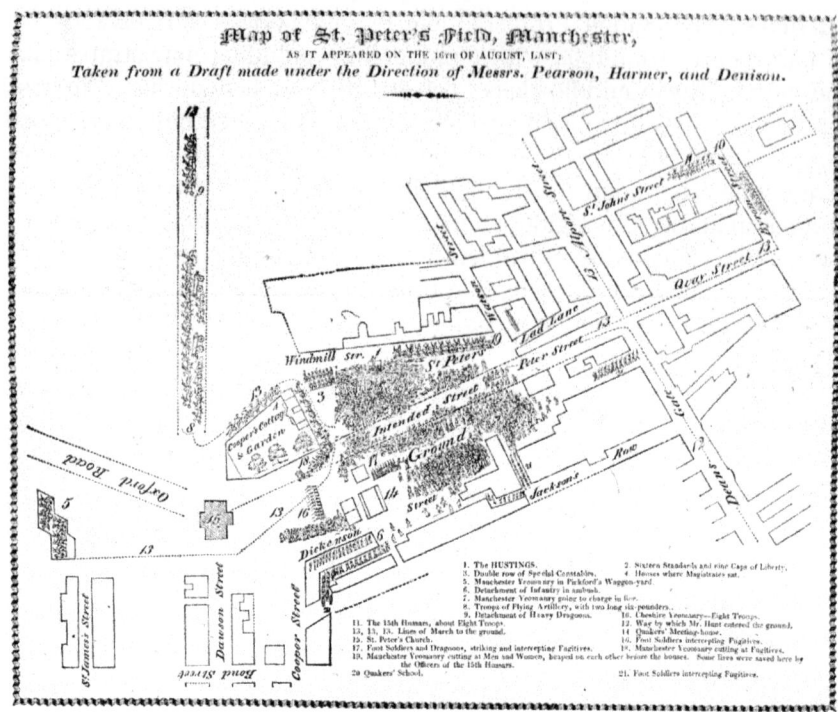

2 Map of St Peter's Field.

violence, particularly following reports of drilling being practised by the marchers in the weeks prior to the meeting, ordered the presence of the hundred or so volunteer members of the MYC, 420 members of the Cheshire Yeomanry and approximately 1,000 regular troops, including the Fifteenth Hussars, many of them veterans of Waterloo.[25] The magistrates authorised the arrest of Hunt and the other leaders once the meeting had begun, instructing the MYC to carry out the arrests. It was after the arrests had been made that most of the violence occurred as the MYC began to cut a swathe through the crowd having found themselves hemmed in.[26] The Fifteenth Hussars arrived to disperse the people, pushing them back with the flat side of their sabres, resulting in more than 300 sabre wounds: 'fifteen a minute for twenty minutes'.[27] Many were trampled by the horses. The true scale of the injuries will never be known as many victims were too scared or too poor to seek medical help. The relatively small number of fatalities is due to luck rather than the actions of the troops. As Poole notes, 'the radicals of Lancashire planned for Victory Square, only to find themselves in Tiananmen Square.'[28]

Manchester
PUBLIC MEETING.

A REQUISITION having been presented to the Boroughreeve and Constables of Manchester, signed by above 700 Inhabitant Householders in a few hours, requesting them to call a PUBLIC MEETING " to consider the propriety of adopting the most LEGAL and EFFECTUAL means of obtaining a REFORM in the Commons House of Parliament " and they having declined to call such Meeting therefore the undersigned Requisitionists give NOTICE that a Public Meeting will be held, on the area, near St. Peter's Church, for the above mentioned purpose, on Monday the 16th instant—the Chair to be taken by H. Hunt, Esq. at 12 o'clock.

  ⁎ Major Cartwright—Mr. Wooller—Mr. Pearson—Mr. Carlisle Dr. Crompton—Edward Rushton—Mr. J. Smith—Sir Thomas Smith—will be invited to attend this Meeting.

Manchester, 6th August, 1819.

3 Announcement of 16th August Meeting.

The blame for the 'bloodiest political event of the nineteenth century on English soil' has been attributed to a variety of people and events.[29] The economic conditions and unsuitable law enforcement in Manchester as outlined above were undoubtedly instrumental, as was the lack of a strong leadership within the radical movement. Sir John Byng, the supreme commander of the Northern Forces, was informed by the Manchester magistrates that his presence was not necessary. As a consequence, this absence resulted in the troops being placed under the command of the less experienced Lieutenant Colonel L'Estrange which may have contributed to the chaos and lack of military organisation. Read firmly places the blame with the Manchester magistrates, claiming that Sidmouth had expressly instructed them to avoid violence, whilst also criticising the government for their lack of supervision of the magistrates and the unseemliness of their unequivocal support: 'That the government felt bound to support the Manchester magistrates in general terms was perhaps not surprising. What was much less defensible was the haste and gullibility with which they rushed to their defence in detail.'[30] Thompson's condemnation of the government is even stronger: 'If the government was unprepared for the news of Peterloo, no authorities have ever acted so vigorously to make themselves accomplices after the fact.'[31] Undoubtedly the government was to blame, if not for the specific events of Peterloo, then for the climate of fear and culture of repression which legitimised the maiming and killing of its own citizens.

Moreover, it is the actions of the MYC that attracts the force of Thompson's opprobrium. Their drunkenness and bad horsemanship, as outlined by Marlow, cannot excuse their behaviour and Thompson is indeed correct when he declares: 'The panic was not (as has been suggested) the panic of bad horsemen hemmed in by a crowd. It was the panic of class hatred'.[32] The MYC, described by Belchem as 'inebriated publicans, butchers and shopkeepers' comprised local men out with scores to settle who attacked defenceless people and pursued them as they tried to escape.[33] It is also worth noting that, according to O'Gorman, 'the magistrates and constables were almost all members of anti-reform groups, adding a political slant to their grievances.[34] One of the most telling pieces of evidence to support Thompson's assertion that 'there is no term for this but class war' is Marlow's claim that the MYC were the only forces to send their sabres to be sharpened prior to 16 August. At the inquest into the death of John Lees, one of those killed at Peterloo, Daniel Kennedy testified that he sharpened sixty-three of the yeomanry's swords in July, although he claimed not to know the reason why.[35]

The question, therefore, is why England did not witness a revolution in 1819: its people were starving, the government and monarchy were abhorred and a legitimate, peaceful march had resulted in a massacre. In the months following Peterloo, the government, unmindful of public opinion, swiftly introduced even more draconian laws known as the Six Acts, aimed at tightening the stranglehold on all forms of radical expression. Key figures such as Hunt were imprisoned due to their involvement at Peterloo and there was no effective leadership within the radical movement to capitalise on the sense of national outrage. Institutionalised by factory life and inculcated with the work ethic promulgated by dissenting religions so popular in the manufacturing towns and cities, the urban poor continued to organise and protest but failed to use their collective force to engender fundamental change. For Thompson the legacy of Peterloo is that never again was such force

4 Plaque commemorating the Peterloo Massacre, Manchester. Replacing an earlier plaque that spoke only of the 'dispersal by the military'.

used by the authorities on a peaceful crowd: 'Since the moral consensus of the nation outlawed the riding down and sabreing of an unarmed crowd, the corollary followed – that the right of the public meeting had been gained.'[36] Whether Peterloo was instrumental in achieving parliamentary reform in 1832 cannot be proven. Whilst the Chartists continued to champion Peterloo in the 1830s and 1840s, it was not until 1951, when a mural was commissioned in the newly rebuilt Free Trade Hall, that Manchester provided a memorial to those who had died, although the mural painted by A. Sherwood Edwards, now on an upstairs corridor in the Radisson Hotel, depicts only the aftermath of the event. Nearly 200 years after the event, there is still a campaign 'for a fitting memorial to the martyrs of democracy'.[37]

The response

The battle to control the representation of Peterloo in the public consciousness began before the blood had dried on St Peter's Field. As the only journalist employed by a national newspaper present on that day, John Tyas' eye-witness account published in *The Times* on 19 August helped shape the public response to the massacre.[38] He stresses the peaceful nature of the crowd and the unwarranted violence by the Yeomanry: 'Not a brick-bat was thrown at [the Yeomanry] – not a pistol was fired at them during this period – all was quiet and orderly'. Once arrests had been made, the Yeomanry began 'cutting most indiscriminately to the right and the left.'[39] Eye-witness testimony such as this helped to galvanise public opinion against the government, although such a view was not shared by the anonymous writer in the *Gentleman's Magazine* of the same month, in which the journalist expresses 'our strongest approbation of the conduct of unprincipled individuals, whose only object, under the specious names of patriotism, is to effect a Revolution, and aggrandize themselves on the ruins of their country'.[40]

Unsurprisingly, Tory periodicals such as the *Quarterly Review* and *Gentleman's Magazine* focus on the injuries sustained by the Yeomanry, rather than those inflicted by it upon the unarmed demonstrators. The *Gentleman's Magazine* dispassionately notes: 'four persons were killed', before detailing the injuries of one of the Yeomanry, a 'Mr. Hume'.[41] An article in the *Quarterly* in January 1820 places the blame firmly with the protestors: '[The Yeomanry] were assailed not only with abuse, but with heavy stones and brickbats: several yeomen were felled from their horses; one was hurt mortally.'[42] In the eyes of the Tory press and the administration it upheld, the actions of the Yeomen were justified in the protection of the state from a riotous mob. Sidmouth sent a letter of congratulations to the magistrates and military, highlighting 'the great satisfaction derived by his Royal Highness from their prompt, decisive and efficient measures for the preservation of the public peace.'[43] Despite the assured tone of the letter, the fear of revolution was a very real one.

The response of the radical press

Horrid Massacre at Manchester[44]

Disturbances at Manchester[45]

The first two radical weeklies to respond to Peterloo were *Sherwin's Weekly Political Register* on 21 August and the *Examiner* on 22 August, thereby representing two ends of the radical continuum in response to events in Manchester, as exemplified by the headlines above. Richard Carlile's revolutionary rhetoric in the *Register* is the most extreme radical response and is undoubtedly coloured by Carlile's presence in Manchester on the fateful day. His article begins:

> It is impossible to find words to express the horror which every man must feel at the proceedings of the agents of the Borough-mongers on Monday last, at Manchester. It is out of the pale of words to describe the abhorrence which every true Englishman must feel towards the abetters and the actors in that murderous scene.[46]

For Carlile, the only possible response is for the people to 'arm themselves immediately, for the recovery of their rights'. The outcome of such a conflict is unknown 'but it may with safety be said, that neither this nor any other country ever remained long in such a condition without a revolution.'[47] In an open letter to Sidmouth following the editorial, Carlile continues his revolutionary discourse:

> The people, not only of Manchester, but of the whole country are in duty bound and by the laws of nature imperatively called upon to provide themselves with arms and hold their public meetings with arms in their hands, to defend themselves against the attacks of similar assassins, acting in the true *Castlereaghan* character.[48]

For Carlile, revolution is not only one's duty but also a natural response to the unnatural actions of a despotic regime. Such seditious writing was inevitably going to court the attentions of the authorities. *Sherwin's Weekly Political Register* did not appear after 21 August and, by November, Carlile was in gaol.

Having already served a gaol sentence for libel, Leigh Hunt's editorial in the *Examiner* is more tempered than Carlile's furious invective, drawing on the collective sense of 'astonishment and indignation' expressed by newspapers, with the exception of the *Courier*, which 'dwell[ed] with shuddering sympathy on the wounds of the constables and soldiers'.[49] Having countered the misrepresentations made in the *Courier*, Hunt's rage becomes apparent:

> We lament as much as any human being possibly can the effusion of human blood, and all those first causes of wilfulness and injustice which give rise to it; but the seat-selling violators of the English Constitution can see, with philosophy enough, whole oceans of blood shed for the security of their own guilty power, or the restoration of a tyrannical dynasty; and the interested hypocritical howl raised by their hirelings at the fatal consequences of a disturbance to a few individuals, excites in us nothing but anger and disgust.[50]

Hunt's powerful rhetoric attacks the very foundations of a corrupt regime, in which parliamentary seats are sold and the monarchy is tyrannical. Both Hunt and Carlile argue that such brutality is a violation of the Constitution and the ancient rights of the people. The discourse of English nationalism was to become a feature of Peterloo verse and is explored in more detail in Chapter 2. However, unlike Carlile, Hunt falls short of advocating revolution, or indeed any action on the part of the people.

The headline of the 28 August issue of the *Theological and Political Comet* – 'To the Manchester Bloodhounds' – echoes the *Black Dwarf* three days earlier.[51] The letter 'From the Black Dwarf in London, to the Yellow Bonce at Japan', a well-used conceit by the editor, T.J. Wooler, states that the actions of the Yeomanry, the constables and the magistrates got out of control and was not what was intended by the 'boroughmongers'. 'They have slipped the bloodhounds too soon, and the bloodhounds were more *ferocious* than *wise*.'[52] This hunting motif is replicated in many of the ensuing poems and songs, proving an effective propaganda tool in the demonisation of both the MYC and their huntsmen – Sidmouth and Castlereagh. The direct address to the 'Manchester Bloodhounds' in the *Comet* stresses the unnatural actions of the Yeomanry through a list of rhetorical questions:

> Where is to be found a law that advocates such inhuman deeds, and that authorises such blood-hound whelps as you '*to cut an innocent man to pieces*,' or to have him tried for *high treason*? And, where is there not a law which demands the blood of a murderer, in satisfaction for the blood of murdered innocence?[53]

Such questioning highlights how judicial norms were inverted, as the killers were never brought to justice despite numerous inquests into the deaths. The writer cites the address of Sir Francis Burdett to his electors in Westminster, which was printed in the *Black Dwarf* on 25 August:

> What! Kill men *unarmed*! *Unresisting*!, and, Gracious God! WOMEN too, *disfigured*, *maimed*, *cut down*, and *trampled upon* by DRAGOONS. Is this ENGLAND? THIS A CHRISTIAN LAND! A LAND OF FREEDOM![54]

Burdett's letter is a powerful example of emotive rhetoric and its inclusion in both the *Black Dwarf* and the *Comet* provides a legitimacy and gravitas to their own responses. As an MP, Burdett was part of the British establishment. His vehement address demonstrates to the readers of these radical weeklies that their sentiments are echoed in the wider political arena, giving hope that action may be taken to redress the injustices of the state.

A letter printed in a pamphlet on 7 September 1819 and signed, 'a country gentleman' defends the Yeomanry as 'one of the most respectable classes in England' and attacks Burdett as acting in a manner unworthy of his class: 'Such aspersions might, perhaps be expected from some two-penny scribbler, some wholesale vender of sedition and blasphemy [...]; but, good Heavens! That a man of independence and liberal education should be guilty of so unfounded and barbarous a statement!'[55]

The sharing of discourse and similarities in style across the radical weeklies is an indication of the collaboration between publishers and writers. In the fervent atmosphere of August and September, when the number of radical weeklies was at its height, there was an awareness that the power of response lay in its scale and breadth. Recognition of the significance of the time is demonstrated by the opening address of the first issue of the *London Alfred; or, People's Recorder*, one of the weeklies established to respond to Peterloo. It describes 'the epoch' as 'the most eventful that ever occurred in the annals of British history'.[56] Whilst such a statement may be regarded as hyperbolic, this identification of the importance of the moment is shared by the periodicals and reflected in the urgency of their style and extravagance of their rhetoric.

Radical periodicals

The 1790s and the 1810s saw the proliferation of radical periodicals, spurred on by the ideals of the French Revolution in the 1790s and by the dire circumstances of life under the Liverpool administration in the second half of the 1810s. The French Revolutionary Wars (1793–1802) and Napoleonic Wars (1803–15) fostered waves of patriotism amongst the British and, as a consequence, radicalism declined in popularity from the end of the 1790s. Following the national euphoria surrounding the final defeat of Napoleon at the Battle of Waterloo in 1815, the harsh reality of economic depression led to social unrest and a resurgence in radicalism until 1820, at which point most radical leaders were imprisoned and the periodicals taxed out of existence.

Newspapers and periodicals did not appear in any number until the beginning of the eighteenth century; by 1709 there were eighteen daily London newspapers, with twenty-two provincial ones by 1725. Annual sales of newspapers reached 12.6 million in 1775.[57] The first decade of the eighteenth century also saw the first periodicals or journals. Daniel Defoe, one of the leading journalists of the time, launched the thrice-weekly *A Review of the Affairs of France* in 1704 and, five years later, *Tatler* was launched by the Irish writer and later Whig MP Richard

Steele. As the name suggests, the aim of *Tatler* was to report news and gossip from the London coffee houses, rather than politics. Two years later, Steele was joined by the poet and politician, Joseph Addison, in the publication of the *Spectator*. Although short-lived, the *Spectator* became one of the most significant periodicals of the eighteenth century and its influence is undoubtedly seen in the radical weeklies of the Romantic period.[58] Published daily, the one-page paper comprises a single essay and advertisements. Addison states the aim is 'to enliven morality with wit and to temper wit with morality [...] to bring philosophy out of the closets and libraries, schools and colleges, to dwell in clubs and assemblies, at tea-tables and coffee houses'. By the tenth issue, Addison claimed that three thousand were sold daily but that for each copy sold, at least twenty people would read it.[59] Even if Addison's estimates are a little optimistic, he clearly saw the *Spectator*'s role as influencing the conversations of the coffee houses, rather than just reporting them.

However, just as the newspaper industry began to burgeon, the government sought to restrict its availability through taxation. The first Stamp Act of 1712 imposed a tax of a penny a sheet, thereby pricing the news beyond the means of the working man. By 1797, tax was seven pence a sheet.[60] Journals, magazines and periodicals succeeded in avoiding stamp duty by not directly reporting the news but by commenting on it.[61] Letters, reports and fictional conversations enabled readers to garner the news of the day, whilst publishers kept prices low. This continued until the Six Acts of 1819 when stamp duty was extended to all publications which sold for less than sixpence and contained opinion about the news. What is abundantly clear is that the history of the press in England is paralleled by government action to control and restrict it, something that is arguably still occurring today.

Radical periodicals in the 1790s

England in the early 1790s was a hotbed of revolutionary and anti-revolutionary politics. Events in France had resulted in widespread support for the French in their removal of the corrupt class system and the absolute monarchy of the *ancien regime*. Even parts of the ruling Whig party were in favour of revolution until the advent of war in 1793 saw the public mood change and the government become ever more repressive over what it regarded as sedition. However, in the early years after the revolution, the reform movement in England capitalised on the new ideals of *liberté, égalité, fraternité* in galvanising support for parliamentary reform.

The reform movement in England emerged prior to the French Revolution. The Society for Constitutional Information (SCI) was founded in 1780 by Major John Cartwright, a moderate radical and stalwart of the reform movement until his death in the 1820s. Along with parliamentary reform, the SCI campaigned for the abolition of slavery and the repeal of the Test and Corporations Act, which banned dissenters from entering universities, the armed forces and the professions. The English intelligentsia had been dominated by dissenters since the mid-eighteenth century, including the industrialist Josiah Wedgwood and the scientist Joseph Priestley. In the ensuing decade this domination was continued by, among others, William Godwin, Richard Price, Mary Wollstonecraft and Thomas Paine.

The year 1792 brought the publication of the second part of Tom Paine's *Rights of Man* and the establishment of the London Corresponding Society (LCS) which joined the campaign for parliamentary reform but which sought to attract the labouring classes rather than the middle-class dissenters and reformers who swelled the ranks of the SCI. Key figures in the early years of the LCS were John Thelwall, Thomas Hardy and John Horne Tooke, who were to be famously tried for treason in 1794 and acquitted. The LCS was devoutly Painite and the more moderate SCI was also moving in that direction through the efforts of Horne Tooke. Membership of the LCS was contingent upon an affirmative answer to three questions, the most significant of which asked:

> Are you thoroughly persuaded that the welfare of the kingdoms require that every adult person, in possession of his reason, and not capacitated by crimes, should have a vote for a Member of Parliament?[62]

This demand for universal suffrage, annual parliaments and secret ballots, was to become the cornerstone of the radical reform movement and was printed on the banners carried proudly at Peterloo.

Similar societies sprang up in industrial cities, such as Manchester, Sheffield, Derby and Nottingham, as the reform movement gathered momentum. Many new political periodicals emerged in the 1790s, both moderate and radical, thereby lending their weight to the drive for reform, forming part of the cultural battle of the 1790s. Nevertheless, by the end of the decade the LCS and many of the political periodicals no longer existed. Harsh laws, war with France and the inescapable failures of the French Revolution led to the silencing of many reformers for the next twenty years.

The explosion of the radical press after 1789 was partly a response to the seismic events happening in Europe. The French Revolution had violently and irreversibly removed politics from the hands of the few and put it into the hands of the many. Even if working men and women did not have the vote, they felt entitled to be informed about the new political ideologies that were changing the world. Radical periodicals met that demand, as well as responding to the cultural needs of the labouring classes through the inclusion of poetry and drama in their pages. Their oppositional discourse gave an identity and a nascent class-consciousness to the growing industrial workforce. Literacy levels rose during the eighteenth century with the increase in basic educational provision for the lower classes, particularly through charity and religious schools. Coupled with the rise of print culture, this empowerment of the masses caused great concern to the authorities, which feared that the dissemination of knowledge would lead to political instability. The response of the state was to tax newspapers even more harshly and outlaw meetings where it was likely that radical texts would be read aloud to those workers unable to read, spreading seditious views ever more widely. This moral panic is illustrated by the *Anti-Jacobin Review*, one of the key periodicals established in the 1790s to ride the wave of anti-French sentiment during the Revolutionary Wars:

> We have long considered the establishment of newspapers in this country as a misfortune to be regretted; but since their influence has become predominant by the universality of their circulation, we regard it as a calamity most deeply to be deplored.[63]

Despite such rhetoric and, given the relatively short lifespan of many of the radical periodicals of the 1790s, their influence on the succeeding generation of reformers is apparent.

Politics for the People (1793–95)

Two of the most significant and influential radical weeklies of the 1790s are Daniel Isaac Eaton's *Politics for the People; or, A Salmagundy for Swine* and Thomas Spence's *Pigs' Meat: Lessons for the Swinish Multitude*.[64] Both titles parody Edmund Burke's famous description of the people as the 'swinish multitude'. In his conservative, anti-Jacobin work of 1790, *Reflections on the Revolution in France*, Burke anticipates the disastrous consequences of the revolution 'when ancient opinions and rules of life are taken away [...] Along with its natural protectors and guardians, learning will be cast into the mire, and trodden down under the hoofs of a swinish multitude.'[65] The reform movement seized on this phrase time and again to satirise Burke by showing that the multitude was definitely not 'swinish'.[66] When *Politics for the*

People first appeared in September 1793 it was entitled *Hog's Wash*, a knowing comment on Burke and his anti-Jacobin ideology.

On the opening page of the first issue of *Politics for the People* is printed the following poem:

> Thy magic Rod, audacious Burke,
> Could metamorphize Man to Pork,
> And quench the spark divine;
> But Eaton's Wonder-working Wand,
> By scattering Knowledge through the Land,
> Is making Men of Swine.[67]

This satirical verse not only encapsulates the irreverence behind Eaton's work but also alludes to the underlying philosophy behind his periodical – the enlightenment of the common man through the dissemination of knowledge, one of the greatest fears of the government and of Burke. *Politics for the People* was its mission statement as well as its title. Like Spence, Eaton was a member of the LCS and voiced its views on parliamentary reform in the pages of his periodical. In March 1795, the two-penny *Politics for the People* was replaced by the one-penny *Philanthropist*, a smaller weekly but, for all intents and purposes, a continuation of *Politics for the People*. When the Treasonable and Seditious Practices Act and the Seditious Meetings Act, better known as the two gagging acts, came into force in 1795, Eaton went into hiding and then fled to the United States and by 1796 *Philanthropist* had ceased publication.

Pigs' Meat (1793–96)[68]

Thomas Spence's intention for his new publication in 1793 reads:

> To promote among the labouring part of mankind proper ideas of their situation, of their importance, and of their rights, and to convince them that their forlorn condition has not been entirely overlooked and forgotten, nor their just cause unpleaded, neither by their maker nor by the best and most enlightened of men in all ages.[69]

Throughout his life, Spence saw his role as mainly that of an educator. Once a schoolmaster in his native Newcastle, he spent his life writing lectures and pamphlets, informing readers and listeners of his plans for wholesale reform. He also saw himself as a spokesman for the disenfranchised and the voiceless, reminding them, as he states above, that they are not forgotten. The emphasis on the rights of the people is not just Painite rhetoric but reference to the very heart of Spence's beliefs: the redistribution and common ownership of the land. Inspired by the works of seventeenth-century republicans, such as James Harrington and Algernon Sidney, Spence's views linked the radicalism of the Romantic period to that of the English Revolution, a link which was made even stronger and more explicit by the radical writers of 1819.

As with *Politics for the People*, *Pigs' Meat* is a cornucopia of extracts, poems and letters. Extracts from Harrington's *Oceana* feature regularly, along with the works of John Locke, Richard Price and Jonathan Swift. Poems by Milton and Goldsmith sit alongside songs by Spence. In many of his songs he adopts the tradition of the broadside ballad of stating a known tune, such as 'Rule Britannia' and 'God Save the King' thereby encouraging a collective, communal performance.[70] This technique was used later in the *Black Dwarf* and *Medusa*.

Following his death in 1814, his followers, Thomas Evans, Arthur Thistlewood and 'Dr' James Watson, known as the Spencean Philanthropists, continued his work. Post Waterloo, the ultra-radical Spenceans were the most extreme element of the reform movement, advocating violent insurrection in order to achieve Spence's core belief of the redistribution of land; however, their involvement at Peterloo was negligible. Their influence is more evident in many of the most radical periodicals published in this era.

Radical periodicals in the 1810s

When the euphoria accompanying the British victory at Waterloo and the subsequent demise of Napoleon dissipated, the reality of post-war Britain reignited the reform movement, leading to the brief period of 1815–1819 becoming, in Thompson's words, 'the heroic age of popular radicalism.'[71] The economic hardships, social unrest and government repression have been outlined above in the build up to Peterloo. As the political climate became even harsher for the labouring classes, the need for the oppressed to have a voice became ever more necessary. Inspired by the weeklies of Spence and Eaton, the new generation of publishers sought to rally the people and garner support for the re-energised reform movement. However, whereas publications such as *Pigs' Meat* were driven by ideology, topicality became the motivating force for this new generation. The implicit understanding that it was events rather than ideas that shaped people's opinions is reinforced by the number of periodicals that emerged immediately after Peterloo.

As well as the undoubted influence of Paine, Spence and Eaton on this new generation of writers, the significance of William Cobbett must not be ignored. Kevin Gilmartin maintains that 'the weekly newspaper or pamphlet was the most important print vehicle for early nineteenth-century radical argument and opinion' and credits Cobbett with beginning that trend with the establishment of *Cobbett's Weekly Political Register* in 1802.[72] Initially pro-government, by 1805 Cobbett had turned against the government and began to promote the causes of the working man:

> Gentlemen, We are now all well convinced, that the real cause of the evils, with which our country is affected, is the want of reform on the Commons' House of Parliament; and, therefore, it becomes our duty to take into our serious consideration what we ourselves ought *to do* in order to assist in the producing of such reform.[73]

As is evident above, the *Register* never emulated the radical tones of *Pigs' Meat*; moreover, at the price of just over one shilling, it was beyond the means of its intended readership. In 1816 Cobbett issued an unstamped version of the *Register*, also known as the *Two-Penny Trash*, which, at its height, sold more than 40,000 copies a week.[74] Following the suspension of Habeas Corpus in 1817, Cobbett expected to be arrested and therefore fled to the United States. As a consequence, the popularity and influence of the *Register* declined and it played no role in the radical response to Peterloo.

The *Cap of Liberty*, the *Briton*, the *Medusa*, the *White Hat* and the *Theological and Political Comet* were some of the London-based radical weeklies that proliferated in the aftermath of Peterloo. They were all short-lived, falling victim to the oppressive Six Acts, passed by a threatened government at the end of November 1819 in order to destroy any incipient rebellion. As well as the imposition of sixpence stamp duty, The Newspaper and Stamp Duties Act required printers and publishers to post a bond of £300. In effect, this repressive measure ensured the demise of the majority of the radical weeklies; a price of seven or eight pence per issue would have been beyond the means of the vast majority of the weeklies' readers; however, the legacy of these short-lived publications lies in their dynamic journalism and contribution to the radical debate. The letters, poems, songs and editorials within them mirror the tavern meetings and communal activities of the reform societies throughout the country. Today they provide us with an insight into the turbulence of the times – their irreverence, humour and energy undimmed by the intervening two centuries.

The *Cap of Liberty* (1819–20)

The *Cap of Liberty* ran for eighteen weekly issues from 8 September 1819 until 5 January 1820 and was priced at two pence. It was printed in Smithfield by Thomas Davison, a well-known ultra-radical, who also published *Medusa*, the *Theological and Political Comet*, the

Deists' Magazine and *London Alfred*.[75] The editor was James Griffin, an apprentice surgeon turned bookseller and publisher who had been involved in the London radical underworld since 1817. The content of the revolutionary *Cap of Liberty* is dominated by Peterloo and is aptly described by Paul Keen as 'the aggressive and often raucous voice of ultra-radicalism.'[76] As well as calling for reform, *Cap of Liberty* is also concerned with such issues as the position of Catholics in Ireland, printing several poems celebrating Irish rebel heroes, such as Robert Emmet and Thomas Russell.

The journal's name is taken from the symbol of revolution, also known as the *bonnet rouge*, worn by Jacobins in France during The Terror of 1793 and 1794. Described by John Belchem as a:

> Roman badge of freedom. It was an ancient and revered emblem which had adorned Britannia's spear and the coinage of the realm until the 1790s when it acquired revolutionary connotations as the livery of French anarchy and Jacobin terror.[77]

Caps appeared at the Spa Fields Uprising in 1816 and again at Peterloo where the Manchester and Salford Yeomanry Cavalry regarded them as objects to be seized, along with the banners.[78]

The publisher of *Cap of Liberty*, Thomas Davison, or Davidson, was a republican, a deist and a Painite, who was a member of the ultra-radical Spenceans led by Watson. This group also included Arthur Thistlewood, who was to be executed for his role in the Cato Street conspiracy; the radical preacher and son of a slave, Robert Wedderburn; and the hairdresser turned poet, E.J. Blandford. Davison was a journeyman printer who, according to McCalman, 'became one of London's leading ultra-radical publishers in 1819–20.'[79] In 1820, following the failure of all of his publishing ventures, Davison was sentenced to two-years' imprisonment and £100 fine for blasphemous libel. He spent the last years of his life in penury as a bookseller.

The *Briton* (1819)

The *Briton* is one of the shortest lived of the London radical weeklies to emerge after Peterloo and one of the most mysterious. Costing a penny, it ran for nine issues from 25 September until 20 November 1819, ceasing publication prior to the passing of the Six Acts. Printed in Aldersgate, London, nothing is known about the publisher – J. Turner. The following epigraph appears under the title on the front page of each issue:

> Let us think. Let us act as the brave,
> And die for REFORM if need be;

5 Peterloo banner.

> He's a blockhead, a traitor, a slave,
> Who will not attempt to be free.[80]

The radical, or even revolutionary ideology underpinning the periodical is apparent in this verse in its call for action in the cause of reform. As well as radicalism, the *Briton* also espouses Christianity and is opposed to the 'establishment of Atheism or Deism' which is 'the avowed object of some of the Reformers', in addition to 'counteract[ing] the baneful tendency of such pernicious publications […] [which] is not the only object which the managers of the BRITON have in view. Next to the preservation of Religion, is the preservation of the Rights of Man.'[81] This combination of radicalism and Christianity is unusual in the radical press and perhaps suggests that its publisher was not part of the Spencean coterie of Davison and Shorter.

The title of the *Briton* is an example of what Anne Janowitz refers to as 'oppositional patriotism', a common eighteenth-century stance adopted by radicals whose own brand of patriotism, such as the defence of the British Constitution and ancient Anglo-Saxon rights, was in opposition to the patriotism espoused by a German monarchy and Francophile aristocracy.[82]

The *Medusa* (1819–20)

The *Medusa; or Penny Politician* was one of the most radical of the radical weeklies and one of the more successful. It ran for forty-six issues from 20 February 1819 until 7 January 1820 and cost one penny. Along with *Cap of Liberty* and *Theological and Political Comet*, it was published by Thomas Davison in Smithfield, although the first twelve issues were printed by W. Mason in Clerkenwell Green. Its motto – 'Let's die like Men, and not be sold like Slaves' – is a clear statement of its revolutionary ideals and is taken from the 1795 play *Venice Preserv'd* by John Philip Kemble, seemingly an unlikely source of revolutionary rhetoric.[83] *Medusa's* style is aptly described by Keen as containing 'uncompromising and often belligerent dissent'.[84] It contains a great deal of poetry, including poems by the noted radical poets E.J. Blandford and Allen Davenport. The title, *Medusa*, is an obvious reference to the snake-haired monster from Greek mythology, whose direct stare would turn men to stone. Interestingly, Medusa was a gorgon, the name of another radical weekly published between 1818 and 1819.[85] Davison's choice of title may be an allusion to the power and indestructibility of radical thought.

The *Theological and Political Comet* (1819)

The *Theological and Political Comet* is another radical weekly published by Thomas Davison. Published between 24 July and 13 November 1819, it ran for seventeen issues and cost one and a half pence. 'And Political' was appended to the original title of the *Theological Comet* following Peterloo, an indication of its increased focus on political issues. It was edited by Robert Shorter, who also wrote poetry under the pseudonym Sir John Falstaff, an allusion to the Shakespearean comic character from *Henry IV* and *The Merry Wives of Windsor*. The following was printed at the end of each issue:

> Edited by Sir John Falstaff, editor of the first two numbers of the *Medusa*, the *London Weekly Magazine*, etc. Printed and published by R. Shorter, Strand and sold by all free-thinking booksellers, and Newsmen, who need not be fearful of vending this publication.[86]

It would seem that Shorter was keen to downplay both the role played by Davison and the risks taken by booksellers in selling seditious material.

The accompanying by-line or epigraph to the periodical states: 'It is a shame to trust our souls in the hands of those we should be afraid to trust with our money: – Come, come, venture to think for yourselves.' This exhortation to its readers to think for themselves is carried into the editorial in its first issue, addressed 'To the free-thinking people of England':

> Enlightened as ye are, are ye sufficiently enlightened to see through, and comprehend the meaning of a great, thick book, which is commonly called, and generally known by the name of, THE OLD AND NEW TESTAMENT?[87]

Shorter evidently regards the bible as a tool of social repression and endeavours to enlighten his readers against its pernicious influence. Despite the use of 'theological' in its title, the *Theological and Political Comet* is militantly secular.

The *White Hat* (1819)

Probably the most ephemeral of the radical weeklies, it is unclear how many issues were produced. Keen notes that only one issue appeared on 19 October 1819, whereas Scrivener maintains that the weekly ran for nine issues from 19 October until 11 December 1819.[88] Costing two pence, it was printed and published in Whitechapel by C. Teulon, about whom little is known. The white hat from which its title is taken is a symbol of radical protest, worn with green ribbons and accompanied by a black crepe armband after Peterloo as 'an emblem of class conflict'.[89] The paper describes the significance of the hat:

> The WHITE HAT, worn by so many steady and decided patriots battered by the bludgeons of the special constables, slashed by the sabres of the Yeomanry Cavalry [...] is become a badge too explicit to be mistaken, too honourable to be neglected, and too formidable to be despised.[90]

Along with the cap of liberty, clothing was clearly a signifier of radicalism. The broadside ballad *The White Hat*, in Chapter 2, attributes the wearing of the white hat to both Henry Hunt and Oliver Cromwell, thereby providing a provenance for this radical symbol.

The *Black Dwarf* (1817–24)

Thomas Jonathan Wooler's *Black Dwarf* is the most successful of the radical weeklies to emerge after the Napoleonic Wars. Costing four pence and with a circulation of more than 12,000 in 1819, it sold more than double the number of copies of *The Times* and achieved national circulation.[91] Following the decline of Cobbett's *Political Register* in 1817, Wooler became the most popular journalist in England and the

Black Dwarf 'the nation's most widely read radical journal.'[92] Wooler's trial in 1817 for two counts of seditious libel was a highly publicised event and he defended himself to a packed courthouse. Convicted on one of the two charges, Wooler spent a month in prison before being released following a petition to the House of Commons by Francis Burdett.

From its inception in January 1817, the *Black Dwarf* was satirical in tone and vehement in its advocacy of radical constitutionalism. Partly funded by Major Cartwright, it survived the Six Acts and continued until Cartwright's death in 1824, after which Wooler appears to have faded out of radical politics. According to Jon Klancher it appealed to 'northern miners and urban artisans' who 'tucked the *Black Dwarf* prominently in their hats for all to see' and was one of the few radical weeklies to achieve a national readership.[93] Throughout its eight-year existence, the *Black Dwarf* featured topical poetry as another form of political satire, along with parodies and numerous letters from the eponymous Black Dwarf, which all contribute to the carnivalesque tone of the paper. The title may have been inspired by Walter Scott's 1816 novel of the same name, in which, according to folklore, the black dwarf defended wild animals from hunters.[94] The motto for each issue is from Alexander Pope's poem from 1727, 'The First Satire of the Second Book of Horace':

> Satire's my weapon; but I'm too discreet,
> To run a-muck and tilt at all I meet:
> I only wear it in a land of Hectors,
> Thieves, supercargoes, sharpers, and directors.[95]

Just as Pope had written the imitations of Horace to satirise George II, Wooler's apt choice of motto demonstrates his desire to satirise those in power.

Sherwin's Weekly Political Register (1817–19) and the *Republican* (1819–26)

On 5 April 1817 the eighteen-year-old W.T. Sherwin published the twopenny *Sherwin's Weekly Political Register*, a Painite journal which quickly gained in popularity. The title would appear to be a parody of the more moderate *Cobbett's Weekly Political Register*. Sherwin was joined later in 1817 by Richard Carlile, more used to selling radical pamphlets and periodicals than writing them. Carlile became the publisher, a role which made him, rather than Sherwin, liable for prosecution if the *Register* published anything seditious. Carlile quickly became an important figure in radical circles and was due to speak on the hustings at St Peter's Field on 16 August 1819 alongside Henry Hunt. Unlike Hunt, Carlile managed to avoid arrest and published his eye-witness account of events that day in the 21 August issue of *Sherwin's Weekly Political Register* under the headline 'Horrid Massacre at Manchester'. The following issue of the *Register* was its last and six days later Carlile published the first issue of the *Republican*, which was the name originally used by Sherwin. It continued until December 1826 when dwindling sales forced Carlile to cease publication. Whether the *Register* folded due to the end of Sherwin's involvement or his attempt to escape prosecution is unclear. Little is known of Sherwin after 1819 and he does not appear to have had any involvement in the *Republican*. In the first issue, Carlile states that the new publication is 'merely a continuation' of the *Register*, with its new title needing 'no explanation, nor shall its object be disguised.'[96]

Despite the new periodical, Carlile was on trial in October 1819 charged with several counts of blasphemy and seditious libel for his work in the *Republican* and for publishing the works of Paine. He was found guilty and sentenced to six years in Dorchester Gaol, from where he continued to write the *Republican* which was published by his wife Jane with the help of Davison. Carlile claims that during his trial, sales of the *Republican* reached 15,000 a week. Even though Carlile is perhaps best known for publishing several pirate editions of Shelley's *Queen Mab* in the 1820s, he disliked poetry and, as a consequence, published little of it in the *Republican*.

The *Examiner* (1808–81)

Aptly described by Thompson as 'the weekly of the Radical intelligentsia', the *Examiner*, priced at sixpence, was aimed at a more literary, middle-class readership than the more extreme radical weeklies.[97] It was published by John Hunt and edited by his brother Leigh until 1821. It ultimately ran for 3,813 editions with circulation of around 8,000 in 1812 which declined to about 4,000 by 1818.[98] The *Examiner* is probably best known for publishing the work of some of the Romantic period's greatest writers: Byron, Shelley, Keats and Hazlitt. The *Examiner* was no stranger to controversy. Leigh Hunt was found guilty of libelling the Prince Regent in 1813 and sentenced to two-and-a-half years' imprisonment. This may explain why Hunt did not publish any of Shelley's Peterloo poems, despite Shelley sending *The Masque of Anarchy* to him in September 1819 and the sonnet 'England in 1819', three months later.[99] In fact only two poems directly concerning Peterloo were printed in *The Examiner*.

Hunt sought to distance his publication from the ultra-radical weeklies that sprang up in the weeks and months after Peterloo. In the *Examiner* on 7 November 1819 he accuses the *Cap of Liberty* of being run by government spies, such as the notorious William Oliver who was instrumental in organising the Pentridge Uprising in 1817 in order to rout out revolutionaries:

> There is a weekly publication now before us (the *Cap of Liberty*, for Oct. 20) containing language and sentiments of the most foolish and atrocious kind, – just such language and sentiments as we may reasonably suppose would be used by Oliver and C., to answer their diabolical purposes.[100]

The *Cap of Liberty* issued an angry five-page rebuttal to Hunt's 'wanton charge' on 17 November:

> The sole acknowledged foundation of this charge originates in the fact that the Cap of Liberty has taken a long lead of most of its contemporary publications in the cause of Reform. It has hitherto, and always will, at every hazard, pursue the path from which the Examiner retired in terror and dismay. The prison of which Mr Hunt was an inhabitant for two years […] has clipped his pinions, and he since has soared upon a less aspiring wing.[101]

The accusation that Hunt's radicalism was somewhat tempered following his imprisonment has a ring of truth to it.

The *Manchester Observer*

Founded in January 1818 by the radicals John Saxton, James Wroe and John Knight, the *Manchester Observer* reached a circulation of 4,000 twelve months after its inception and was bought in many industrial towns and cities by working-class readers.[102] Radical and non-conformist, the weekly paper printed news and letters, as well as poems. In March 1819, Wroe, Knight and another part-owner of the paper, Joseph Johnson, formed the Patriotic Union Society and invited Hunt to speak at a meeting in the summer of 1819. They were all present at Peterloo; Saxton, Knight and Johnson were arrested alongside Hunt, with Wroe arrested soon after for publishing a pamphlet detailing the events of the day. Wroe is also famed for coining the term 'Peter-Loo' in the *Observer*, a few days after the event. The *Observer* published the greatest number of Peterloo poems, some of which appeared in other publications a few days later. Thompson claims that the newspaper 'had a greater sense of the *news* of the [radical] movement than any competitor' with circulation figures close to those of the *Black Dwarf* by the end of 1819; however, despite its sales, the paper was beset by financial difficulties, compounded by the repeated libel prosecutions meted out against its editors.[103] In March 1821, the *Manchester*

Guardian was established and the *Observer* ceased publication shortly afterwards.

The broadside ballad[104]

Alongside the verse published in the radical press in response to the Peterloo Massacre, numerous broadside ballads appeared on the streets of Manchester and London. Poems and songs have a longstanding tradition within English vernacular culture as a swiftly produced and widely disseminated method of information, commemoration and protest. The radical press in 1819 sought to replicate the immediacy and accessibility of the broadside as part of a wider cultural response to the events in Manchester, as well as contributing in innovative ways to the English tradition of protest poetry.

Broadside ballads have been in existence since the early sixteenth century, soon after Caxton's invention of the printing press. A broadside is a single sheet of paper, usually quarto (10" by 8"), with printing in two columns on one side, often accompanied by a woodcut at the top. They were quick to print and cheap for ballad singers and peddlers to sell at markets and fairs throughout the country. Stationers would pin them on the walls outside their shops and innkeepers would paste them on tavern walls to be enjoyed by their customers. At prices ranging from half a penny to sixpence, they were accessible to the majority of the labouring classes, for whom they were printed and to whom they were sold. Prose broadsides were also printed, often as a way of disseminating news; however, it is the broadside ballad, with its diversity of subject matter and accessibility of style, that was the cornerstone of vernacular culture from Tudor times until the mid-Victorian era, when the increase in newspapers led to its decline.

As Mark Booth notes, 'the broadside ballad is a great meeting ground for orality and literacy'.[105] Folk tales and ancient romances with their origins in oral culture would routinely be printed as broadsides. Tales of Robin Hood and Jack the Giant Killer were perennial favourites, together with the Elizabethan ballad of *Chevy Chase* which narrates events surrounding a conflict between the English Earl Percy of Northumberland and the Scottish Earl Douglas resulting in the Battle of Otterburn in 1388, in which both noblemen died. Towards the end of the sixty-eight stanzas, the respective kings are informed of the deaths:

The news was brought to Edinburgh,
Where Scotland's king did reign,
That brave Earl Douglas suddenly
Was with an arrow slain.

> 'O, heavy news!' King James did say,
> 'Scotland may witness be,
> I have not any captain more
> Of such account as he!'
> Like tidings to King Henry came,
> Within as short a space,
> That Percy of Northumberland,
> Was slain in Chevy Chase.[106]

As with so many ballads, *Chevy Chase* narrates a significant event in British history as a way of commemorating it as well as passing on the tale to future generations. The form of this ballad is one of the most common; the four-line stanzas with alternate iambic tetrameters and trimeters and an *abcb* rhyme scheme is a form frequently used by ballad writers, as is the tune.

The tunes of the ballads are often stated at the top of the broadside, reliant upon the knowledge of the reader, as musical notation would have been prohibitively expensive to print and illegible to most of the buyers of broadsides. The use of traditional tunes for new ballads was commonplace and is evident in a number of the Peterloo poems. By printing poems and songs from oral culture, the broadside would provide a degree of stability to the text, moving it from the fluidity of oral transmission to the more concrete form of print culture; however, the transmission between oral and print culture worked two ways: newly composed ballads would be assimilated into oral culture, as many people would learn them by ear as opposed to reading the text. Familiarity with the tune would facilitate this process, enabling the listener to learn a new ballad with remarkable ease.

Ballads were largely rooted in vernacular culture with ballad singers and hawkers on the very margins of society, frequently on the wrong side of the law and often arrested as vagrants. As well as disseminating news and retelling folktales, ballads were often used as a form of social protest and political propaganda. Aware of the many pro-Royalist broadsides being printed during the English Revolution, Oliver Cromwell outlawed the printing and selling of ballads in 1647. When the law was revoked during the Restoration, there was a proliferation of ballads and songs with Samuel Pepys becoming a keen collector.[107] Despite such notable collectors, the ballad was still regarded as a low form of culture at the beginning of the eighteenth century. In 1708 the *Dictionarium Anglo-Britannicum* defined the ballad as: 'a common song sung up and down the streets.'[108] Samuel Johnson's 1755 *Dictionary of the English Language* was equally as condescending. The ballad 'once signified a solemn and sacred song [...] but now it is nothing but trifling verse.'[109] By the end of the century, however, the ballad was regarded with more suspicion than disdain:

> BALLAD: a kind of song, adapted to the capacity of the lower class of the people; who being mightily taken with the species of poetry, are thereby not a little influenced in the conduct of their lives. Hence we find, that seditious and designing men never fail to spread ballads among the people, with a view to gain them over to their side.[110]

This rather alarmist definition from the *Encyclopaedia Britannica* suggests that by the 1790s the ballad was regarded as a potentially dangerous text that contributed towards the spread of political literacy in the years following the French Revolution. Its reference to the politicisation of 'the lower class' through the dissemination of the ballad by 'seditious' men is indicative of both the fear of the 'mob' and the understanding of the ballad as part of a movement against the state due to its accessibility. The inclusion of ballads in periodicals of the 1790s was partly due to the familiarity of the reader, whether middle class or labouring class, with the form: 'the simple stanza-plus-refrain acquired a poetic responsibility which it had not previously had.'[111] The adoption of the broadside ballad by Spence and other radical poets of the 1790s highlights how the reform movement sought to utilise vernacular culture as a means of urging people to support the campaign for parliamentary reform.

The antiquarian movement

Despite this suspicion of the ballad as a weapon of subversion, during the eighteenth century it underwent a gentrification process, with the more traditional ballads becoming *de rigeur* among the middle classes. The antiquarian, Thomas Percy, is often credited with the revival of the ballad through the publication of the three-volume work, *The Reliques of Ancient English Poetry* in 1765, but in fact renewed interest in the ballad and vernacular English culture can be traced back to the beginning of the eighteenth century and the pages of the *Spectator*. In two essays published in May 1711 Joseph Addison champions the ballad's simplicity of style arguing that it 'pleases all Kinds of Palates', even those who 'have formed to themselves a wrong artificial Taste upon little fanciful Authors and Writers of Epigram'.[112] This attack was part of a counter movement to the domination of neoclassicism at the time. The strict rules and influence of Greek and Roman culture stifled literary expression, and Addison's argument on the merits of the ballad was a way of asserting an English cultural identity. Within these two essays Addison encapsulates the fundamental qualities of the ballad in its appeal across time and social class as a result of its accessibility of language and closeness to nature.

Another key figure in the eighteenth-century ballad revival is Joseph Ritson, whose work, *A Select Collection of English Songs*, published in 1783, was in direct competition with Percy's *Reliques*. The rivalry between these two key figures of the ballad revival is highly significant as it embodies the political competition over the appropriation of the ballad form. Percy's aim, according to Susan Oliver, was the redemption of an 'oral ballad culture that had latterly become associated with vulgar street culture and popular protest', motivated by class politics and a 'response to urbanisation'.[113] Through his inclusion of songs and poems from Shakespeare, Chaucer and Spenser, Percy was attempting to canonise vernacular poetry by giving it literary credentials; however the vernacular poetry selected by Percy was centuries old, such as *Chevy Chase* and the old Scottish ballad of *Barbara Allan*. By locating the ballad in the past, Percy hoped it would gain acceptance as a literary genre free from a political and social message. Nevertheless, this very attempt to both de-politicise and canonise the genre is in itself a political act and evidence of Percy's conservative agenda. As a consequence, Percy's efforts in reclaiming the past resulted in some fabrication in the editing process with the omission of stanzas deemed too bawdy and even the insertion of new verses written by Percy himself.

Ritson was highly critical of Percy, stating: 'Forgery and imposition of any kind, ought to be universally execrated, and never more when they are employed by persons high in rank or character, and those very circumstances are made use of to sanctify the deceit.'[114] Ritson feared that the domination of antiquarianism by the elite would lead to a distortion of popular culture. His own most widely read work, *Robin Hood: A Collection of all the Ancient Poems, Songs and Ballads, now Extant, relative to that celebrated English Outlaw*, published in 1795, not only draws on a staple from traditional, oral culture but also demonstrates his anti-authoritarian views. Ritson's collections are more varied than Percy's and his radical sentiments are evident in his selections just as Percy's more conservative tendencies are in his. This contesting of the past was the focus of the debate between the two antiquarians and the battle over the rights to edit the ballads and appropriate the past.

Whereas Bishop Percy was very much a figure of the establishment, dedicating his book to the Countess of Northumberland and including ballads relating to the ancient family of Percy, Ritson, a conveyancer from Newcastle, was well known as a radical, friend to both William Godwin and Thomas Spence. When Ritson's *English Songs* first appeared in 1783, it was published by Joseph Johnson with engravings by Blake. However, despite his radicalism, in 1800 Ritson was instrumental in helping Scott to collect material for his *Minstrelsy of the Scottish Border*, demonstrating perhaps that his regard for the preservation and distribution of traditional poetry outweighed his political allegiances.

Betty Bennett argues that the Napoleonic Wars were key to popularising the ballad in the late eighteenth century, more so than *Reliques*, due to the large number of ballads being published at the time, which were aimed at 'addressing and educating the populace on a vital national question.' It is interesting to note that none of the 350 poems in Bennett's collection was published by the radical press, despite the popularity of periodicals such as *Pigs' Meat* at the time.[115] For Maureen McLane both the collaboration and competition amongst the balladeers ensured that 'eighteenth-century balladeering was thus already polemical'.[116] Percy regarded ballads as a reinstatement of the ancient chivalric code and the celebration of English feudalism in the face of growing uncertainty at home, a sentiment shared by Scott, whereas Ritson's idea of the ballad as a radical, popular form of expression was adopted by the young Romantic poets Robert Southey and Samuel Taylor Coleridge. The inclusion of more recent ballads within Ritson's collection highlights the living nature of the genre as opposed to Percy's relics of the past. However, it is the versatility of the ballad as demonstrated by both Percy and Ritson that enabled writers as diverse as Scott and Spence to appropriate the genre and utilise it as a vehicle for their own political views.

The protest ballad

The historic union between ballad and protest dates back to Norman times, with one of the first extant ballads dated 1540 featuring the controversial figure of Thomas Cromwell as its subject matter.[117] Murray Pittock defines the ballad as a 'major political weapon' with more than three million in circulation by the late sixteenth century.[118] *The Poore Man Payes for All* first appeared as a broadside in 1630 with accompanying woodcuts depicting a rich nobleman and a poor labourer. It was to be sung to the tune of 'In slumbring sleepe I lay'. Following a traditional dream narrative, the narrator's imaginary world reflects the harsh reality of the times:

Me thought I saw how wealthy men
Did grind the poore men's faces,
And greedily did prey on them,

> Not pittying their cases:
> They make them toyle and labour sore
> For wages too-too small;
> The rich men in their taverns rore,
> But poore men pay for all.[119]

This song concerns the perennial problem of the division between rich and poor in society. The proto-socialist understanding of the way in which the poor have no control over their labour and produce was to become an even stronger theme in an industrial society where a rural economy was largely replaced by an urban one. Over 150 years after *The Poore Man Pays for All* was sold on the streets, Spence returns to its theme in 'The Rights of Man for Me' to be sung to the tune of 'Maid of the Mill' and published in *Pigs' Meat* in 1795:

> This world for the poor they say never was made,
> Their portion in the heav'ns be,
> And say that they envy them their happy lot,
> So certain's their felicity;
> But thank them for naught, if the heav'ns they could lett
> Few joys here the poor would e'er see,
> For *rents* they must toil and for *taxes* to boot,
> The Rights of Man then for me.[120]

Spence explores the role of religion in the suppression of the poor and how the rewards of heaven are used to pacify and assure them of happiness after death. As the song continues, Spence extends his argument, encouraging the people to 'shake off all vile slavery' and follow the example of France in reclaiming the rights of freedom and democratic representation.

The influence of the broadside ballad on Spence's song is evident. The naming of a familiar tune encourages the reader to perform the song, enabling it to be transmitted both through print and oral culture. There are also examples of ballads appearing in radical weeklies and as broadsides. *Distress of the Poor* appears both as a broadside in Manchester and in *Sherwin's Weekly Political Register* in 1818. As the broadside is undated, it is unknown where it first appeared but it is clear evidence of the borrowing and movement of songs between the two media. The song was to be sung to the tune of 'Derry Down', one of the most widely used tunes and one which dates back to the sixteenth century.[121] As with the two ballads considered above, *Distress of the Poor*, as its title suggests, also explores the lives of the poor:

> The spinners of Manchester loudly complain
> How toilsome their labour, how trifling their gain;

The hatters, the dyers, the weavers also,
Are starving with hunger you very well know.
Derry Down, &c.

We fondly did hope when the wars were all o'er,
That hunger and thirst we should never feel more,
But woeful experience shews us the reverse,
That the peace only served to complete our distress.[122]

It is interesting to note that this song is rooted in both time and place; it depicts the lives of the cotton workers in Manchester in the aftermath of the Napoleonic Wars, where the low wages were resulting in starvation.

An adequate price for our labour we want,
But this our proud gentry never will grant;
So far they from striving our wrongs to redress,
They laugh at our sufferings, and mock our distress.

Your cringing, soliciting never will do,
Too oft it has proved unsuccessful to you;
I could tell you a way to relieve your distress,
But I can't bring the words in to metre my verse.[123]

Unlike Spence, this writer refrains from employing revolutionary rhetoric but the implication is clear. Fear of prosecution may have tempered the song but the final line – 'Unite in the cause, and you're sure of the prize' – is suggestive of revolutionary action.

As well as the countless ballads that appeared in the 1790s championing reformist and even revolutionary sentiments, the ballad as a moral tale was used as a vehicle for conservative propaganda by the Evangelical Hannah More in the 1790s. Her *Cheap Repository Tracts*, published between 1795 and 1798, sold more than two million copies in a year.[124] Specifically aimed at moralising the labouring classes, and thus laying the foundations for Victorianism, they contain poems, stories and essays that are fiercely anti-Jacobin. Her social narratives show how hard work and morality are rewarded. More was consciously appropriating the culture of the chapbook which she regarded as part of a pagan tradition and one she wished to replace with moral, Christian instruction.[125] By subsidising the tracts, she was able to sell them more cheaply than the chapbooks, a marketing move that proved successful.[126]

The ballad was of huge significance within the wider cultural sphere of the eighteenth and early nineteenth century. The appropriation of vernacular culture was a war being waged on both a class and a political level. Percy and Ritson, among others, were contesting the representation of oral culture, with Percy wishing it to be seen as suitable for a middle-class readership, whilst Ritson strived to maintain its lower-class affiliation. Conservatives such as Hannah More and radicals such as Spence used the cheapness and popularity of the ballad and chapbook as a highly effective weapon in the propaganda war of the 1790s. In 1819 the ballad writers, journalists and poets were well aware of the power of the ballad in spreading news and galvanising support, a knowledge they exploited to the full as the following poems and songs demonstrate.

Notes

1. S. Bamford, *Passages in the Life of a Radical*. 3 vols. (Manchester: Heywood, 1842), vol. 1, p. 208.
2. Over 300 eye-witness accounts of Peterloo survive, with Bamford's being the best known (R. Poole, 'What We Don't Know About Peterloo', in R. Poole (ed.), *Return to Peterloo. Manchester Region History Review*, 23 (2014), p. 2).
3. M. Bush, *The Casualties of Peterloo* (Lancaster: Carnegie Publishing, 2005), p. 90.
4. I am indebted to the work of Joyce Marlow, Robert Reid, Donald Read, R.J. White, Robert Poole, Michael Bush and E.P Thompson, among others, for their detailed accounts of Peterloo, its causes and effects.
5. *Manchester Observer* (21 August 1819), p. 687.
6. R. Reid, *The Peterloo Massacre* (London: Heinemann, 1989), pp. 199, 26, 15.
7. Timmins notes the inaccuracy of population statistics prior to the national census in 1801. The figure for 1801 is for both Manchester and Salford (in A. Kidd and T. Wyke (eds), *Manchester: Making the Modern City* (Liverpool: Liverpool University Press, 2016), pp. 30, 2). By 1802, Manchester had more than fifty cotton-spinning mills (T. Wyke, 'Rise and Decline of Cottonopolis', in *Ibid.*, pp. 69–117 at p. 72).
8. Michael E. Rose, 'Voices of the People', in Kidd and Wyke (eds), *Manchester*, p. 181.
9. Frank O'Gorman, 'Manchester Loyalism in the 1790s', in Poole, ed., *Return to Peterloo*, p. 21; S. Hylton, *A History of Manchester* (Andover: Phillimore, 2010), pp. 18, 53.
10. R.J. White, *Waterloo to Peterloo* (London: Heinemann, 1957), pp. 106, 125–6.
11. E.P. Thompson, *The Making of the English Working Class* (Middlesex: Penguin, 1980), pp. 733, 723.
12. *Ibid.*, p. 683.
13. Reid, *The Peterloo Massacre*, p. 110; White, *Waterloo to Peterloo*, p. 146; D. Read, *Peterloo: The Massacre and its Background* (Manchester:

Introduction 35

14. Manchester University Press, 1958), p. 35; J. Belchem, *Orator Hunt: Henry Hunt and English Working-Class Radicalism* (Oxford: Clarendon, 1985), p. 7.
14. J. Marlow, *The Peterloo Massacre* (London: Rapp and Whiting, 1969), pp. 66–7.
15. Hylton, *A History of Manchester*, p. 85.
16. M. Krantz, *'Rise Like Lions': The History and Lessons of the Peterloo Massacre of 1819* (London: Bookmark Publications, 2011), p. 1.
17. C. Horner 'The Rise and Fall of Manchester's "Infernal Set of Miscreants": Radicalism in 1790s Manchester', *Manchester Region History Review*, 12 (1998), pp. 18–26.
18. Reverend William Hay and Reverend Charles Ethelstone, two of the Peterloo magistrates, were Orangemen (K. Navickas, 'Lancashire Britishness: Patriotism in the Manchester Region During the Napoleonic Wars', in *Return to Peterloo*, ed. R Poole, p. 46–7).
19. P. Mason, *Live Working or Die Fighting: How the Working Class Went Global* (London: Harvill Secker, 2007), p. 16; A. Clark, *The Struggle for the Breeches: Gender and the Making of the British Working Class* (London: Rivers Oram, 1995), pp. 159–60. See the introduction to Chapter 3 for more information.
20. Hylton, *A History of Manchester*, p. 84; Marlow claims the crowd was between 10,000 and 30,000 (*The Peterloo Massacre*, p. 60).
21. The marchers were named 'Blanketeers' as they intended to march wrapped in a blanket (Hylton, *A History of Manchester*, p. 84–5).
22. Marlow, *The Peterloo Massacre*, p. 60. Poole has written on the significance of the wakes tradition to Peterloo: R. Poole, 'The March to Peterloo: Politics and Festivity in Late Georgian England', *Past and Present*, 192 (2006), pp. 109–53; Krantz, *'Rise Like Lions'*, p. 1. Marlow states that estimated numbers range from 30,000 to 150,000 with 60,000 as being generally accepted ('The Day', p. 4). The *Manchester Observer* of 21 August 1819 states 120,000 were present (p. 687).
23. The announcement for the meeting was published in the *Manchester Observer* on 7 August 1819, p. 670.
24. The announcement appeared in the *Manchester Observer* on 14 August 1819, p. 678.
25. Reid, *The Peterloo Massacre*, pp. 154–7.
26. According to Bush, the MYC pursued its victims with one woman, Mary Jones, being sabred a mile away from St Peter's (*The Casualties of Peterloo* (Lancaster: Carnegie Publishing, 2005), p. 47).
27. R. Poole, 'By the Law and Sword: Peterloo Revisited', *History*, 91:302 (2006), p. 263.
28. *Ibid.*, p. 276.
29. Poole, 'What We Don't Know About Peterloo', p. 2.
30. Read, *Peterloo*, p. 183.
31. Thompson, *The Making of the English Working Class*, p. 750.

32 Marlow, *The Peterloo Massacre*, p. 98; Thompson, *The Making of the English Working Class*, p. 752.
33 Belchem, *Orator Hunt*, p. 13.
34 O'Gorman, 'Manchester Loyalism in the 1790s', p. 27.
35 *Coroner's Inquest into John Lees* (London: Hone, 1820), p. 161.
36 Thompson, *The Making of the English Working Class*, p. 780.
37 This is being led by the Peterloo Memorial Campaign www.peterloomassacre.org [accessed 19 November 2017]. George Cruikshank designed a memorial depicting a soldier on horseback with sabre raised and poised to attack a woman holding a baby.
38 Tyas was arrested alongside Henry Hunt. This account was reprinted in the *Examiner* on 22 August, entitled 'Dispersal of the Reform Meeting at Manchester by a Military Force' (608, pp. 539–43).
39 Tyas, 'Dispersal of the Reform Meeting', p. 2.
40 'Manchester Meeting', *Gentleman's Magazine & Historical Chronicle*, 89 (1819), pp. 171–4, at p. 171.
41 *Ibid.*, p. 173.
42 'State of Public Affairs', in *Quarterly* (January 1820), p. 502.
43 Quoted in P. McKeiver, *Peterloo Massacre 1819* (Manchester: Advance Press, 2009) p. 111.
44 *Sherwin's Weekly Political Register* 10:5 (1819), p. 237.
45 *Examiner* 608 (1819), p. 529.
46 *Sherwin's Weekly Political Register*, 10:5 (1819), p. 237.
47 *Ibid.*
48 *Ibid.*, p. 239. Lord Castlereagh was the Foreign Secretary, hated by many for his merciless reprisals following the failed 1798 uprising in Ireland.
49 *Examiner* 608 (1819), p. 529.
50 *Ibid.*, pp. 529, 530.
51 P. Keen, (ed.), *The Popular Radical Press in Britain 1817–21*. 6 vols. (London: Pickering and Chatto, 2003), vol. 6, p. 47.
52 *Black Dwarf*, 3:34 (1819), p. 551. Original emphases.
53 Keen, *The Popular Radical Press*, vol. 6, p. 48. Original emphases.
54 Following publication, Burdett was convicted for seditious libel, sentenced to three months' imprisonment in Marshalsea Prison and fined £2000 (*DNB*). Original emphases. *Black Dwarf* 3:34 (1819), p. 550.
55 *Hay Portfolio*, 60.
56 Keen, *The Popular Radical Press*, vol. 6, p. 145.
57 K. Williams, *'Read All About it': A History of the British Newspaper* (London: Routledge, 2010) pp. 49, 54.
58 The original *Spectator* ran for 555 issues from March 1711 until December 1712. It was briefly revived in 1714, 1715 and 1753. Today's *Spectator* dates back to 1828.
59 The *Spectator*, 10 (1711), p. 1.
60 A sheet comprised four pages. Between 1712 and 1815 newspaper taxes increased by almost 800 per cent (Williams, *'Read All About it'*, p. 62).

61 J. Black, *English Press in the Eighteenth Century* (London: Routledge, 2010), p. 73.
62 Quoted in Thompson, *The Making of the English Working Class*, p. 19.
63 Quoted in Williams, 'Read All About it', p. 81.
64 Salmagundy is a dish containing cold meat, fish, eggs and onions (*OED*). As was common with radical weeklies, Spence and Eaton served as printers, publishers and editors.
65 Burke, *Reflections on the Revolution in France* (Oxford, Oxford University Press, 1993), pp. 116–17.
66 There are numerous references to Burke's phrase in the poems in this collection.
67 *Politics for the People* (London: 1794), vol. 1, p. 1.
68 William St Clair estimates that 1,500 copies of *Pigs' Meat* were sold each week (*The Reading Nation in the Romantic Period* (Cambridge: Cambridge University Press, 2004), p. 574.)
69 T. Spence, *Pigs' Meat; or Lessons for the Swinish Multitude*, vol. 1 (London: 1793). n. pag.
70 Spence's song 'Jubilee Hymn' to the tune of 'God Save the King' was to be 'sung at the commencement of the millennium, when there shall be neither lords nor landlords; but God and Man will be all in all' (*Pig's Meat* (1793), vol. 1, pp. 42–3. Also see number 8 in Chapter 1.
71 Thompson, *The Making of the English Working Class*, p. 661.
72 K. Gilmartin, *Print Politics: The Press and Radical Opposition in Early Nineteenth-Century England* (Cambridge: Cambridge University Press, 1996), p. 73.
73 *Cobbett's Weekly Political Register*, 30:22 (1816), p. 673. Original emphases.
74 M. Scrivener (ed.), *Poetry and Reform: Periodical Verse from the English Democratic Press, 1792–1824* (Michigan: Wayne State University Press, 1992), p. 23.
75 McCalman suggests that William Mason, a printer and radical, was Davison's main financier, along with George Cannon, the publisher of *The Theological Enquirer*, who supported Davison when he was jailed for publishing Cannon's works (pp. 155–60). I. McCalman, *Radical Underworld: Prophets, Revolutionaries and Pornographers in London, 1795–1840* (Cambridge: Cambridge University Press, 2004).
76 Keen, *The Popular Radical Press*, vol. 4, p. 11.
77 J. Belchem, 'Manchester, Peterloo and the Radical Challenge', in *Peterloo Massacre, MRHR*, pp. 9–14, at p. 11.
78 J.A. Epstein, *Radical Expression: Political Language, Ritual, and Symbol in England, 1790–1850* (Oxford: Oxford University Press, 1994), pp. 70–86.
79 McCalman, *Radical Underworld*, p. 133.
80 Keen, *The Popular Radical Press*, vol. 4, p. 297.
81 *Ibid.*
82 A. Janowitz, *Lyric and Labour in the Romantic Tradition* (Cambridge: Cambridge University Press, 1998), p. 86.

83 Keen, *The Popular Radical Press*, vol. 5, p. 225; J. Kemble, *Venice Preserv'd* Act 3, scene 1, l.352.
84 Keen, *The Popular Radical Press*, vol. 5, p. 1.
85 *The Gorgon* was published and printed by various men, including Richard Carlile and W.T. Sherwin. According to Gilmartin, the radical reformer, Francis Place, also had some involvement (p. 150). *The Gorgon* ran from May 1818 until April 1819 and was one of the few radical weeklies that did not publish poetry.
86 Keen, *The Popular Radical Press*, vol. 6, p. 14.
87 *Ibid.*, p. 7.
88 Keen, *The Popular Radical Press*, vol. 6, p. 251; Scrivener, *Poetry and Reform*, p. 226.
89 Epstein, *Radical Expression*, p. 95.
90 Keen, *The Popular Radical Press*, vol. 6, p. 254.
91 Scrivener, *Poetry and Reform*, p. 23; Gilmartin, *Print Politics*, p. 30.
92 Epstein, *Radical Expression*, p. 37.
93 J. Klancher, *The Making of English Reading Audiences, 1790–1832* (Wisconsin: University of Wisconsin Press, 1987), p. 102.
94 In 1818 John Hunt emulated Wooler by naming his short-lived periodical *The Yellow Dwarf*.
95 *Black Dwarf* 34:3 (1819), p. 550; *The Poetical Works of Alexander Pope* (Glasgow: 1773), p. 135, ll. 69–72.
96 *Republican*, 1 (1819), p. 1.
97 Thompson, *The Making of the English Working Class*, p. 741.
98 G.D. Stout, 'Political History of Leigh Hunt's *Examiner*', *Washington University Studies*, 19 (1949), pp. 5, 37.
99 On 23 September 1819, Mary Shelley noted in her journal: 'S's poem goes to Hunt' (M.W. Shelley, *The Journals of Mary Shelley: 1814–1844*, eds. P.R. Feldman and D. Scott-Kilvert (Oxford: Clarendon, 1987), vol. 1, p. 298). Shelley sent the sonnet to Hunt on 23 December, stating: 'I do not expect you to publish it, but you may show it to whom you please' (P.B. Shelley, *The Letters of Percy Bysshe Shelley*, ed. F.L. Jones (Oxford: Clarendon Press, 1964), vol. 2, p. 167.
100 *Examiner*, 619 (1819), p. 707.
101 Keen, *The Popular Radical Press*, vol. 4, p. 184.
102 S. Harrison, *Poor Men's Guardians: A Survey of the Struggle for a Democratic Newspaper Press* (London: Lawrence and Wishart, 1974), pp. 52–3.
103 Thompson, *The Making of the English Working Class*, p. 742. Original emphasis.
104 Although today a ballad generally refers to a narrative poem, in the eighteenth century it signified any form of popular verse or song. It is used here in that more general sense.
105 M. Booth, *The Experience of Songs* (New Haven CT and London: Yale University Press, 1981), p. 113.

106 *The Famous History of Chevy Chase* (Lincoln, 1795), p. 23.
107 Palmer notes that Pepys' collection comprised 1671 ballads (R. Palmer (ed.), *A Ballad History of England from 1588 to the Present Day* (London: Batsford, 1979), p. 6).
108 J. Kersey, *Dictionarium Anglo-Britannicum: or, A General English Dictionary* (London, 1708), n. pag.
109 Samuel Johnson, *Dictionary of the English Language* (London: 1755), vol. 1, n. pag.
110 *Encyclopaedia Britannica* (Dublin: 1790–98), vol. 2, p. 768.
111 B. Bennett, *British War Poetry in the Age of Romanticism: 1793–1815* (New York: Garland, 1976), p. 1.
112 The *Spectator*, 70 (1711), p. 1.
113 S. Oliver, *Scott, Byron and the Poetics of Cultural Encounter* (Hampshire: Palgrave, 2005), p. 32.
114 J. Ritson, *A Select Collection of English Songs* (London: 1783), vol. 1, pp. x, v.
115 Bennett, *British War Poetry*, p. 51.
116 M. McLane, *Balladeering, Minstrelsy and the Making of British Romantic Poetry* (Cambridge: Cambridge University Press, 2008), p. 52.
117 R. Palmer, *The Sound of History: Songs and Social Comment* (London: Pimlico, 1988), p. 1.
118 M. Pittock, *Poetry and Jacobite Politics in Eighteenth-Century Britain and Ireland* (Cambridge: Cambridge University Press, 1994), p. 111.
119 Palmer, *Ballad History*, p. 16.
120 *Pigs' Meat* (1795), pp. 249–50.
121 See number 11 in Chapter 5 for more information.
122 Scrivener, *Poetry and Reform*, p. 212.
123 Central Library Collection of Ballads, vol. 2, 169.
124 *DNB*.
125 A chapbook is a small pamphlet comprising a single sheet folded into eight, twelve or more pages. It contains poems, folk tales and nursery rhymes decorated with woodcuts, as well as being almanacs and political and religious tracts. They were cheap to print and buy and were popular throughout the seventeenth and eighteenth centuries.
126 St Clair, *The Reading Nation in the Romantic Period*, pp. 352–3.

1

'Rise Britons, rise now from your slumber': the revolutionary call to arms

> Rise like lions after slumber
> In unvanquishable number –
> Shake your chains to earth like dew
> Which in sleep had fallen on you –
> Ye are many – they are few.[1]

Shelley's famous refrain in *The Masque of Anarchy*, written furiously and frantically in the ten days following his receipt of news from Manchester, is undoubtedly the most famous piece of poetry associated with Peterloo. Described by Robert Poole as 'perhaps the most powerful of all political poems', in Salford this verse can still be seen on Transport House, the former regional headquarters of the Transport and General Workers' Union.[2] Echoes of this invocation can also be found in the socialist anthem, 'The International', written by a transport worker, Eugene Pottier, after the crushing of the Paris Commune by the French government in 1871:

> Arise ye workers from your slumbers
> Arise ye prisoners of want
> For reason in revolt now thunders
> And at last ends the age of cant[3]

What is less well known is that Shelley and Pottier are, consciously or otherwise, utilising a trope that features in ballads and broadsides dating back to the sixteenth century.[4] This chapter begins by briefly examining the historical provenance of this trope and its significance within radical culture prior to Peterloo, as well as those written in the immediate aftermath of the massacre, thereby highlighting the intertextual dialogue between the poems which is illustrated not only by an ideological unity but also by the commonality of motifs, forms, styles and even tunes. The urging of the people to wake from their apathy and subjugation to rise against their oppressors became part of the radical discourse in late 1819 and early 1820. The urge to act against the intolerable oppression of the Liverpool administration captured the *zeitgeist* of the months following Peterloo when, it was truly believed, revolution would occur.[5] The hoped-for revolution did not come to pass but the poems gathered here evince a powerful sense of collectivity and common purpose with the repeated exhortations to arise and awaken redolent of those turbulent times.

Another famous use of the awakening and arising trope features in Milton's *Paradise Lost*, first published in 1667. In the first book, following their expulsion from Heaven, Satan calls upon his Angels to 'Awake! – arise! – or be forever fallen', appealing to them with the possibility of re-entering Heaven or founding a new kingdom.[6] When Richard Carlile pirated Shelley's 1812 *Declaration of Rights*, containing Satan's exhortation, in the *Republican* on 24 September 1819, its contemporaneous resonance with the readership would not have been missed.[7]

The earliest example of an exhortatory ballad that I have discovered dates to 1557. *Arise and Awake* was to be sung to the tune of 'Rogero':

> Aryse and wak, for Christi's sake,
> Aryse, I say again;
> Awake, all ye that synfull be,
> Awak, for fear of payn.[8]

Here the speaker urgently seeks to awaken the sleeper from the dangers of sleep. The repetition of 'aryse' and 'awak' creates a sense of desperation and implies that unconscious sleep is dangerous and safety will come with consciousness. The poems in this chapter depict sleep as compliance with tyranny and call on the people to awaken in order to act, as shown in 'Address to Britons':

> Too long beneath an abject yoke
> We basely bowed nor dar'd complain.[9]

During the English Revolution of the 1640s, there are examples of the trope of awakening being used on both sides of the conflict. 'A New Ballad, Called a Review of the Rebellion, in Three Parts' to the tune of 'When the King Enjoys His Rights Again' was written by the well-known ballad writer, Martin Parker, and published in 1647. As would be expected from a Royalist, Parker calls upon the British to wake from the sleep they have been lulled into by the Parliamentarians and return to an absolute monarchy under Charles I:

> Britaines, awake from your six yeares dreame,
> And listen to this deare bought theame,

> Which shewes how you fast asleep were lulled,
> And by what magick spells so gulled.[10]

This lengthy ballad narrates an exclusively Royalist view of the revolution before concluding that the only course of action is:

> Then must king Charles alone
> Be set upon his throne.[11]

Two years later Charles was dead and Cromwell's Commonwealth had replaced the monarchy. However, there was still resistance to the landowning gentry, notably by the Diggers, led by Gerrard Winstanley. The Diggers opposed the enclosure of common land and, in 1649, they occupied an area of wasteland at St George's hill, using it as a platform to argue for the equitable redistribution of land. 'The Digger's Song', written by Winstanley in 1649, exhorts the people to 'stand up now' against the Cavaliers and gentry and reclaim the land unjustly taken from them:

> With spades and hoes and plowes stand up now,
> Your freedom to uphold, seeing Cavaliers are bold
> To kill you if they could, and rights from you to hold.
> Stand up now, Diggers all.[12]

The command to 'stand up' implies that the Diggers needed to assert their presence and, in parallel with the command to rise, suggests emergence from a state of compliance. The reference in the poem above to 'spades and hoes and plowes' not only alludes to the agrarian activities of the Diggers but also carries the implication that these farming tools could quickly become weapons in what was rapidly becoming a class war.

The appeal to defend ancient or natural rights permeates the poems of the 1790s and 1810s and can be seen in several of the poems in this chapter, including 'Patriotic Song', in which the chorus declaims:

> Steady, boys, steady
> We claim all our rights and we'll have them again.[13]

However, calling on the people to rise is not just the province of English radicals. Charles Mackay includes 'Welcome, Charlie, O'er the Main' in his 1861 collection, *Jacobite Songs and Ballads of Scotland from 1688–1746*; the song had also been published in the *Scots Magazine* in 1817, although its championing of 'Royal Charlie' suggests it was written around the time of the 1745 Jacobite Rebellion in which Charles Edward Stuart, the Young Pretender, marched his troops to within a hundred miles of London. The song begins:

Arouse, arouse, each kilted clan!
Let Highland hearts lead on the van,
And forward wi' their dirks in han'[14]
To fight for Royal Charlie.[15]

As with many of the songs employing this trope, the exhortation to rise or awaken comes at the beginning, acting as a call-to-arms with the voice in the song leading the people to action.

Such revolutionary fervour was also expressed by English poets, including Richard 'Citizen' Lee, a fervent supporter of the French Revolution, given his nickname. Lee was a radical publisher and poet who probably met Spence through the London Corresponding Society, of which they were both members. Lee's poem, 'The Triumph of Truth and Liberty', was published in *Pigs' Meat* in 1794 at a time when revolutionary fervour in England was fading, with many becoming disillusioned with the way in which the libertarian ideals of the revolution were being replaced by the savagery of Robespierre's Reign of Terror. 'The Triumph of Truth and Liberty' is uncompromising in its tone and style:

Rouse, indolent mortals! Why will ye remain
Thus neuter in LIBERTY'S cause?
With one noble effort unrivet the chain,
That binds you to tyranny's laws![16]

In contrast to Shelley's appeal for the people to 'shake your chains to earth', Lee's use of the industrial 'unrivet' conveys both the power of those chains and the possibility of overcoming them. The wrathful tone of the poem hints at the desperation felt by many radicals that, by 1794, England was not going to follow in France's revolutionary footsteps.

In the months leading up to Peterloo, radical poets commanded the people to arise as tensions rose and the government became ever more repressive. *Medusa* and the *Black Dwarf*, significant publishers of Peterloo songs, both printed exhortatory songs in the early months of 1819. 'Invocation to Britain' by C.P. was published in *Medusa* in May 1819:

Sons of Albion, ye suff'rers of rapine and wrong,
Arise from the slumbers yo[u]'ve lain in too long;
Proclaim to the world, that by birth ye were free,
And your watch word shall 'FREEDOM and LIBERTY' be.[17]

This republican poem later draws parallels with both the English Revolution and Glorious Revolution, reminding its readers 'How Charles lost his HEAD, and how James lost his CROWN' before calling on them to 'regain the charter / Tyrants long ago have sold.'[18] 'To Britons', written by 'Caledonius' and published in the *Black Dwarf* in March 1819, also refers to Charles I, 'stripped at once of life and crown' and James II, 'a brother tyrant'. In parallel with the poem above and *Masque of Anarchy*, the poem begins:

> Awake from your slumbers, ye true sons of freedom!
> Awake all the Patriots, ye bards of the lyre![19]

Not only does the poem call on the people to wake, it also calls on poets to awaken them with poetry and song. This bardic role of a cultural leader and recorder within radical verse is highly significant. In the following poems and songs, the poet is a knowing and powerful presence, commanding the reader to act and driving the reader from apathy and ignorance to engagement and knowledge.

As with the examples cited above, the poems and songs in this chapter are examples of the apostrophe or exhortatory ballad. The apostrophe takes the form of a literary address to a person or object, perhaps the most famous example being Faustus' apostrophe to Helen of Troy in Marlowe's 1594 play *Doctor Faustus*; the apostrophe famously begins: 'Was this the face that launched a thousand ships?' This genre has dramatic scope and employs rhetorical devices to increase its force and effect. Unlike Faustus' apostrophe to Helen, the poems below have a nameless speaker, thereby increasing the emphasis on the object of the address, whether the Prince Regent or the people of England. Similarly, the exhortatory ballad directly addresses its audience but, unlike the apostrophe, calls upon the object of its address to act in some manner. It is evident why these genres were adopted by many radical poets in the immediate aftermath of Peterloo at a time of heightened tensions and expectations. Their sense of immediacy and direct call to action are attempts to capitalise on the collective sense of outrage and also demonstrate an awareness of the significance of the time.

Interestingly, this urging of the people to act is not replicated in the prose articles of the radical weeklies in which these poems appeared. They all share rage and disgust at the actions of the authorities and are open in their condemnation but they do not explicitly call for revolution or revenge. The epigraph of *Medusa*: 'Let's Die like Men, and not be Sold like Slaves', is an undeniable use of revolutionary rhetoric and yet this is not apparent in its articles and letters concerning Peterloo. The first edition of the *White Hat* states: 'The voice of the country, as that of one man, should cry aloud for radical reform', which stops somewhat short of the calls for vengeance present in many of the exhortatory poems.[20] It would appear that the poems within the radical weeklies contain a more overt radicalism, the reason for which may be that it was hoped by the editors and publishers that revolutionary rhetoric within the form of a song or poem would be deemed less seditious by the authorities than the same ideals expressed in prose. However, it is these poems and songs that would have been more widely disseminated due to their accessibility and focus on collective performance. With familiar tunes and easily remembered refrains, it is their revolutionary sentiment that would have been heard in the taverns and meeting houses of London and beyond, as part of the 'communitarian lyric', as described by Anne Janowitz, in which the ballad was central to the plebeian culture of the time through its combination of political, poetic and community.[21] The following poems are contributing to the tradition of radical verse established in the seventeenth century. At times of national crisis, poets have employed this trope, often drawing on those past events to prove that, if England could get rid of two kings, it could certainly get rid of a third.

1 'Address to the Prince Regent'

This apostrophe is addressed to George, Prince of Wales (1792–1830), who became Regent in 1812 due to the illness of his father, George III. The Prince Regent was almost universally despised due to his debauched life and disregard for his people. On his death in 1830, *The Times* commented: 'There never was an individual less regretted by his fellow creatures than this deceased king. What eye has wept for him? What heart has heaved one throb of unmercenary sorrow? ... If he ever had a friend – a devoted friend in any rank of life – we protest that the name of him or her never reached us' (quoted in *DNB*). Caricaturists such as James Gillray and George Cruikshank produced numerous cartoons of the prince, ridiculing his obesity and dissipated lifestyle.

In the aftermath of Peterloo, the government chose to ignore the protests of many of the newspapers and the outrage emanating from the British public by sealing its support of the Manchester magistrates with a public letter from the Prince Regent thanking the authorities for their actions. Both the *Cap of Liberty* and the *Briton* printed addresses or letters to the Prince Regent, berating him for taking advice from 'a wicked cabinet' and causing insult to the British people through his support for the Manchester authorities. This poem was first published in the *Manchester Observer* on 2 October 1819 and appeared four days later in the *Cap of Liberty* immediately following the second letter to 'his Royal Highness the Prince Regent'.[22] The writer of the letter, J. Griffin, a regular contributor to the periodical, asks the Regent: 'Can you, Sir, imagine that you will be allowed to proceed in this course?

Can you persuade yourself that Englishmen will bow the neck and bend the knee before a throne supported by military despots?'[23] The sentiments in the letter are continued in the poem, although it is not clear whether the poem was written by Griffin. 'Address to the Regent' calls upon the prince to atone for the massacre in Manchester by seeing justice is done. As with the preceding letter, underpinning the poem is a threat to the prince that the already unpopular monarchy is perilously close to being overthrown by the people and any lack of action with regard to events in Manchester will almost undoubtedly result in revolution.

> While the Throne thou hast not mounted,
> Stands – but totters to its base;
> And the hordes thou hast not counted
> Give thee yet a breathing space!
> While the PEOPLE yet permit thee
> Take thy 'vantage now or never,
> Ere the arm of vengeance hit thee,
> Wake! – arise! – or fall forever!!!
>
> This is now no time for dallying,
> While the gathering tempests lour;
> The mighty shouts of armies rallying,
> Soon may meet on RAGLEY Bower.[24]
> *Thread-bound* hangs our scant allegiance –
> Wilt thou the last *tie dissever!*
> Dost thou fear no banded legions?
> Wake! – arise! – or fall forever!!
>
> Trust'st thou Soldiers?[25] Vain the trust is
> Hirelings soon or late betray:
> MANCHESTER calls loud for Justice –
> Wipe her crimson tears away!
> Ere her griefs and wrongs estrange her,
> Ere she try the damn'd endeavour –
> Sta[u]nch her blood-drops – meet thy danger –
> WAKE! ARISE! Or fall forever!!!

2 'The Appeal of Blood'

This poem by S.L. calls on Britons to rise in order to avenge the deaths at Peterloo, many of which were caused by sabre wounds. Framed by an unidentified narrator, the middle four verses are a direct appeal by the personification of the blood spilt on St Peter's field. The voice argues that revenge is justified because justice is on the side of those who combat oppression and corruption. It was published on the final page of the 16 October issue of the *Briton*.[26]

> Blood, unrevenged, stains the ground;[27]
> Its cries from heaven to earth resound;
> And he must have a heart of steel,
> Who does not hear the just appeal.
>
> Rise, Britons, rise a noble band,
> With justice arm'd go hand in hand;
> Convict the wretches of their guilt,
> Revenge the blood that's basely spilt.
>
> Your children, friends, your husbands, wives,
> Are sabred; some have lost their lives;
> To you they call; avenge their woes,
> As we've been served, so treat our foes.
>
> Determin'd, resolute and brave,
> Obtain your rights, or else the grave;
> With steady, unremitted zeal,
> Restore the sacred public weal.[28]
>
> With truth and justice be allied,
> When struggling for your nation's pride;
> Nor bend beneath oppression's sway,
> Altho' corruption stem thy way.
>
> Blood calls 'Revenge!' ye, Britons, hear;
> Stop murderers in their wild career;
> Or else, perhaps your doom may be,
> To live and die in infamy.

3 'Song to Liberty'[29]

Written under the pen-name 'Cleomenes',[30] this song was published on the final page of the *Briton* on 23 October 1819.[31] As with the previous poem, this song takes the form of an apostrophe. Its call to arms is undoubtedly revolutionary and it champions English radical nationalism in which Britons are called upon to fight tyranny for liberty.

> RECITATIVE[32]
> Rouse thee, Britannia![33] Shake the quiv'ring lance,
> And plume thyself in all thy martial pride;
> Thy gallant sons bid to the field advance, –
> To honour and to victory allied.

SONG

Britons,[34] to arms! The trumpet sounds,
'Tis the great call of liberty!
From Albion's[35] rocks the shout rebounds,
Its hills return it to the sky.
Britons, to arms! The cannons' roar
Shall blaze our noble deeds on high;
And echo, breaking on our shore,
Shall tell the glorious victory.

Britons, to arms! 'tis HAMPDEN[36] calls,
Fight for insulted liberty!
Before the tyrants, England falls
Again, unless your force is nigh
Britons, to arms! The cannons' roar,
Shall blaze your noble deeds on high;
And echo, far as fame can soar,
Shall tell the glorious victory!

4 'Patriotic Song'[37]

Published in *Medusa* on 4 December 1819, this song is to be sung to the tune of 'Hearts of Oak'.[38] Also known as 'Heart of Oak', the song was composed by Dr William Boyce with lyrics by the actor David Garrick. The song first appeared in Garrick's pantomime *Harlequin's Invasion* in 1759. It was intended to celebrate British military successes in Africa, Europe and North America during 1759, culminating in the capture of Quebec. The tune was appropriated by John Dickinson for 'The Liberty Song' published in Boston in 1768, which supported American liberation from Britain. The similarities between the opening verse and chorus of 'Patriotic Song' and 'Hearts of Oak' demonstrate that the radical song was closely modelled on the original, harnessing the motifs of freedom and slavery as a call to rebel against the tyranny of the British government and reclaim true British freedom. The jaunty anapaestic tetrameter of the original adds to the satirical tone of 'Patriotic Song', where the upbeat tempo is in stark contrast to the sentiment.

Come, cheer up, my lads, 'tis to glory we steer,
To add something more to the wonderful year;
To honour we call you, as freemen not slaves,
For who are so free as the sons of the waves?

Chorus:
Heart of oak are our ships, jolly tars are our men,
We always are ready; steady, boys, steady!
We'll fight and we'll conquer again and again.[39]

In the original song, 'heart of oak' refers to the British ships, although the oak tree has been a long-established trope of English steadfastness and endurance and is still used today as the emblem of the Conservative party. The tune of 'Hearts of Oaks' remains the official march of the British Royal Navy.[40] The opening verse and chorus of Garrick's song state:

> Come cheer up my lads, we will prove Britons still,
> And boldly advancing our duties fulfil;
> Resist every tyrant who dauntingly braves
> The voice of the people and bids them be slaves.
>
> CHORUS
> British hearts we have yet.
> Let us show we are Men!
> For Freedom we're ready;
> Steady boys, steady
> We claim all our rights and we'll have them again.
>
> No longer shall Liberty be but a name,
> The spark in our breasts shall burst forth in a flame;
> Whose fire overpow'ring, shall o'erthrow that race
> Whose deeds have fill'd England with shame and disgrace.
> British hearts, & c.
>
> No power can controul those that dare to be free,
> Success must attend, if united we be;
> Then join hand and heart, let us strain ev'ry nerve,
> We'll prove to our foes that we Freedom deserve.
> British hearts, & c.
>
> Arise! Let us break that confederate band,[41]
> Whose crimes have debas'd this once glorious land;
> Let us shew the vile crew Retribution is near, –
> See Justice already at them points her spear.[42]
> British hearts, & c.
>
> Her arm is outstretched, very soon shall the blow,
> Descending resistless lay Tyranny low,
> Then Britons again shall dear Freedom enjoy,
> And tyrants no more shall her blessings destroy
> British hearts, & c.

The selection of the tune for these two radical songs (see number 5 below) suggests its widespread familiarity, as well as a desire to subvert a song designed to celebrate British military success.

5 'A New Song'[43]

As with number 4 above, this song was also to be sung to the tune of 'Hearts of Oak'; it was published in the *Theological and Political Comet* on 13 November 1819.[44] This song anticipates a better future following the defeat of the 'demons' by Britons who have fought to reclaim 'your rights and your laws'.

> Rouse, rouse, loyal Britons, your fame to maintain
> Nor tamely submit to wear slavery's chain;
> Like Britons stand firm in humanity's cause,
> Asserting with spirit your rights and your laws,
>
> CHORUS
> Thus united and free,
> May we never agree;
> And man view each other
> As friend and as brother;
> And may Britons be happy, as happy can be!
>
> By justice supported, with rapturous eye,
> See the banners of liberty waving on high;[45]
> Her sons are all rallying round at her call,
> Resolv'd by her standard to stand or to fall.
> Thus united & c.
>
> To the traitors' perdition, whose merciless plan
> Is, by Tyranny's force to destroy Rights of Man,[46]
> Your freedom to shackle, your rights to invade,
> And, by state-craft and trick, make religion a trade.
> Thus united & c.
>
> Not long shall the demons o'er Briton have sway,
> Not long on her vitals these vultures shall prey;[47]
> United and firm all their efforts withstand,
> And Oppression and Anarchy[48] chase from our land.
> Thus united & c.
>
> While Nature, in plenty, her riches doth pour,
> And Providence kindly is blessing the store,
> With the feelings of Britons, how shall we endure
> To see Pride and Cruelty[49] starving the poor?
> Thus united & c.
>
> Old England, my country, may Heaven thee defend,
> On each patriot heart all thy blessings descend;
> Thy foes all confounded, they triumphs secur'd,

That the sun of thy glory be never obscur'd!
Thus united & c.

6 *A New Song. On Peterloo Meeting*

This broadside is one of the Manchester Central Library Collection of Ballads.[50] It is undated but the references to Henry Hunt and Sir Charles Wolseley demonstrate that it was written shortly after 16 August 1819. The use of 'Peterloo' in the title is an indication of how widely the term was used. The ballad narrates the events of 16 August and pays homage to Hunt's bravery. It was to be sung to the tune 'Parker's Widow'.[51]

RISE Britons, rise now from your slumber,[52]
Rise and hail the glorious day.
Come and be ranked with the number,
With true Friends of liberty,
Don't you see those heroes bleeding,
Lying in their crimson gore,
Briton's sons who died for freedom,
Alas who fell to rise no more.

CHORUS
Come my lads let's all be true,
And never, never for to rue,
Come join my lads and all be free,
With shouts of Hunt and Wolseley.[53]

It was on the 16th day of August,
That thousands met on Peterloo plain,[54]
Where we arrived of fear, regardless
Little we know their dreadful schemes
When, lo, we spied them near advancing,
With swords drawn on mischief bent,
Rushed through the crowds with horses prancing
It would make a heart of stone relent.

But matchless Hunt that valiant hero,
His name it shall recorded be,
[....] be my friends I will never leave you,
Thou death should be my destiny.
Straight to New Bailey,[55] then they brought him,
In a dungeon close confined,
Then to Lancaster[56] they did send him,
For conspiracy as I have been told.

Britannia's sons so famed for bravery,
Who fought so bold for freedom's cause,

Now your doom'd to cruel slavery,
Opprest by so many laws.
So Britain lets no longer greet them
But endeavour to be free,
And let the air resound and echo,
With shouts of Hunt and Wolseley.

7 'Song'

This song, to be sung to the tune 'Roncesvalles', was published in the *Republican* on 3 December 1819 under the authorship pf 'W.L.'[57] It was one of only two songs or poems published in the *Republican* that are of direct relevance to Peterloo. Roncesvalles, in northern Spain, was the location for two famous battles. The first, in 778, saw the defeat of Charlemagne's forces and the death of their commander, Roland. The second was in 1813 during the Peninsular War when the Anglo-Portuguese army was defeated by the French. One of the British commanders at the 1813 Battle at Roncesvalles was Field Marshal Sir John Byng, who was Commander of the Northern District of England in 1819.[58]

Literary references to Roncesvalles are numerous. *The Song of Roland* or *Chanson de Roland* is an eleventh-century epic poem and the oldest surviving French literary text. Felicia Hemans, whose brothers fought in the Peninsular War, wrote poems about both battles. 'The Battle of Roncesvalles' narrates the story of Roland's defeat, whilst 'England's Dead' deals with the 1813 battle:

> But let the storm rage on,
> Let the fresh wreaths be shed,
> For the Roncesvalles' field is won –,
> There slumber England's dead[59]

References can also be found in Byron's *Don Juan*, Scott's *Marmion* and *Don Quixote* by Cervantes. Although I have not been able to discover the tune 'Roncesvalles', the poem, 'The Admiral Guarino', written by Matthew Gregory Lewis in 1808 narrates Roland's defeat in the battle of 778 and has the same form as 'Song':

> Hark and heed me, deeds reciting
> Sad to hear and sad to tell
> How, at Roncesvalles fighting,
> Charles choicest warriors fell[60]

Matthew Lewis is best known for his Gothic novel, *The Monk*, which was first published to great success in 1796.

The combination of rhetorical question and imperative renders this a forceful and passionate poem intent on rousing the people to fight for freedom rather than a 'glorious doom'.

BRITONS, from this fatal slumber,
Rouse, your country succour craves!
Woes beset you without number,
Rouse! Nor crawl a race of slaves.

Hark! The voice of Freedom calls you,
For your dearest rights to stand!
Lest worse ills than these befall you,
Drive your tyrants from the land.

Will you yield to die with hunger?
Shall the dungeon hide each head?[61]
Shall the scoundrel Borough-monger[62]
Rob you of your hard-earn'd bread?

Once Colombia's mighty People[63]
Pined in fetters tight as we,
But, resolved base power to cripple,
Won the blessing, Liberty.

Let bold Cromwell's name inspire ye,
Emulate his glorious worth;[64]
Let these bright examples fire ye,
Drive your despots from the earth.

Let not the villain threats confound ye,
Fear not gaols nor gibbets dire;
Lo! Your infants starving round ye,
Vengeance deep their cried inspire.

Brave, in Freedom's cause to perish
Mean, of plagues or want at home;
Then the generous impulse cherish,
Freedom, or a glorious doom.

8 'The Watch Word of Britons'

Published in the *Medusa* on 25 September 1819, this song is to be sung to the tune of 'Rule Britannia'.[65] The lyrics for 'Rule, Britannia!' were written by the Scottish poet, James Thomson, and set to music by the composer, Thomas Arne, who was also responsible for the revival of another patriotic song, 'God Save the King'.[66] The song formed part of David Mallet's masque, *Alfred*, which was first performed on 1 August

1740 for Frederick, Prince of Wales at Cliveden, his summer retreat in Kent. The masque embodies a jingoistic Whig patriotism and seeks to compare the very German Prince of Wales with the very English King Alfred, who was also a figurehead for English radicals. The song achieved widespread popularity following its performance at the Drury Lane theatre in 1745 when the British army was engaged in the Jacobite Rebellion.[67] The song was quickly adopted by radicals and became a favourite with the Jacobites who wrote a parody with the chorus:

> Rise, Britannia! Britannia, rise and fight
> Restore your injured monarch's right.[68]

Murray Pittock notes that parodies were written as a way of reclaiming the song and were 'an attempt to recapture the Stuart image of Britannia from the clutches of the Hanoverian James Thomson's "Rule Britannia"'.[69] In the 1790s the tune made several appearances in Spence's *Pigs' Meat*. The songs 'The Progress of Liberty', 'A Song' and 'The Liberty of the Press' all state that they are to be sung to the tune of 'Rule, Britannia!'.[70] Epstein comments that many of the bands at Peterloo played 'Rule Britannia'.[71] Today the original 'Rule Britannia' is performed every year at the BBC's Last Night of the Proms amid much flag waving and general celebration of Britishness.

The choice of patriotic tunes for radical songs dates back to the mid-eighteenth century when 'Rule Britannia' and 'God Save the King' were written. They were selected by radical balladeers to intensify the satire of the lyrics. These radical songs subvert the jingoistic, imperial tenor of the original and convey ideals of liberty from oppression and tyranny. The song, with its message of death or liberty, promises a place in history and immortality for those prepared to fight.

> Arouse! Arouse! Ye freemen brave,
> And claim the rights your fathers held:
> Prepare, prepare, these rights to save
> Tyrants basely have withheld.
>
> CHORUS
> This is our Watch word, our watch word this shall be
> 'Or give us death or liberty'
> Too long beneath an abject yoke[72]
> We basely bowed nor dar'd complain;
> The magic charm the spell is broke
> And tyrants shall no longer reign.
> This is & c.

Can monarchs quench their rising flame
Which grows in ev'ry patriot's breast?
Shall freedom still be but a name,
Untamely we be still oppressed?
This is & c.

Are the bloodhounds[73] in the shape of men
Allow'd to slay a harmless race?
Shall they imbrue[74] their hands again,
And we permit the foul disgrace?
This is & c.

Oh Freedom be thou still our guide,
Still ev'ry heart be fixed on thee;
For gods behold with joy and pride,
A nation struggling to be free!
This is & c.

The man who nobly joins thy band,
And fearless dare thy foes engage,
Immortalised his name shall stand
Enroll'd in hist'ry's brightest page!
This is & c.

9 'Address to Britons'

This anonymous poem was published in *Medusa* on 20 November 1819 and placed immediately following a letter to Sir John Bailey, a judge of the Court of King's Bench, from Henry Hunt. In the letter, Hunt claims that the law is now for sale in Britain, thereby denying the poor access to justice. Hunt cites the Magna Carta in support of his argument, 'We will not SELL justice'.[75] The criticisms of the state expressed in the poem below as corrupt and guilty of misrule resonate more strongly on reading Hunt's letter.

Ye Sons of Albion, rise united
Disdain to live in Slavery;
No longer let your prayers be slighted
But shew the world you dare be free.
Too long has Britain felt, bewailing,
The woes inflicted by misrule:
Then never let your ardour cool
While wretches are your rights assailing.
To – to –.[76]

Behold Corruption fain would banish
The freedom your forefathers gam'd,

And bid their hopes delusive vanish,
Their vile attempts must be restrain'd.
Shall Britons tamely wait their ruin,
And bending at some tyrant's nod,
Like cowards basely kiss the rod,
The instrument of then undoing?
To – to – .

Shall licens'd murders[77] be committed
By tyranny's obsequious tools,
And shall such murd'rers be permitted
To taunt you as insensate fools!
Arise! Display a British[78] spirit,
Let ev'ry energy appear;
Shew Freedom still to you is dear,
By 'warding[79] them the doom they merit.
To – to –.

10 'The Manchester Massacre, or Adieu to Slavery'

This song was to be sung to the tune 'Scots wha hae wi' Wallace bled', the lyrics to which were written in 1793 by Robert Burns and take the form of a speech given by Robert the Bruce to his troops on the eve of the Battle of Bannockburn in 1314 when the Scots defeated the English. Burns used a traditional Scottish tune, 'Hey Tuttie Tatie', which, it was widely believed, was played by Bruce's army at Bannockburn. As Pittock demonstrates, Burns' 'Scots wha hae' can be interpreted as a criticism of the contemporaneous oppressors of the Scots – the Hanoverians – as well as the historical oppression of the Plantagenets.[80] The sentiment behind the song can be seen as both Jacobite and Jacobin as it calls on the people:

Lay the proud Usurpers low!
Tyrants fall in every foe!
Liberty's in every blow!
Let us do or die!!! (ll. 21–4)

Perhaps surprisingly, the song was published under its original title 'Bruce's Address to his Troops, at the Battle of Bannockburn' in the *Morning Chronicle* on 8 May 1794. It was anonymous but the accompanying note states: 'If the following warm and animating ode was not written near the time to which it applies, it is one of the most faithful imitations of the simple and beautiful lyric of the Scottish Bards we ever read, and we know but one living Poet to whom to ascribe it'.[81]

'Scots Wha Hae' is the stated tune for 'A Song' by Allen Davenport published in *Medusa* on 5 June 1819. It begins:

> Britons rise, the time is come,
> To strike the opposition dumb,
> For though we are opposed by some,
> Our wish is to be free[82]

As with 'The Manchester Massacre', this poem unites the tune with the exhortatory ballad. 'Scots Wha Hae' remains the anthem of the Scottish Nationalist Party and is sung each year at the close of its national conference.

'The Manchester Massacre' was published c. 1820 in *The Radical Reformers' New Song Book: Being a Choice Collection of Patriotic Songs*, a chapbook published by John Marshall, a Newcastle radical and printer. Its precise publication date is not known.[83]

> England, roused as from a sleep,
> Finds abundant cause to weep,
> Sees her Sons in blood lie deep,
>   With horror and dismay.
> Her Daughters too, do not go free,
> But in the common blood-shed see,
> Children share the same mercy,
>   From the Cavalry.
>
> Can Britons see this awful sight,
> And not cry out, We'll boldly fight,
> So long as blood doth give us might,
>   To gain our Liberty.
> See yon Scots! How dear the name,
> Who with Wallace[84] nobly came,
> To fight for Freedom was their aim;
>   Behold your Pattern.
>
> Britons' rights you must maintain,
> Let freedom be your only aim,
> Now throw off your heavy chain;
>   Adieu to Slavery.
> To see Sir Francis,[85] or the Star,
> To join your force he will prefer,
> Then let your actions now declare
>   You worthy of your head.

Notes

1 P.B. Shelley, *The Poems of Shelley*, ed. Jack Donovan, Cian Duffy, Kelvin Everest and Michael Rossington (London: Longman, 2011), vol. 3, p. 63, ll. 372–6.
2 See Appendix for the full poem.
3 https://www.marxists.org/history/ussr/sounds/lyrics/international.htm [accessed 19 November 2017].
4 See the Introduction for information on broadsides, pp. 27–9.
5 Thompson notes that 'in the months of October and November Radical constitutionalism itself took a revolutionary turn' (E.P. Thompson, *The Making of the English Working Class* (Middlesex: Penguin, 1980), p. 759).
6 J. Milton, *The Complete Poems*, ed. J. Leonard (London: Penguin, 2008), p. 129.
7 *Republican*, 1:5 (1819), p. 78.
8 T. Wright (ed.), *Songs and Ballads* (London, 1860), pp. 168–9.
9 Number 9 below.
10 M. Parker, 'A New Ballad', *Political Ballads: Early English Poetry, Ballads and Popular Literature of the Middle Ages*, ed. T. Wright (London: Richards, 1861), vol. 3, p. 13.
11 *Ibid.*, p. 25.
12 R. Palmer (ed.), *A Ballad History of England from 1588 to the Present Day* (London: Batsford, 1979), p. 23.
13 Number 4 below.
14 Dagger.
15 C. Mackay (ed.), *Jacobite Songs and Ballads of Scotland from 1688 to 1746* (London: Griffin, 1861), pp. 306–7.
16 R. Lee, 'The Triumph of Truth and Liberty', *Pigs' Meat* (1794), pp. 176–7.
17 P. Keen (ed.), *The Popular Radical Press in Britain 1817–21*. 6 vols. (London: Pickering and Chatto, 2003), vol. 5, p. 95.
18 'The charter' refers to Magna Carta, one of the main constitutional documents in British history. It was signed in 1215 by King John under pressure from his barons to limit the powers of the king. Along with the Bill of Rights (1689), Magna Carta was regarded as one of the cornerstones of English liberty by radicals.
19 *Black Dwarf*, 3:10 (1819), p. 153.
20 Keen, *The Popular Radical Press in Britain*, vol. 6, p. 253.
21 A. Janowitz, *Lyric and Labour in the Romantic Tradition* (Cambridge: Cambridge University Press, 1998), pp. 27, 33.
22 *Manchester Observer* (2 October 1819), p. 734. It was not uncommon for radical weeklies to reprint poems from other newspapers or periodicals. A number of the poems in this anthology first appeared in the *Manchester Observer*. It may have been that the London-based weeklies wished to disseminate poems from the Manchester press to a wider readership.
23 Keen, *The Popular Radical Press in Britain*, vol. 4, pp. 88–92.

24 Ragley Hall in Warwickshire was home to the Marquis of Hertford, whose wife Isabella was the Prince Regent's mistress from 1807 until 1819. Their relationship was satirised by George Cruikshank, most notably in *An Excursion to Ragley Hall* printed in 1812, in which the devil is depicted driving the Prince Regent and the Marchioness to Hertford's country home. Her horned husband is riding the donkey at the front. The Marchioness was believed to have been instrumental in changing the Regent's political allegiance from the Whigs to the Tories (J. Wardroper, *The Caricatures of George Cruikshank* (London: Gordon Fraser, 1977), pp. 37–8, 51, 90). The reference to Ragley in the song implies a threat to the Regent, suggesting the massed ranks of the people will hunt him down unless he stands up for justice.

Griffin's letter to the Regent, mentioned above, also refers to Ragley Hall: 'Ragley Park is not a place for dallying away useful time, while ferocious ruffians, after butchering some hundreds of English people, are perverting law and justice, to endeavour to screen themselves from the punishment due to their villainy' (Keen, *The Popular Radical Press in Britain*, vol. 4, p. 91). Griffin is clearly accusing the Regent of neglecting his duties in favour of pleasure.

25 Many hundreds of regular soldiers were employed at Peterloo under the command of Lieutenant-Colonel George L'Estrange. These included the 15th Hussars, infantry from the 31st and 88th regiments and a detachment of the Royal Horse Artillery. The poet is implying that hired soldiers cannot be trusted to be loyal to the king.

26 *The Briton*, 1:4 (1819), p. 32.

27 The poignant image of the blood-soaked land is present in many Peterloo poems, as well as other war poems where it serves as a memorial to the dead and injured. One of the most powerful uses of this image is by Lord Byron in the second Canto of *Childe Harold*, where he describes the dead bodies on the battlefield at Talavera in Spain, site of one of the fiercest battles of the Napoleonic Wars (G. Byron, *Lord Byron: The Major Works*, ed. J. McGann (Oxford: Oxford University Press, 1986), p. 80, ll. 900–8):

> Let their bleached bones, and blood's unbleaching stain,
> Long mark the battle-field with hideous awe:
> Thus only may our sons conceive the scenes we saw!

28 The welfare of a country and especially its people. It can also be used as a synonym for 'commonwealth', and, given the links between radical poetry in the years following the Napoleonic Wars and poetry of the English Revolution, this meaning may be more applicable to the poem above (*OED*).

29 Keen, *The Popular Radical Press in Britain*, vol. 4, p. 336.

30 Cleomenes was the king of Sparta for approximately thirty years prior to his death in 491 BC. He waged almost continual war in the region to strengthen Sparta's power. The name of the poet using this pseudonym is not known, although the choice of a gifted military leader complements the rabble-rousing tone of the poem.

31 It is common practice for poems in the radical weeklies to be placed on the final page of the issue. Their sense of collectivity appears an apt conclusion to the preceding articles and letters.

32 'A style of musical declamation intermediate between singing and ordinary speech, used especially in the dialogue and narrative parts of an opera or oratorio' (*OED*).

33 Britannia has been the symbol for Great Britain since Roman times, appearing on coinage from the first century AD until 2008. During the eighteenth century she became closely associated with Liberty and a Whiggish patriotism (as demonstrated by 'Rule, Britannia!') and was depicted in Roman battle dress carrying a shield. By the end of the eighteenth century, however, Britannia was often portrayed in caricatures as being in distress or under attack, and Britain was more commonly symbolised by the ruddy-faced yeoman, John Bull (T. Hunt, *Defining John Bull: Political Caricature and National Identity in Late Georgian England* (Hampshire: Ashgate, 2003), pp. 121–3). George Cruikshank's 1819 caricature *Death or Liberty* depicts a skeletal man wearing a cloak with the words 'radical reform' upon it attempting to rape Britannia. Many radical poets adopted Britannia and portrayed her, as in the poem above, as a strong, warrior-like woman.

34 Many radical poems use the term 'Britons' to refer to the English. As with Albion (see below), the ancient association of the word alludes to the ancient rights and customs of England and its inhabitants.

35 Albion is the oldest name for the island of Great Britain and is often used in literature to represent England or Britain, most notably in William Blake's 1793 poem, *Visions of the Daughters of Albion*. The use of Albion rather than England in many radical poems is often used as part of the radical ideology in which Anglo-Saxon England is regarded as the golden age of freedom.

36 John Hampden (1595–1643) was one of the leaders of the Parliamentarians during the English Revolution and a cousin of Thomas Cromwell. For more information, see pp. 69–70.

37 Patriotism was a contested concept in the late eighteenth and early nineteenth centuries. Radicals used the term to underpin their belief that a true Englishman defended his ancient rights and liberties against the foreign monarchy and Francophile aristocracy. Many of the radical associations at the time of Peterloo included the word 'patriotic' in their titles, such as the Manchester Patriotic Union Society, whose leader Joseph Johnson invited Henry Hunt to speak at St Peter's Field on 16 August 1819 (D. Read, *Peterloo: The Massacre and its Background* (Manchester: Manchester University Press, 1958), pp. 35–6).

38 *Medusa*, 1:42 (1819), p. 234. The song was also published in 1833 in a chapbook entitled *Harp of Liberty*, part of a collection of ephemera on Peterloo in the Working-Class Movement Library in Salford (AG-Songs).

39 C.M. Simpson, *The British Broadside Ballad and its Music* (New Jersey: Rutgers University Press, 1966), pp. 299–301).

40 http://anthem4england.co.uk/anthems/heart-of-oak/ [accessed 19 November 2017].
41 State authorities which could include government, justice system and monarchy; 'confederate' is used in the pejorative sense of 'one leagued with another or others for an unlawful or evil purpose; an accomplice' (*OED*).
42 Lady Justice dates back to Ancient Egypt and is typically portrayed as blindfolded and carrying a sword in one hand and a set of balances in the other to indicate the impartiality, power and fairness of justice respectively. Luca Giordano's *Justice*, dating to the 1680s, is a prime example of the depiction of Justice in art. Probably the most famous statue of Justice is that outside the Old Bailey in London.
43 'A New Song' is a common title in vernacular poetry and is often accompanied by the name of the tune, thereby enabling a reader, or listener, to quickly engage with the song. The generic title is also an indication of the topicality of the song and speed with which it has been written.
44 Keen, *The Popular Radical Press in Britain*, vol. 6, pp. 137–8.
45 There were many banners at St Peter's Field and they were targeted by the MYC as trophies which they publicly burnt. Banners carried slogans such as 'Universal Suffrage', 'No Taxation Without Representation' and 'Liberty or Death'. Royston Female Union had a banner declaring: 'Let us die like men and not be sold like slaves', an exact copy of the strap-line of the *Medusa* (J.A. Epstein, *Radical Expression: Political Language, Ritual, and Symbol in England, 1790–1850* (Oxford: Oxford University Press, 1994), pp. 65–6). One of the original Peterloo banners is housed at the Rochdale Arts and Heritage Service (see Figure 5).
46 The capitalisation of 'Rights of Man' may allude to Thomas Paine's radical treatise published in 1791 and 1792, or may be a more generic reference to the destruction of men's rights by the Tory government.
47 This is a possible reference to the Greek myth in which Prometheus was punished for stealing fire from the gods in order to help man. Zeus sentenced him to eternal damnation by being tied to a rock and having his entrails eaten every day by an eagle. Prometheus came to symbolise the striving of man for a better life, notably in Shelley's lyrical drama *Prometheus Unbound*, which was published in 1820.
48 Anarchy is used here to mean disorder and chaos. The poem maintains that both too much government and too little are undesirable.
49 Personification is used extensively in the song and contributes to its visual aspect. This personification of abstract nouns may have been a way to avoid using specific names, creating a sense of universality rather than directly relating the song to Peterloo.
50 Manchester Central Library, *Collection of Ballads*, vol. 2, no. 169.
51 According to Palmer, 'Parker's Widow' was written as a lament for Richard Parker who was executed in 1797 for his part in the naval mutiny at the Nore (R. Palmer, *A Touch of the Times* (Middlesex: Penguin, 1974), p. 298). Palmer includes a ballad entitled 'The Death of Parker' in *Ballad History*, in

which Parker's widow laments the death of her husband (p. 82). Following the failed mutiny, Parker was arrested, court-martialled and hanged from the yardarm on his ship, HMS Sandwich. His wife, Anne McHardy Parker, worked tirelessly to get her husband pardoned, including petitioning the queen. After Parker's execution, Anne and several other women exhumed his body and succeeded in obtaining a Christian burial at St. Mary Matfelon Church in Whitechapel (J. Dugan, *The Great Mutiny* (London: Andre Deutsch, 1965), pp. 364–9).

52 Shelley's refrain from *The Masque of Anarchy* bears a striking resemblance to the ballad's opening line: 'Rise like lions after slumber'.

53 See the Introduction for information on Henry Hunt. Sir Charles Wolseley (1769–1846) was a leader of the reform movement and founder, along with Major Cartwright, of the Hampden Clubs. He helped the victims of Peterloo and their families and attended some of the trials. Following a speech he gave at Stockport in June 1819 in which he advocated universal suffrage and annual parliaments, he was convicted of treason and sedition in 1820 and sentenced to eighteen months' imprisonment (*DNB*, R.J. White, *Waterloo to Peterloo* (London: Heinemann, 1957), p. 180).

54 Several poems on Peterloo use the term 'plain' to describe St Peter's Field, notably in the alliterative phrases 'Peterloo plain' or 'the Plain of Peterloo', thereby using the archaic definition of 'plain' as denoting 'the field of battle' (*OED*). Its use suggests it was a well-used phrase, indicating that Peterloo was the people's Waterloo.

55 Henry Hunt was arrested at St Peter's Field along with others, including journalists Joseph Johnson and John Sexton. They were confined in the New Bailey Prison in Salford on a charge of 'assembling with unlawful banners at an unlawful meeting for the purpose of inciting discontent' (Read, *Peterloo*, p. 139).

56 Hunt was moved to Lancaster Gaol on 27 August. He was tried at York in 1820, found guilty of seditious conspiracy and sentenced to two-and-a-half years' imprisonment. He was incarcerated in Ilchester Gaol where he wrote *Memoirs of Henry Hunt, Esq., Written by himself in his Majesty's Jail at Ilchester.*

57 *Republican*, 1:15 (1819), p. 228.

58 Byng was not present at Peterloo, as the magistrates told him that he was not needed (Read, *Peterloo*, p. 101).

59 J. Harland (ed.), *Lancashire Lyrics: Modern Songs and Ballads of the County Palatine* (London: 1866), p. 293, ll. 37–40).

60 S. Moore (ed.), *The Pictorial Balladist: A Collection of Ballads of Various Ages and Countries etc* (London:1860), p. 813, ll. 1–4.

61 A reference to the imprisonment of nine men and two women arrested at or shortly after Peterloo.

62 One who trades in parliamentary seats for boroughs.

63 In 1819 Gran Colombia became an independent state, liberated from Spanish rule by the Venezuelan political activist, Símon Bolívar.

64 Cromwell is an ambivalent character for radicals. It is evident in this song that the author admires him as one who drove away tyranny. *The White Hat* in Chapter 2 directly compares Cromwell and Hunt, suggesting that regicide should be championed in 1819 as it was in the 1640s. However, Nora Crook notes that radicals, including Godwin who began writing a biography of Cromwell in 1818, generally regarded Charles as a traitor and Cromwell as a tyrant (N. Crook, 'Shelley's Late Fragmentary Plays: "Charles the First" and the "Unfinished Drama"', in A. Weinberg and T. Webb (eds), *The Unfamiliar Shelley* (Hampshire: Ashgate, 2009), p. 300). It is more common for radical poems and songs of this period to celebrate the Republican martyrs Hampden and Sidney, as demonstrated in number 5 in Chapter 2.
65 *Medusa*, 1:32 (1819), p. 252.
66 See Chapter 6, number 2.
67 P. Scholes, *The Oxford Companion to Music* (Oxford: Oxford University Press, 1970), pp. 897–8.
68 W. Chappell, *The Ballad Literature and Popular Music of the Olden Time* (New York: Dover Publications, 1965), pp. 686–9.
69 M. Pittock, *Poetry and Jacobite Politics in Eighteenth-Century Britain and Ireland* (Cambridge: Cambridge University Press, 1994), p. 83.
70 T. Spence, *Pigs' Meat* (1793), vol. 1, pp. 280–1; (1794) vol. 2, pp. 67, 151–2.
71 J. Epstein, *Radical Expression*, p. 83.
72 The Norman Yoke refers to the colonisation of England by the Normans in the eleventh century and the subsequent erosion of ancient rights. For more information, see pp. 67–8.
73 The bloodhound motif features in several of the Peterloo poems and is used to symbolise either the Yeomanry, as in this poem, politicians or the Manchester magistrates. The first article to mention Peterloo in the 28 August issue of the *Theological and Political Comet* is entitled 'To the Manchester Bloodhounds'. It condemns the 'villainous' actions of the authorities before concluding 'I have yet much more to say to your bloodhoundships; but, at present, no more than that, I am ONE only of your *many* and *reasonable* despisers' (Keen, *The Popular Radical Press*, vol. 6, pp. 47–9). The motif dehumanises the Manchester authorities who unfeelingly hunted down the people at Peterloo like prey.

In *The Political Showman at Home*, published in 1820 by William Hone and illustrated by George Cruikshank, the bloodhound is described thus: 'It hunts down those who endeavour to regain their Liberty [...] it has an exquisite smell for blood'. The accompanying illustration depicts a dog devouring a woman, surrounded by human bones and with a figure swinging from a gallows in the background (n. pag). Hone and Cruikshank symbolise tyranny in the bloodhound with references to its existence in Spain and Ireland, broadening its relevance from England, although the savaging of a woman has clear connotations with Peterloo.
74 To stain, especially with blood.

75 Keen, *The Popular Radical Press*, vol. 5, p. 326.
76 It is unclear from the poem what words have been omitted in the final line of each verse.
77 The murders at Peterloo are 'licensed' because they were authorised by the state.
78 Unusually for a radical poem of this era, the word 'British' rather than 'English' is used. The rhyming in each verse is different (although the rhyme scheme is the same) again giving no indication of the missing words.
79 This is a contraction of 'awarding', done in order for the line to scan.
80 M. Pittock, *Poetry and Jacobite Politics*, pp. 218–19.
81 R. Burns, 'Bruce's Address to His Troops, at the Battle of Bannockburn', the *Morning Chronicle*, 7670 (1794), p. 3.
82 Keen, *The Popular Radical Press*, vol. 5, pp. 135–6.
83 Palmer dates the chapbook to c. 1820 (*Song*, pp. 260, 331). I received a copy of the song from Brian Maidment.
84 Sir William Wallace was one of the leaders of the Scottish Wars of Independence, defeating the English at the Battle of Sterling Bridge in 1297 before being defeated at the Battle of Falkirk the following year. He was later arrested, tried and executed for high treason. He is widely regarded as a Scottish patriot and hero. He features in other radical poems, such as 'To Britons', written by Caledonius, 'the muse of Scotia', and published in the *Black Dwarf* on 10 March, 1819:

> Awake from your slumbers, ye true sons of freedom!
> Awake all the Patriots, ye bards of the lyre!
> Ye spirits of Washington, Wallace and Hampden,
> Shed wide o'er their bosoms your generous fire! (p. 153)

Here Wallace is linked with John Hampden and George Washington, other republican heroes, thereby uniting the English, Scottish and American causes. According to John Tyas' report in *The Times*, one of the banners at Peterloo 'was inscribed [with] the motto of Sir William Wallace, "God armeth the Patriot"' (19 August 1819, p. 2). Both the tune and the lyrics of 'The Manchester Massacre' equate the Scots' fight for freedom from the English with the English people's fight with their oppressors.
85 Sir Francis Burdett, independent MP for Westminster. For more information, see pp. 4 and 12.

2

'Ye English warriors': radical nationalism and the true patriot

Radicalism and nationalism would appear to be unlikely bedfellows, given that they tend to be placed on opposite ends of the political spectrum; yet this chapter demonstrates how many of the radical poems and songs written after Peterloo are underpinned by a radical English nationalism, with poets making a clear distinction between the un-English characteristics of a tyrannical state and monarchy and the true English patriot fighting for lost freedoms. Although the ideology of nationalism emerged in the revolutionary fervour of the late eighteenth century, this chapter establishes the nature of English radical nationalism and how the championing of English national identity has resonances with the republicanism of the seventeenth century, the heroes and martyrs of which were a regular presence in the radical press.

The nineteenth century witnessed the expansion and global success of the British Empire. Despite the loss of the American colonies in 1783, Great Britain's victory in the Napoleonic Wars demonstrated to the world the might of the Royal Navy, instrumental in fulfilling Britain's imperial ambitions. As a nation, in 1819, Great Britain was little more than a century old, created by The Act of Union with Scotland in 1707. The later Act of Union with Ireland in 1800 established the United Kingdom of Great Britain and Ireland. Despite the dominance of England in the United Kingdom, geographically, economically and politically, Englishness was under threat. As Benedict Anderson observes, within the naming of the union is an obscuring of nationality; England, together with Scotland and Wales, was subsumed into the new imperial Great Britain.[1] For postcolonial scholars, such as Edward Said, it is imperialism that begets nationalism, manifested through the creation of Self and Other, particularly for colonised peoples who need to create a sense of Self in the face of the imperial aggressor.[2] This argument necessarily leads to the questioning of England's role within the British Empire. Katie Trumpener notes that Englishness was underdeveloped due to the centrality of England to the Empire, as it was concerned with other cultures rather than its own.[3] It could also be argued that this underdevelopment of Englishness was due to the erosion of English national identity within Great Britain, consequently resulting in the creation of a radical nationalism as observed by Said in the experiences of colonised peoples as a way of asserting identity. Throughout history, the Welsh, Scots and Irish have striven to preserve their cultures and display their national identity; however, the English remain uneasy, unsure of where Britishness ends and Englishness begins, with many struggling to find an English identity beyond the culturally loaded flag of St George appropriated by football fans and the far right.

'Nationalism' is a complex term, weighed down by the negative associations with war and fascism which dominated so much of the political landscape in the twentieth century; however, in the hands and minds of radicals, nationalism was and continues to be a way of asserting an identity threatened by the enemy within: the state. The first recorded usage of 'Nationalism' in Britain was 1774 and is defined as the 'advocacy of or support for the interest of one's own nation, especially to the exclusion or detriment of the interest of other nations [...] Whereas *patriotism* usually refers to a general sentiment, *nationalism* now usually refers to a specific ideology.'[4] As a replacement for the long-established patriotism or 'love of or devotion to one's country', nationalism, through the use of the term 'ideology' can be interpreted as the politicisation of patriotic sentiment.

Eric Hobsbawm locates the impetus for nationalism as rooted very firmly in the late eighteenth century, due primarily to the French Revolution: 'France provided the first great example, the concept and vocabulary of nationalism'.[5] This view is echoed by Anderson who includes the American Revolution as another model for nationhood, the rhetoric of which, due to the advances made in printing, could be widely disseminated and read.[6] The French and American Revolutions rejected the national identity imposed on a people by a monarchy and instead gave sovereignty to the people. The eradication of the ruling elite in both nations provided the people with a *carte blanche* to create their own national identity forged through the struggle for liberty.

For Said, central to national identity is narration, with the state, whether real or imagined, being reaffirmed through stories as 'the method colonised people use to assert their own identity and the existence of their own history.'[7] In parallel with this view, Gerald Newman regards culture as significant and notes that it is mainly through culture that a nation defines itself, a view shared by Trumpener, who states that it is the changes wrought upon the land and the consequent direct threat to cultural memory and tradition that provide a catalyst for nationalism.[8] Indeed the rise of the antiquarian movement across Europe in the eighteenth century fed this need to protect cultural memory through the collecting and publication of stories of historic deeds and national heroes.[9] The role of imagination and narration within English nationalism is central. The twin pillars of radical English nationalism throughout the centuries are the tropes of the Norman Yoke and the Anglo-Saxon Constitution. Whilst the Norman Conquest undoubtedly occurred, the lauded liberties and constitution of the Anglo-Saxon nation it colonised became mythologised over the centuries.[10]

Christopher Hill locates the origins of the trope of the Norman Yoke in a thirteenth-century text, *The Mirror of Justices*, probably written by Andrew Horn, a fishmonger and later Chamberlain of the City of London. Re-published in Latin in 1642 and in English in 1646, Hill claims this text was the catalyst for the adoption of the Norman Yoke by dissenting radicals such as the Levellers and Diggers opposed to both King and Cromwell.[11] According to Timothy Morton and Nigel Smith, the origins of English nationalism can be traced back to these dissenting radicals of the English Revolution.[12]

The concept of the Norman Yoke is that the Norman Conquest resulted in the demise of Anglo-Saxon liberty established in the six centuries prior to the Battle of Hastings. Under Anglo-Saxon law, or the mythical constitution, all men were free and equal, ruling themselves through democratic institutions. Crimes were dealt with through trial by jury comprising twelve of the defendant's male neighbours. The tyrannical foreign monarchy and aristocracy imposed by the Normans still had its legacy in the seventeenth century and must be opposed in order to re-establish the ancient rights of the English people.[13] As Hill observes, the theory of the Norman Yoke bears little resemblance to fact but 'as a rudimentary class theory of politics, the myth had great historical significance' and had probably existed as part of the oral tradition since 1066.[14]

The utilisation of the trope of the Norman Yoke is evident in the writings of Gerrard Winstanley, leader of the Diggers, a small radical group intent on the reclamation and distribution of the land during Cromwell's Commonwealth. *A Digger Declaration* in 1649 regarding their cultivation of the wasteland at St George's Hill states:

> Seeing the common people of England by joynt consent of person and purse have caste out Charles our Norman oppressour, wee have by this victory recovered ourselves from under this Norman yoake and the land is now to returne into the joint hands of ... the commonours.[15]

The association of Charles I with Norman oppression demonstrates how the trope of the Norman Yoke was used by the Diggers to forge a strong sense of national identity through their portrayal of the monarchy as an alien imposition upon the English people.

Thomas Spence shared the views of the Diggers and the republican James Harrington on the colonisation of the English and unlawful seizure of land.[16] Spence's poem, 'The Downfall of Feudal Tyranny', begins:

> That conquering blade, who did us invade,
> Ev'n William the Norman by name,
> Among his proud band, he divided our land,
> Nought leaving but slav'ry and shame.[17]

Janowitz notes 'though in places Spence relies on the narrative of the Norman Yoke, with its shadowy and magical ideal of an original Anglo-Saxon constitution, he reasons together issues of natural right and custom'.[18] Here Spence provides a bridge between the traditional radicals such as Major John Cartwright with his firm belief in the Anglo-Saxon Constitution and Paine, who denied its existence.[19] Echoing Janowitz's observations, Epstein states: 'The appeal of the Anglo-Saxon Constitution, while historical in form, was often a simultaneous appeal to some notion of natural law – the assumption being that the lost liberties of Anglo-Saxon England had embodied notions of original right'.[20] This view is aptly illustrated by the 'Reformer's Song of Liberty':[21]

> Our ancient rights we ask, and ask no more,
> Our birthrights which the tyrants now withhold;

The utilisation of a historical precedent, combined with the theory of natural rights, strengthened the radical movement, providing it with gravitas and authority.

Whereas the Diggers advocated a radical English nationalism based on natural rights and the redistribution of land, it was the dissenting Levellers and their leader, John Lilburne, who were more widely known during the Romantic era. Fear of levelling beliefs in the 1790s was acute; the Association for the Preservation of Property Against Republicans and Levellers was established at this time and is suggestive of a widespread understanding of such ideology, with the term 'Leveller' having such negative connotations that even radicals appear to have avoided specific reference to this discourse.[22] According to Edward Vallance, radical writers of the 1790s, such as Catherine Macaulay, William Godwin and Mary Wollstonecraft 'preferred to applaud ... men like John Hampden, Henry Vane and Algernon Sidney, rather than the Levellers'.[23]

In her *History of England*, of the year 1642, Macaulay writes:

> The genius of the nation, which had been long improving by a taste for Freedom, now exempt from the fetters of tyranny, was risen to a very exalted height, and ranged itself on the side of its parent Liberty. It was from the elocution of Pym, the unbounded knowledge and persuasive talents of Hampden, the profound sagacity of young Vane, &c. that it owed its greatest success.[24]

This may explain the lack of reference to Lilburne in the Peterloo poems and the inclusion of John Hampden, who is mentioned in six poems in this collection.[25] In fact, two John Hampdens are referenced, both of whom are republican heroes: the elder John Hampden (1595–1643) was one of the leaders of the Parliamentarians during the English Revolution and a cousin of Thomas Cromwell.[26] Disillusioned with the arbitrary monarchy of the Stuarts and fearful of a 'popish plot', he opposed the imposition of Ship Money in 1636 and was later instrumental in drafting the Grand Remonstrance, a list of over 200 grievances against Charles I.[27] In November 1641, it was passed by the House of Commons but, after several weeks' delay, rejected by the king. It is one of the key events leading to the English Revolution. Hampden died in the Battle of Chalgrove Field in 1643 and later became a favourite figure amongst eighteenth- and early nineteenth-century English radicals. His grandson, John Hampden (1653–96), was a Whig MP and shared his grandfather's distrust of the Stuarts and, in particular the Catholic James, heir to Charles II. Hampden supported the rival claim to the throne of Charles' illegitimate son, Lord Monmouth, and, along with Algernon Sidney (1623–83) and William Russell (1639–83) plotted to ambush Charles and James on their way to London from the races at Newmarket. The plan was foiled and the three of them arrested. Although Hampden was pardoned, Russell and Sidney were executed in 1683 and subsequently became republican martyrs. The fame of the Hampdens among radicals continued into the nineteenth century, partly through Major Cartwright's eponymous Hampden Clubs established in 1812.

These republican martyrs feature regularly in radical poems. The Spencean Robert Wedderburn, a self-styled preacher and Jamaican-born son of a black slave and a Scottish plantation owner, had long believed that the 'liberation of West Indian slaves and English working people were inseparable causes.'[28] Testament to the radical belief that nationalism was concerned with ideals rather than race, Ian McCalman notes Wedderburn's use of English Revolution references within his writings.²⁹ In his poem, 'An Englishman's Domestic View of his Political Situation, Addressed to the Partner of his Bosom', published in *The People* in 1817, Wedderburn laments the loss of English land and rights:

> Deep is the grave where traitors fall;
> High is the block prepar'd –
> O! Hampden – Russell – Sydney – all!
> Your manes shall be heard.³⁰

Similarly, a broadside ballad of the same period entitled *Anticipation; or, Albion's Republic* evokes the names of the martyrs in an imagined English republic where tyrants have been banished:

> With Hampden and Sidney – those heroes repose,
> Who died in the cause – and to joy turn'd the woes
> Of Albion's Republic, the Isle of the brave.³¹

In both poems, Hampden, Sidney and Russell are lauded for endeavouring to save England from tyranny and, as such, are portrayed as patriots, inspiring subsequent generations to fight for liberty:

> In patriot bands we'll join with bravery,
> Break the chains of tyrants' knavery,
> Let our cry be – Down with slavery –
>   Liberty or death!³²

The role of the patriot within radical poetry is explored by Janowitz: 'In the earlier radical and reform poems, the image of the patriot is narrated as a figure of identity within an historical community saturated with popular power.'³³ Within English communities, Janowitz maintains, the patriot uses the language of the Norman yoke and Anglo-Saxon liberty to support radical sentiment, as well as deriving identity from what his (or her) country once was and should be again, even taking on the role of the revolutionary.³⁴ This figure of the patriot is exemplified in 'The Voice of Britannia', where the symbol of nation is employed to condemn the actions of her people:

> Can those, I pray, be true-born sons of mine,
> Who hurl their darts at Freedom's sacred shrine?
> No, no! They are my most mischievous foes,
> Who strive, O Freedom, to depress thy cause;³⁵

Repeatedly, these poems and songs present the actions of the Manchester and Salford Yeomanry Cavalry, magistrates, politicians and churchmen as tyrannical and, through the establishment of an ancient English identity, unpatriotic. As Scrivener aptly notes:

The myth of the Norman Yoke was appealing because it discovered in Saxon history a precedent for democratic innovation, so that reform would not be innovation at all but restoration. Moreover, the monarchic and aristocratic domination of government could be ascribed to a foreign usurpation, un-English.[36]

Through the discourse of Anglo-Saxon rights and republican ideology, these radical poets strive to turn the stalwarts of the British establishment into the feared and hated Other on which nationalism depends.

1 'Britons Who Have Often Bled'

This is one of only two poems relating to Peterloo to be published in the *Republican*,[37] despite the fact that Carlile witnessed the massacre and wrote about it extensively in prose.[38] It is not known whether Carlile authored the poem, although the rhetoric is very much in keeping with his prose style. 'Britons Who Have Often Bled' appeared in the seventh issue of the *Republican* on 15 October 1819, the same month in which Carlile was put on trial for seditious libel. The poet depicts a choice for the people between revolution, slavery or death, and calls on the reader to fight the unnamed tyrant for the causes of God and Liberty.

> Britons who have often bled
> In the cause that Hampden[39] led,
> Welcome to your gory bed,
> Or to Victory.
>
> Now's the day, and now's the hour,
> See the front of battle lour,[40]
> See approach your Tyrant's power,
> Chains and slavery.
>
> Who would be a traitor knave?
> Who would fill a coward's grave?
> Who so base as to be a slave?
> Traitor, coward, turn and flee!
>
> Who at Liberty's sweet cry
> Freedom's sword would raise on high?
> Freeman stand, or freeman die,
> Hark! Your chief cries, 'on with me!'
>
> By Oppression's woes and pains,
> By your sons in servile chains,
> We will drain our dearest veins,
> But they shall be free!

Lay your proud oppressors low!
Tyrants fall in every blow!
For the cause of God below,
In the cause of Liberty!

2 'An Address to "The Rabble"'

Appearing in the same issue of *Medusa* as the poem, 'Manchester Yeomanry Valour', on 30 October 1819, 'An Address to "The Rabble"' begins by invoking events of the seventeenth century to embolden its readers and remind them of the legacy of the Parliamentarians who executed one king and deposed another, thereby demonstrating that tyrannical monarchs do not have to be tolerated.[41] The self-deprecating 'rabble' in the title is illustrative of how many radical writers appropriated the language of conservative writers to satirical effect. As Janowitz observes, the poem 'invokes a collective and interventionist poetic voice against the massacre'.[42] Unlike many poems in this chapter, which espouse a radical English nationalism, this poem supports the strength of the union between England, Scotland, Wales and Ireland as the way to defeat slavery.

> Ye English warriors (glorious name)
> Great heirs of freedom and of fame,
> Who bears the scars of war:[43]
> Ye great descendants from those men
> Who shortened tyrant Stuart's reign,[44]
> Oh! Prove what yet ye dare.
>
> To feed each starving family,
> To rescue all from slavery,
> Now grasp th' avenging –[45]
> Methinks each infant thus complains,
> E'er long we must in tyrant's chains
> The pang of slavery feel.
>
> Britons, be mindful of your fame.
> Britons (Oh! Eternal shame,)
> The brave Lancastrians[46] bleed.
> See them, in peaceful council, lie
> Slaughter'd by hell-hounds![47] See, they die,
> Englishmen, meed for meed.[48]
>
> Britons, now your voices join;
> Britons, with your souls combine,
> T' avenge the infernal deed.
> Let not th' adjacent nations[49] view,

In Albion's[50] Sons a dastard crew,
That dare no slaves exceed.

Britons, can you tamely bear
The tyrants' insult? Can you wear
Degrading slavery's chains?
Can you, like Afric's injured sons,[51]
Whose blood 'neath tyrant's lashes runs,
Live in perpetual pain?

With brazen[52] throat Fame thund'ring cries,
'To deeds of glory, Britons, rise,
And act a Briton's part;
Stand boldly forth upon that ground
Where fame eternal Hampden crown'd,
And bravest Patriots[53] bled.'

And while collectively you stand,
To free from slav'ry Britain's Land,
Let Union rule supreme;[54]
Without her aid no strength can be,
No brilliant crowns of victory
Can grace the Patriot's brow.

O! England's primest flower, be firm, and hear –
All, all's at stake to Britons dear;
And soon will twine around the English name
Eternal Glory, or Eternal Shame!

3 The White Hat[55]

This broadside ballad is part of the Hay Portfolio at Chetham's Library, Manchester.[56] Although it is undated, it is clear from the text that it relates to Peterloo. The ballad directly links the events of the 1640s during the English Revolution with 1819 through the comparison between Oliver Cromwell and Henry Hunt, both of whom were renowned for wearing a white hat, which, in the poem, symbolises both revolution and regicide. There is a degree of ambiguity in this poem. Through the invocation of Leveller ideology, the poem demands the reform of both the church and the state, so often regarded as colluding in the repression of the people; however, there is a degree of cynicism directed at Hunt and, through the comparison with Cromwell, the poet appears to be suggesting that Hunt would adopt the trappings of monarchy just as Cromwell did.

In sixteen hundred and forty one,[57]
The radicals had some famous fun;

Till with King CHARLES they so merrily sped,
The first took his Crown and then his Head.
    Then hey for Radical Reform,
    To raise in England a glorious storm;
    Till every man his dinner has got,
    For Twopence the Loaf and a Penny the Pot![58]

Hampden[59] and Pym,[60] with their radical sheers,
Cropt the Bishops and sliced the Peers;
While OLIVER kick'd the mace with an air,
And set his own rump in the Speaker's Chair.[61]
    Then hey for Radical Reform, &c.

Oliver wore a broad-brimm'd Hat;
It was not white; but no matter for that;
For so very broad his brim was grown,
That it cover'd the Altar and capp'd the Throne.
    Then hey for Radical Reform, &c.

OLIVER then grew proud and high;
He looked on his comrades rather shy;
He spit in their faces, and cut them all,
Till they humbly cried – GOD SAVE KING NOLL![62]
    Then hey for Radical Reform, &c.

In Eighteen Hundred and Nineteen
Again shall be what before has been,
Until we reform both Church and State
As in Sixteen Hundred and Forty-eight.[63]
    Then hey for Radical Reform, &c.

HAMPDEN and PYM were not half as good
As *Doctor* Watson and THISTLEWOOD;[64]
And Lawyer PEARSON as learnedly spoke,
As ever did Solicitor COKE.[65]
    Then hey for Radical Reform, &c.

And there's Henry Hunt, the Cock of us all,
Will do the job much better than NOLL;
Whose Beaver was never so broad and flat,
As our King HARRY the Nineth's White Hat.[66]
    Then hey for Radical Reform, &c.

And OLIVER had not HARRY's way,
In making harangues from a one-horse chay:[67]
Or, when he had reach'd his private ends,
In cutting his inconvenient friends.[68]
    Then hey for Radical Reform, &c.

And then the Puritan Paper, MERCURIUS
POLITICUS,⁶⁹ 'gainst the Crown so furious: –
For heavy prose and lumpish rimes,
What was it compared to our own TIMES?
  Then hey for Radical Reform,
  To raise in England a glorious storm!
  For never a Journal, Rebel, or Roundhead,
   Like MERCURY TIMES in malice abounded.

We'll have no Pension, Place, nor Court,
No King, no Regent to support;
No Priests to feed, no taxes to pay,
And we'll go to the Devil our own way.
  Then hey for Radical Reform,
  To raise in England a glorious storm;
  Till every man his dinner has got,
   For Twopence the Loaf and a Penny the Pot!

A Parliament shall be held once a year,
Without the Presence of Bishop or Peer;
And every man his own Law-maker,
In right of his single vote and acre.⁷⁰
  Then hey for Radical Reform, &c.

Reform like this we Radicals chuse,
Who have something to gain and nothing to lose;
Unlike Sir FRANK,⁷¹ and the Whiggish Train,
Who have something to lose and nothing to gain.
  Then hey for Radical Reform, &c.

Now march, my boys in your Radical rags;
Handle your sticks, and flourish your flags;
'Till we lay the Throne and the Altar flat,⁷²
With a whisk of HARRY the Nineth's White Hat!⁷³
  And hey for Radical Reform,
  To raise in England a glorious storm;
  And level each purse-proud Aristocrat,
   With a whisk of HARRY the Nineth's White Hat!

4 'Song'⁷⁴

This song, to be sung to the tune of 'Scots wha hae wi' Wallace bled',⁷⁵ is accompanied by the following introduction:

> A friend of ours, and a Norfolk freeholder, favoured us with the expostulation of 'a poor but honest' Whig, to the assembled HOWARDS,⁷⁶

RUSSELLS,[77] KEPPELS,[78] COKES, ANSONS,[79] &c at Hulkam, on the late Massacre (as it were,) of birds[?] at that place.

It is not known to whom the 'Norfolk freeholder' refers and there appears to be no link between this song and 'The Norwich Declaration' in Chapter 5. It appears coincidental that 'Song' appeared in the *Manchester Observer* on 9 October 1819, the same day of the Norwich Declaration. However, all of the names above refer to Whig politicians, some of whom were outspoken in their condemnation of the massacre. The song reports or imagines a meeting at Holkham Hall in Norfolk, ancestral home of the Earls of Leicester. Thomas William Coke was the first Earl of Leicester and also a Whig MP who spoke out against the government response to Peterloo.

> Whigs! Whose ancestors were wont
> Of fruitless power to stand the brunt,
> Nor leave, like you, to shoot, or hunt*,
> > Sweet Freedom's cause.
>
> Cause, by the virtuous HAMPDEN[80] led –
> Cause, for which SYDNEY,[81] RUSSELL,[82] bled,
> When e'en o'er you its glory shed –
> > Oh, turn and pause!
>
> Peers! Gentlemen! Can ye lie by
> When vultures* hover in the sky?
> When, without Inquest†, Freemen die?
> > Untimely fall.
>
> Can ye make *game* your only care,
> Nor, from your toil one moment spare,
> To question *other massacre*!
> > Rouse, one and all!

* If it were not too obvious an anachronism, one would suppose Patriot HUNT, rather than the sport was alluded to.

* The honest Songster is here rather obscure. It is not easy to say by 'vultures', he alludes to our *saintly* Ministers, our *humane* Magistratcy, our *brave* Yeomanry Cavalry, our *virtuous* Boroughmongery, or our *ultra* Democracy – Perhaps to all of them in *due degree*.

† This was not so in *Denmark:* there were *something like* Inquests, unstifled by combinations of Ministers, Magistrates, Surgeons, Apothecaries or Police Constables.

'First Clown. – What! Is this Law?
'Second Clown. – Aye, marry, is it Crowned Quest law.
'First Clown. – How can that be?
'Second Clown. – Why, 'tis so found; the Coroner hath sat, and finds it Christian burial – accidental death. It cannot be else, for here lies the point – If I kill myself unwittingly, it argues an accident, and an accident hath three branches – not to act, not to do, and not to perform. Argat he killed himself accidentally.

> 'First Clown. – Give me leave, Clown, here lies the matter – good; here stands the man – good. If the man go to the sabre and slay himself, it is willy-nilly. He goes – mark that; but if the sabre come to him and slay him, why he slays not himself. Argat, he that is not guilty of his own death shortens his own life.
> Hamlet, in Manchester Fustian[83]

5 'Sonnet'[84]

Although the sonnet is generally regarded as a 'high' cultural genre, it is widely used in the radical press. The sub-genre of the political sonnet dates back to Milton, who is mentioned in the poem, and was also used to great effect by both Wordsworth and Shelley in the Romantic period. This anonymous sonnet, published in the *White Hat* between October and December 1819 is Miltonic in both style and subject matter. Written in a version of a Shakespearean form,[85] it is addressed in an elevated style to the 'Muse of old Albion', exhorting it to 'Wake! Arise!' thereby utilising the tradition of English nationalism found within poetry and song at a time of crisis together with the Romantic and radical trope of awakening.[86] The author believes that poetry of heroic past deeds can invigorate the cause of freedom and prevent a lapse into tyranny.

> Muse of old Albion! In whose deep ton'd lyre
> Dwell the recording songs of lasting fame,
> Thou that dost cleanse by thy celestial fire
> From earthly dross, the patriot's holy name,
> And lift it into glory! Wake! Arise!
> Sing of our fathers – their bold manly words
> Their still more manly daring and the prize
> Of freedom won by their victorious swords –
> For the old beldam[87] tyranny is rife,
> And shall our lip turn slave, and kiss the rod?[88]
> Ours, of the land that gave a Milton[89] life,
> The land of Sydney's heart and Hampden's[90] strife?
> No, muse of Albion! Tread we as they trod,
> And our high cause confide in our protecting God?

6 'The Measure of Ministers'[91]

Subtitled 'A Song of Similes' and published in the *Cap of Liberty* on 22 December 1819, this satirical poem does not deal explicitly with Peterloo but ridicules the government's introduction of new legislation, known as the Six Acts, intended to stifle radicalism by, among other things, restricting the freedom of the press.[92] The extensive use of word play adds to the humorous effect.

All England's been wond'ring what would come to pass,
In the present queer state of the nation;
Their *measures* the Ministers *cut out* at last,
And *straight-jackets* must prove our salvation.

They'll strike at the *root* with a new sharpen'd *Bill*,
Which they're *grinding* the Parliament's wish on,
For *Radicals*, by their new method of *drill*,[93]
Are *sowing* the *seeds* of Sedition.

A treacherous *bait* now *floats* in the stream,
Which thro' both houses quickly is *gliding*;
They're *trolling*[94] for *Pikes*, by their *nets* it would seem,
And their great skill in *angling*[95] they've pride in.

A large *standing army* they're trying to raise,
The Radical *train-bands*[96] to kill;
And their *quick steps* are certainly worthy of praise,
For the *awkward squad's*[97] constant at *drill*.

The nation's *old coat* they'll endeavour to *patch*,
Tho' much mending more 'twill not bear;
Of heavy *oat-cakes** they are *baking a batch* –
And *hard of digestion*, I fear. –

Its once boasted freedom the *Press* now must lose,
Or at least will become a *dead letter*:
If they turn a *new leaf*, or a fresh *page compose*,
I hope it will read something better.

*Alluding to TITUS OATS[98]

7 Untitled[99]

This untitled poem was printed with an accompanying letter in the *Briton* on 13 November 1819. The letter, signed 'D.F.D.' and addressed to the editor, states:

> The following Dialogue, between a father and son, was written for the instruction of youth; and I wish that every parent would teach it to his child, and thus implant in the tender mind, a knowledge of truths worthy of being remembered and *practised*.

The poem takes the form of a Socratic dialogue in which the son questions his father on the relationship between a ruler and his people. It could also be seen as imitating or subverting the catechistic method of education widely used at the time with the child as the questioner rather than the adult. The poem stresses the sovereignty of the people

> Sir, what is a Ruler?, come, say,[100]
> Now speak without fear or delay.
> He is, son, a man – ONE OF US;
> And is a great blessing or curse.
>
> Pray, what has a Ruler to do?
> To guide, to protect, me and you:
> To keep enemies off from our shores,
> And poverty out of our doors.
>
> Can Rulers like Tyrants rave,
> And make every subject a slave?
> No! though Kings, they're UNDER CONTROUL:
> They reign FOR THE GOOD OF THE WHOLE.
>
> *To whom does the power belong?*
> *To make one as chief from the throng?*
> To the People, the People at large;
> They MAKE Kings, and Kings they DISCHARGE.
>
> *Supposing the Ruler won't reign*
> *By laws which he swore to maintain:*
> *If he tax e'en the beer and the corn,*[101]
> *And treat all petitions*[102] *with scorn: –*
>
> Then the people who LENT him the sway,
> Can SEND him in justice away:
> Can banish, like James the misled;
> Like Charles, they can cut off his head.

8 'Manchester Heroes'[103]

Addressed to the spirit of 'Old England', the poet, writing under the pseudonym Demophilus,[104] provides a stark contrast between the noble deeds of the past and the shameful present. The poem suggests that a wrathful, Old Testament God will seek vengeance for the violation of his laws. Written in Manchester, it was published in the *Manchester Observer*[105] on 18 September and in the *Cap of Liberty* on 29 September 1819.

> Is this, then, the land that humanity boasted,
> Whose natives the sabre once rais'd but to save?
> As the murd'rers den through the universe posted,
> Is this the country which held both the good and the brave!

Yes; stained is thy name, and all sullied thy glory,
Old England! My theme once, my boast and my pride!
Accused thou standest in every story,
And savages learn the foul deed, and deride.

What! Thou, whose quick aid was ever extended
To each nation oppress'd and its tyrants down hurl'd;
What! Thou, whose high honour has never descended
To approve of the despots who darken'd the world!

Couldst thou glut thy sword in the breast of the friendless,
And e'en slaughter the aged, the mother and child?
Such, alas! Was thy deed, and its memory, endless
Will mark on thee what would have demons defil'd.

And a Prince of the line, with rapture regarded,
Could applaud the dread butchers, besmear'd with such gore![106]
The blood of the female! Whose virtues retarded,
The approaches of pain, and joyed the hearts' core.

But, oh! Will *his* thanks give to them the great blessing
Of a bosom of ease, of a conscience of joy?
No; if *men* they can be, their mind most distressing,
Shall, with all the Creator has given, e'er cloy.

Will HIS thunders sleep, when HIS laws are invaded,
And HIS precept of justice is scoff'd at with scorn?
'No Murder!' He said, when the Light'ning he braided,
He on Zion's[107] steep stone at the world's early morn.

Wherever their steps bend, the cries most appalling
Of the widows and orphans they cruelly made,
Shall scream their deep curses, for ever recalling
The graves, where the murder's in peace are now laid.

All fiends as they are, fellow-fiends, when their pillows
They vainly shall seek, shall howl in their ears,
In accents more dread than the storm-heaving billows
The torments of hell, and even add to its fears.
Manchester

9 'National Songs – No. 1'[108]

By the Minstrel of the British People

This song was printed in the 23 October issue of the *Manchester Observer*, immediately before 'Reformer's Song of Liberty'.[109] The tune is stated as 'See the Conquering Hero Comes', which was written by Handel in 1747 for his oratorio, *Joshua*, but was added to his 1746 oratorio, *Judas Maccabaeus*, in 1751. *Maccabaeus* was written for Prince William Augustus, Duke of Cumberland, who commanded the Loyalist troops to victory at the Battle of Culloden in 1746, defeating the Jacobites, led by Charles Edward Stuart, the Young Pretender. According to Michael Bush, the band played this tune when Hunt arrived at the hustings.[110] The tune can be found in various broadside ballads, including *The Chairing Song* of 1790 and is also shared with 'Peterloo' in Chapter 6.[111]

> Britons, once the pride of earth,
> Shall we shame our noble birth?
> Shall we galling fetters wear,
> And bend our heads in mute despair?
>
> Hark! Our fathers' sprits cry,
> 'Can our sons in bondage die?
> Do the rights we bled to gain
> Our children view with cold disdain?'
>
> No! ye spirit of our sires,
> Freedom still each Briton fires;
> Still our choral song shall be,
> 'O *who* would live that lives not free?'
>
> Tyrants! Vainly do you rave!
> Dungeons, chains, and death we brave;
> Ne'er shall base, perverted law
> Our course suspend, our bosoms awe.
>
> Dare not hope your hostile arms
> Shake our breasts with dire alarms!
> Thou your thousands crowd the field,
> Our native rights we ne'er will yield.
>
> Bid your sabres gleam around!
> Wake your cannons thundering sound;
> Sabres' gleam and cannons' roar
> But rouse our British courage more.
>
> Tyrants! Short will be your hour;
> Soon must end your gloomy power;
> Soon shall Vengeance hear our call,
> And shouting millions hail your fall!
> *London*   ALFRED[112]

10 'Reformer's Song of Liberty'

As with many of the songs in Chapter 2, 'Reformer's Song of Liberty' unites the call for liberation with a strident British nationalism, invoking the image of a mourning Britannia in the opening verse before vowing to defeat tyranny in the battle for the reinstatement of British laws and rights. Appearing alongside 'National Songs – No. 1' in the *Manchester Observer* on 23 October 1819 (see 9 above), this song is also a rallying cry to the oppressed for whose cause national ideals are central.

> Britannia mourns, for see our freedom lie
> Mangled, at our tyrant's fell command;
> But hark! What is that life-reviving cry?
> Our brothers vow to free our native land!
>
> CHORUS
> In patriot bands we'll join with bravery,
> Break the chains of tyrants' knavery,
> Let our cry be – Down with slavery –
> Liberty or death![113]
>
> Our ancient rights we ask, and ask no more,
> Our birthrights which the tyrants now withhold;
> But we will shew them that their day is o'er,
> For British freedom never shall be sold.
> Chorus, &c.
>
> Ye British fair – to us, ah! Doubly dear,
> Continue our endeavours to beguile;
> Still shed with us the sympathetic tear,
> Still crown each noble effort with a smile.
> Chorus, &c.
>
> Then cease Britannia, mourn not for our cause,
> For thy lov'd liberty – admit no fears;
> Thy sons declare they *will* possess their laws,
> And *thus* declare it by these hearty cheers.
>
> (Three cheers, after which)
> Now we're joined to combat knavery,
> We're resolv'd to act with bravery,
> We still will cry – down with slavery –
> Liberty or death!

11 'The Voice of Britannia'[114]

Printed in the *Manchester Observer* on 13 November 1819, the voice of Britannia, the personification of the nation, mourns the death of the Peterloo victims, withdrawing British identity from the murderers and condemning them to hell. Through the poetic persona, the poet, 'L' predicts that history will remember these events and those who attacked the freedom so dearly valued by Britain.

'———. He who contends for Freedom,
Can ne'er be justly deem'd his Sovereign's foe.'[115]

Ah! Still I see the plains of Peter's field, –
Still, still I hear the groans the dying yield!
A band of creatures, in the shape of men,
Intent on mischief, furious leave the den;
They onward rush with a tremendous sweep,
The thirsty ground in human gore to steep!
Fraught with satanic pride, around they stare, –
They slash, they stab – nor age nor sex they spare.
Shame! Shame! Ye monsters! Oh! Eternal stain!
You on your foreheads bear the mark of Cain![116]
Ye blood-hounds![117] Never call me mother more –
Oh! Father call me strumpet, bawd, or whore![118]
Th' historic page shall unborn nations tell,
What numbers by your *matchless prowess* fell;
This I'll proclaim – and thro' my loudest horn –
You've slain the flock that had too long been shorn!
Shall you, unpunish'd, 'gainst the laws rebel?
Then farewell, Justice! Freedom, fare-thee-well!
How can you rest, tho' laid on downy beds,
With such a pressure on your guilty heads?
If no compunction for such deeds you feel,
Your hearts are harder than the hardest steel –
Can those, I pray, be true-born sons of mine,
Who hurl their darts at Freedom's sacred shrine?
No, no! They are my most mischievous foes,
Who strive, O Freedom, to depress thy cause;
Yet Truth and thou, shall, in your foes' despite,
Around the globe diffuse your cheering light;
While Error hence, with Slavery, shall go
To reign over demons in the shades below!

Notes

1. B. Anderson, *Imagined Communities: Reflections on the Origin and Spread of Nationalism* (London: Verso, 2nd edn, 1991), p. 2.
2. E. Said, *Culture and Imperialism* (London: Vintage Books, 1993), pp. 330, xiii.
3. K. Trumpener, *Bardic Nationalism: The Romantic Novel and the British Empire* (Princeton: Princeton University Press, 1997), pp. 15–16.
4. *OED*.
5. E. Hobsbawm, *The Age of Revolution: 1789–1848* (London: Abacus, 1962), pp. 73–4.
6. Anderson, *Imagined Communities*, pp. 81–2.
7. Said, *Culture and Imperialism*, p. xiii.
8. G. Newman, *The Rise of English Nationalism: 1740–1830* (Hampshire: Macmillan, 1997), p. 56; Trumpener, *Bardic Nationalism*, p. 25.
9. The two main protagonists in the English antiquarian movement are Thomas Percy and Joseph Ritson. For more information, see pp. 29–31. For Murray Pittock, antiquarianism was used as a way of expressing protest which would not have been allowed in the publication of new texts (p. 103).
10. The English Constitution never existed as a document. Magna Carta and The Bill of Rights are often cited as part of the constitution.
11. C. Hill, *Puritanism and Revolution* (London: Mercury Books, 1965), pp. 53–6.
12. T. Morton and N. Smith (eds), *Radicalism in British Literary Culture, 1650–1830* (Cambridge: Cambridge University Press, 2002), pp. 1–21.
13. The theory of the Norman Yoke is explored by Epstein and Wood among others.
14. Hill, *Puritanism and Revolution*, p. 53.
15. Quoted in *Ibid.*, p. 77.
16. Spence's periodical *Pigs' Meat* contains many extracts from Harrington's works, such as *Oceana* (*Pigs' Meat* (1793), p. 212).
17. *Pigs' Meat* (1795), pp. 250–1.
18. Janowitz, *Lyric and Labour in the Romantic Tradition*, p. 73.
19. Paine's belief in natural rights, shared with both Spence and the Diggers, places him firmly within the tradition of English radicalism. In the first part of the *Rights of Man*, written in 1791, Paine asserts: 'No such thing as a constitution exists', in response to its appropriation by Edmund Burke's *Reflections on the Revolution in France*. However, whilst denying the existence of the fabled constitution, Paine does acknowledge the reality of the Norman Yoke: 'Conquest and tyranny transplanted themselves with William the Conqueror from Normandy into England, and the country is yet disfigured with the marks' (T. Paine, *The Rights of Man, Common Sense and Other Political Writings*, ed. Mark Philip (Oxford: Oxford University Press, 2008), pp. 123, 127). Here Paine acknowledges the legacy of French

imperialism on the English as a scarring presumably of both the people and the land.
20 J.A. Epstein, *Radical Expression: Political Language, Ritual, and Symbol in England, 1790–1850* (Oxford: Oxford University Press, 1994), p. 21.
21 See number 10 below.
22 Lilburne achieved prominence in 1817 when the satirist, William Hone, on trial for blasphemous sedition, modelled his defence on the trial of Lilburne in 1649 for high treason. According to Marcus Wood, Hone owned more than eighty tracts by or about Lilburne along with many others by the Diggers and Levellers (M. Wood, *Radical Satire and Print Culture: 1790–1822* (Oxford: Clarendon, 1994), pp. 125, 121).
23 E. Vallance, *A Radical History of Britain* (London: Abacus, 2009), p. 198.
24 C. Macaulay, *The History of England from the Accession of James I to the Elevation of the House of Hanover* (London: Dilly, 1772), vol. 3, p. 335.
25 See numbers 1, 2, 3, 4 and 5 in this chapter and number 3 in Chapter 1. Both Hampdens are referred to in these poems.
26 Scrivener only refers to the elder Hampden; however, I argue that it is the younger Hampden referred to alongside Sidney and Russell (M. Scrivener (ed.), *Poetry and Reform: Periodical Verse from the English Democratic Press, 1792–1824* (Michigan: Wayne State University Press, 1992), p. 18).
27 Due to the parlous state of his finances, Charles decided to levy a tax, traditionally applied only to maritime counties in times of emergency, on all counties in 1636. Hampden opposed what became known as Ship Money, as he was suspicious of the motives of the king, believing he was trying to make himself independent of parliament in order to return the country to Catholicism (E. Vallance, *A Radical History of Britain* (London: Abacus, 2009), p. 135–6).
28 I. McCalman (ed.), *Robert Wedderburn: The Horrors of Slavery and Other Writings* (Princeton: Marcus Wiener, 1991), p. 1.
29 I. McCalman, *Radical Underworld: Prophets, Revolutionaries and Pornographers in London, 1795–1840* (Cambridge: Cambridge University Press, 2004), p. 142.
30 Scrivener, *Poetry and Reform*, p. 192.
31 http://ballads.bodleian.ox.ac.uk/static/images/sheets/10000/07333.gif [accessed 19 November 2017]. Printed by Marshall in Newcastle between 1810 and 1831.
32 Number 10 below.
33 Janowitz, *Lyric and Labour in the Romantic Tradition*, p. 84.
34 *Ibid.*, pp. 82–4, 87.
35 Number 11 below.
36 Scrivener, *Poetry and Reform*, p. 18.
37 *Republican*, 7:1 (1819), p. 112. The other poem is 'Song' by W.I. (Chapter 1, number 7).
38 For examples of Carlile's prose style, see the Introduction, p. 11.
39 For Hampden, see p. 69.

40 Look threatening.
41 See number 3. P. Keen (ed.), *The Popular Radical Press in Britain 1817–21*. 6 vols. (London: Pickering and Chatto, 2003), vol. 5, p. 300.
42 Janowitz, *Lyric and Labour in the Romantic Tradition*, p. 101.
43 This could allude to the Napoleonic Wars, in which hundreds of thousands of Englishmen fought, or to a war on tyranny.
44 The reigns of two Stuart kings: Charles I and James II were cut short.
45 Scrivener suggests the missing word is 'steel', which would rhyme with 'feel' in the last line of the verse (*Poetry and Reform*, p. 246).
46 The majority of those present at Peterloo were from Lancashire which, at the time, included Manchester and Salford. The term also has connotations of the Wars of the Roses, fought between the Houses of Lancaster and York in the fifteenth century.
47 The use of 'hell-hounds' correlates with the naming of the MYC as 'bloodhounds' in the 28 August issue of the *Theological and Political Comet* and the *Black Dwarf* three days earlier. (For further information, see pp. 12 and 63n.73.)
48 Recompense.
49 A reference to the other nations within the United Kingdom of Great Britain and Ireland, particularly as the poet singles out 'Albion's sons' as the object of this sentence.
50 Unusually, the poet interchanges English, Britons and Albion throughout the poem. For Albion, see p. 60n.35.
51 This is the only direct comparison between the English and African slaves in these poems. The slave trade was abolished in the British Empire in 1807 after a thirty-year campaign by the Committee for the Abolition of the Slave Trade but it was not until 1833 that slavery was abolished.
52 In this usage, 'brazen' means 'strong' rather than the more usual meaning today of 'shameless'.
53 John Hampden is often cited alongside Algernon Sidney and William Russell as a great English patriot. See p. 69 for more information.
54 The union of Great Britain and Ireland. The union between England, Wales and Scotland dates back to 1707; Ireland joined the union in 1800.
55 The white hat was a symbol of radical protest. For more information, see p. 23.
56 *Hay Portfolio*, 128. Revd. William Robert Hay (1761–1839) was a clerical magistrate and Chairman of the Salford Quarter Sessions up until 1823. He was one of the magistrates who acted on 16 August 1819 and, according to Read, was one of the men 'directly responsible for the Peterloo Massacre' (D. Read, *Peterloo: The Massacre and its Background* (Manchester: Manchester University Press, 1958), p. 74).The portfolio contains both pro and anti-radical broadsides and newspaper cuttings relating to the Peterloo Massacre. Samuel Bamford's poem, 'Ode to a Plotting Parson' is addressed to Hay.
57 In November 1641, the House of Commons passed the Grand Remonstrance,

'Ye English warriors'

a list of over two hundred grievances against Charles I, which, after several weeks' delay, he rejected. It is one of the key events leading to the English Revolution. John Hampden was instrumental in drafting the Grand Remonstrance.
58 A pot of beer.
59 This refers to the elder John Hampden, see p. 69 for more information.
60 John Pym was an MP and one of the Five Members, along with Hampden, whom Charles I tried to have arrested for treason in January 1642. Pym was a staunch opponent of the king and the Catholic Church. He was to become responsible for the finances of the Parliamentarians until his death in 1643.
61 Unhappy that the fruits of the revolution were not being implemented by the Rump Parliament, Cromwell ordered troops to clear the Commons in 1653 and he took away the Speaker's Mace.
62 'Noll' is a diminutive of Oliver and often used in reference to Cromwell. Cromwell became Lord Protector in December 1653 until his death in 1658, when his son Richard succeeded him. As Lord Protector, Cromwell courted disapproval from many who regarded such an office, with the power to dissolve parliament, as akin to monarchy.
63 Charles I was actually executed in January 1649.
64 Watson and Thistlewood were ultra-radical Spenceans who organised the Spa Fields Rising in 1816. At the first meeting, held on 15 November, Henry Hunt and Francis Burdett addressed a crowd of about 100,000 and the event passed off peacefully. However, Thistlewood and Watson's son, James, wanted to enflame the crowd in order to take the Tower of London and Bank of England. Despite Watson Snr's opposition, the meeting went ahead but the crowds were dispersed by troops. Watson Snr and Thistlewood were arrested and tried for treason in 1817. When it was revealed that the prosecution's main witness was an *agent provocateur*, John Castle, Watson was acquitted and the case against Thistlewood and others was dropped (*DNB*; D. Worrall, *Radical Culture: Discourse, Resistance and Surveillance, 1790–1820* (Hertfordshire: Harvester, 1992), pp. 97–113).
65 This is a probable reference to two lawyers in the seventeenth century. Alexander Pearson was a barrister and judge who was appointed by Cromwell and the Commissioner of Judicature in 1653. Sir Edward Coke had an illustrious career in both justice and politics during the reigns of Elizabeth I, James I and Charles I. Under Charles' reign he served as an opposition and, along with Pym, opposed many of Charles' proposals. In 1628, he drew up the Petition of Right, in which he protected many ancient legal rights of Englishmen which Charles wished to abolish. Coke was a great advocate of Magna Carta, using it as evidence against the autocracy of Charles.
66 Hunt is also referred to as 'Harry the Nineth' in the poem 'Harry the Nineth's Apology' where reference is also made to Hunt's white hat. (*Morning Post*, 15221 (1819), n. pag).
67 Chaise or carriage.

68 Following Hunt's triumphant procession into London on 13 September, accompanied by Watson and Thistlewood, the divisions within the radical movement soon appeared, with the ultra-radicals failing to capitalise on the 'potentially fertile collusion with Hunt' (Worrall, *Radical Culture*, p. 144). Bamford describes Hunt's procession through Lancashire cotton towns with James Moorhouse, another of those arrested at Peterloo, while awaiting trial: 'Hunt sat on the box seat [...] continually doffed his hat, waved it slowly, bowed gracefully, and now and then spoke a few words to the people; but if some five or ten minutes elapsed without a huzza or two [...] he would rise from his seat, turn around, and cursing poor Moorhouse in limbs, soul, or eyes, he would say, "Why don't you shout man? Why don't you shout?"' (Bamford, *Passages in the Life of a Radical*, vol. 2, p. 21).

69 *Mercurius Politicus* was a weekly journal published between 1650 and 1660 and edited by Marchamont Nedham. The journal supported Cromwell's government and opposed monarchy.

70 This echoes the radical demands of an annual parliament and universal male suffrage.

71 Sir Francis Burdett. See pp. 4 and 12.

72 A literal reference to Leveller ideology.

73 By giving Hunt the name of a king, the author is suggesting that Hunt is acting in a kingly manner, as did Cromwell once he had gained power.

74 *Manchester Observer* (9 October 1819), p. 742.

75 This tune was also used for 'The Manchester Massacre' in Chapter 1.

76 This may refer to Henry Howard, the thirteenth Duke of Norfolk, and Whig MP.

77 A possible reference to Lord John Russell, a Whig politician and the sixth Duke of Bedford. His mother was Lady Elizabeth Keppel, sixth daughter of William Anne Keppel, second earl of Albemarle.

78 William Charles Keppel, fourth Earl of Abermarle and Whig MP. His daughter, Anne, married Thomas William Coke in 1822, despite being fifty years his junior.

79 Thomas Anson, the first Earl of Lichfield, was the Whig MP for Great Yarmouth between 1818 and 1819.

80 John Hampden (1653–96). For more information, see p. 69.

81 Algernon Sydney or Sidney was the great-nephew of the Elizabethan soldier and poet, Sir Philip Sidney and second son of the Second Earl of Leicester. Brought up as a Protestant and humanist, Sidney fought with the Parliamentarians during the 1640s; however, despite opposing the rule of Charles I, he questioned his execution as unlawful and regarded Cromwell as a tyrant. One of Sidney's major works, *Discourses Concerning Government*, published between 1681 and 1683, in which he details his republicanism and championing of liberty, was reissued by Joseph Johnson in 1795. This may explain his popularity with radicals in the Romantic era.

82 William Russell was a founder member of the County Party, a forerunner

of the Whigs. As an ardent anti-Catholic, he opposed James, Duke of York, as the successor to Charles II, supporting Lord Monmouth, Charles' illegitimate son instead.
83 This is a parody of Act Five, scene one in *Hamlet* when the two clowns, or gravediggers, debate whether Ophelia is to have a Christian burial following her suicide. Despite their lowly status, they question the coroner's decision regarding Ophelia's burial and, through humour and intelligence, highlight the flawed logic of the decision. The poet is using this Shakespearean scene as a satirical attack on the coroners who did not find the deaths of the marchers unlawful. Fustian is a kind of coarse cloth made of cotton and flax – an indication that the Manchester *Hamlet* concerns the labouring classes.
84 The only version of this poem I have discovered is in *Poetry and Reform*. Its publication date is not stated, only the page reference (p. 96) which indicates that it appeared towards the end of the nine-issue run of the periodical in December 1819 (*Poetry and Reform*, pp. 226–7). For further information, see p. 23.
85 The rhyme scheme is *ababcdcdefeeff*, a slight departure from the Shakespearean form of *ababcdcdefefgg*.
86 See Chapter 1 for examples of exhortatory poems and songs.
87 Witch or hag.
88 Accept punishment submissively.
89 Disliked by the Augustans for his republicanism, John Milton came to symbolise the revolutionary bardic prophet for both canonical and non-canonical poets in the Romantic era. Ian Haywood observes that for anti-Jacobites 'Milton represented the regicidal reality of political revolution' (I. Haywood, *Bloody Romanticism: Spectacular Violence and the Politics of Misrepresentation, 1776–1832* (Hampshire: Palgrave, 2006), p. 77).
90 See note 81 above.
91 Keen, *The Popular Radical Press*, vol. 4, p. 272.
92 For the Six Acts, see p. 214n.55.
93 'Drill' refers both to military drill and a seed drill.
94 As well as meaning 'walking about', in slang 'trolling' describes the walk of a homosexual or cruising for a sexual encounter. If this is indeed a connotation used in the poem, the use of 'pikes' in the same line may refer to penises as well as weapons and fish, thereby heightening the bawdiness of the poem.
95 'Angling' meaning both to entrap and to catch fish.
96 Militia or citizen army in contrast with the regular troops of the 'standing army' in the line above.
97 The first definition of this phrase dates to Charles James' work, *A New and Enlarged Military Dictionary; or, Alphabetical Explanation of Technical Terms*, published in 1802: 'The aukward squad consists not only of recruits at drill, but of formed soldiers that are ordered to exercise with them, in consequence of some irregularity under arms' (*OED*).
98 Titus Oates, 'an unusual figure in British history', was an ordained Church

of England minister who later converted to Catholicism. In 1678 Oates claimed to have uncovered numerous popish plots to assassinate the king, Charles II and his brother James. Despite many contradictions in his evidence, Oates was believed and numerous trials ensued, resulting in the executions of more than thirty men. By 1681, Oates' story was discredited and in 1684 he was arrested. The following year he was convicted of perjury, sentenced to life imprisonment, defrocked and pilloried, although he was released from prison in 1688 following the Glorious Revolution (*DNB*). The reference to Oates in 'oat-cakes' may be suggesting that the government is fabricating evidence of a plot against the king, as Oates did, in order to enable further repressive legislation.

99 Keen, *The Popular Radical Press*, vol. 4, p. 360.
100 The italics denote when the son is speaking.
101 The 1815 Corn Law stated that no foreign corn could be imported until the domestic price reached the exorbitant price of eighty shillings per quarter. The poor harvests after the end of the Napoleonic Wars caused the price of corn to increase but not sufficiently to enable the import of cheaper corn, thus leading to starvation for many, particularly the urban labouring classes, who were unable to grow their own food.
102 The right to petition the monarch was regarded as a cornerstone of English democracy and widely used in the eighteenth and nineteenth centuries as a form of protest. A successful petitioning campaign contributed to the abolition of the slave trade in 1807; however, the vast majority of petitions in the early part of the nineteenth century met with failure. The radical MP Francis Burdett submitted over 500 petitions to the House of Commons containing over a million signatures. They were all rejected, mainly because they were either printed or because they were on the same issue as petitions that had previously been rejected (O. Smith, *The Politics of Language 1791–1819* (Oxford: Clarendon, 1984), p. 33). Similarly, in 1817 Major Cartwright collected 130,000 signatures for his petition in support of extending suffrage to tax payers and annual parliaments. It was dismissed due to the unsuitability of the language in which it was written, leading Olivia Smith to conclude that 'the disenfranchised could not write in a language which merited attention' (*Ibid.*, p. 30).
103 *Cap of Liberty*, 1:3 (1819), p. 48.
104 Demophilus was a military commander at the Battle of Thermopylae in 480BC. Its adoption as a pseudonym by this poet is more likely to be based on a literal translation of the name meaning 'lover of the people'. A letter to the Editor of the *Briton* in the 25 September issue, four days before 'Manchester Heroes' appeared in *Cap of Liberty*, was signed 'Demophilus'. The letter maintains that events in Manchester are yet another erosion of English rights, including the suspension of *habeus corpus*. Demophilus warns that the people cannot continue to endure such repression and yet admits that the people have 'ever been slow in punishing the abusers', citing examples from history where they have failed to rise up against

oppression; however he also warns that 'there is a point beyond which oppression and cruelty cannot extend' (Keen, *The Popular Radical Press*, vol. 4, pp. 301–3).
105 The poem is untitled in the *Manchester Observer* (18 September 1819), p. 718.
106 The Prince Regent congratulated the Manchester Magistrates on their handling of Peterloo. See the Introduction for further information.
107 Jerusalem.
108 *Manchester Observer* (23 October 1819), p. 188.
109 According to Epstein, this column was begun by John Stafford, a poet and weaver from Ashton-under-Lyne (*Radical Expression*, p. 219). See Chapter 3, number 6 for more information.
110 M. Bush, 'The Women at Peterloo: The Impact of Female Reform on the Manchester Meeting of 16 August 1819', *History* 89:294 (2004), p. 221.
111 http://ballads.bodleian.ox.ac.uk/static/images/sheets/25000/24774.gif [accessed 19 November 2017]. See Chapter 6, number 1.
112 King Alfred was a favourite amongst radicals of the 1790s and 1810s as a symbol of English nationalism and Anglo-Saxon rights, replacing Edward the Confessor as a model king for radicals (Hill, *Puritanism and Revolution*, pp. 96–7). Pittock remarks on the widespread appeal of Alfred as an icon of liberty: 'By the 1790s, even Scottish radicals were appealing to notions of liberty claimed to be derived from King Alfred' (M. Pittock, *Poetry and Jacobite Politics in Eighteenth-Century Britain and Ireland* (Cambridge: Cambridge University Press, 1994), p. 141). The radical weekly, *London Alfred, or People's Recorder* ran from 25 August until 17 November 1819. Its title is evidence of the radical symbolism of King Alfred.
113 Banners bearing the inscription 'Liberty or Death' were taken to Peterloo. See Chapter 6, note 1.
114 *Manchester Observer* (13 November 1819), p. 812. For more information on Britannia, see p. 60n.33.
115 This quotation is from Act One, scene one of the tragedy *Edward and Eleonora* written by the poet and playwright James Thomson (1700–48) in 1739 (Thomson, *Edward and Eleonora* (London, 1739), p. 3). Based on the lives of the thirteenth-century monarch, Edward I, and his wife Eleanor of Castile, Thomson's play, first performed in 1775, was banned by the Lord Chamberlain due to some controversial passages in which the king is warned about his evil ministers.
116 Genesis Chapter 4 narrates the story of Cain and Abel. Following the murder of his brother, Cain is an outcast: 'And the Lord said to him, "Therefore, whoever kills Cain, vengeance shall be taken on him sevenfold." And the Lord set a mark on Cain, lest anyone finding him should kill him' (Genesis, 4:15).
117 For information on the use of the bloodhound motif in the Peterloo poems, see pp. 12 and 63n.73.
118 Depictions of Britannia first appeared in the first century AD to illustrate

the conquest of Britain. Although she is not a goddess from the Greco-Roman or Celtic mythologies, she could be linked to the Celtic goddess Brigantia or the Greek goddess of war, Athene, daughter of Zeus. However, the reference to 'Father' may allude to God.

3

'Base brat of reform': the victimisation of mother and child

Of the estimated eighteen people believed to have been killed at Peterloo, four were women and one was a child. Margaret Downes was sabred; Mary Hays was trampled by the Manchester Yeomanry Cavalry; Sarah Jones was hit on the head with a truncheon; and Martha Pilkington was thrown into a cellar. Two-year-old William Fildes was the first victim on 16 August 1819 when he was trampled to death by the horses of the yeomanry whilst they were on their way to St Peter's field.[1] Of the 654 recorded casualties, 168 were women. Thirty-one were sabred; 23 were struck by truncheons; one was bayoneted, and another was shot.[2] These statistics demonstrate that more than a quarter of all casualties at Peterloo were women, even though they comprised only 12 per cent of those present.[3] It would appear that women were deliberately targeted by the Manchester and Salford Yeomanry Cavalry (MYC), with many of the wounds 'savagely inflicted with the intention of disfiguration of the victim', leading Robert Poole to conclude that 'women suffered disproportionately to men' and were twice as likely to be sabred due to the hatred of female reformers.[4] This apparent victimisation of women by the yeomanry resulted in the widespread use of the motif of mother and child across a range of poems, other print media and cultural artefacts produced in response to Peterloo.[5]

One of Peterloo's most enduring cultural representations is George Cruikshank's caricature, *Massacre at St. Peter's or 'Britons strike home'!!!* (see Figure 6). Published by Thomas Tegg in 1819, it plays a pivotal role in the iconography of Peterloo. The corpulent middle-aged yeomanry dominate the image, yet central to the composition is the depiction of a young woman holding a baby and pleading for her life with the puffing buffoon, who bears an uncanny resemblance to the portrayal of the Prince Regent in graphic satire, poised to bring down a sabre on her head. The yeoman's raised sabre is set against the Union Jack, symbol of nation and empire, thereby explicitly linking

6 *Massacre at St Peter's or 'Britons strike home'!!!* by George Cruikshank.

the British state with violence perpetrated against its own, unarmed, people.

This trope of the mother and child pervades the cultural representations of Peterloo, its widespread use leading to an intensification of impact rather than a dilution through repetition. Even though this chapter comprises only eight poems, the trope of woman and child as victims is present in many of the other poems in this collection, as well as in newspaper articles, graphic satire and other artefacts, resulting in a powerful discourse due to the sense of collectivity engendered by its repeated use. This introduction provides examples of how the representations of Peterloo depicted women and children, illustrating that the poems should be read alongside the caricatures and images printed on handkerchiefs and pottery in order to fully understand the power and resonance of this single trope.

Despite the portrayal of women as innocent victims of the brutal and callous MYC, the number of women present at Peterloo indicates the popularity and importance of the female reform movement in 1819. As Bush maintains, the involvement of predominantly working women at Peterloo 'represents the earliest expression of organised female activity in British politics'.[6] Labouring-class women had been involved in radical politics since the end of the Napoleonic Wars and were often present at rallies and demonstrations across the north, as well as joining friendly societies and taking part in strikes. Driven by hunger and poverty, women turned to radical politics, establishing female reform societies during 1819 in northern towns such as Blackburn and Stockport as a way of showing solidarity with their fathers, husbands and sons, campaigning for a universal suffrage demanded solely for men.[7]

> Some females fair in white and Green near the hustings stood,
> And little still we did expect to see such scenes of blood.[8]

During the summer of 1819, women drilled on the moors and on 16 August, dressed in white, carrying banners and caps of liberty they marched together 'redolent of the vestal virgins of ancient Rome but also of the women in white associated with the Festivals of Reason organised in revolutionary France in the mid-1790s.'[9] As Mather observes, 'women in protest had long alternated between the characters of meek, delicate femininity and strong, determined Amazon.'[10] The extension of the female role beyond the mere supporter of men to an active agent on St Peter's Field 'enraged the magistrates and aroused the cavalry's bloodlust. In this respect, the massacre was partly as a consequence of the female presence.' This perceived threat to male rule, through the transgression of gender roles, resulted not only in the deliberate targeting of women but also in the recognition that women did have a role to play in politics.[11]

Whilst the image of women and children as victims dominates the cultural artefacts of Peterloo, the representation of female reformers as 'viragos and whores' in graphic satire immediately preceding the massacre exemplifies the view held by many men, including the Manchester Magistrates and MYC. Although Cruikshank's *Massacre at St Peter's* is one of the best-known portrayals of the cavalry's violence towards women and children, his caricature, *The Belle Alliance, or The Female Reformers of Blackburn* (see Figure 7), printed just a few days before the massacre, depicts a very different view of women. Described by Diana Donald as 'blowsy sluts or viragos in breeches', the fat, ugly women on the hustings are objects of ridicule, their language full of sexual innuendo.[12] Similarly, J.L. Marks' image, *Reform Among Females*, printed shortly before his *Massacre at Peterloo* (see Figure 8), portrays the female reformers as little more than sexual creatures, holding phallic rolled-up petitions in their hands and referring to 'assist[ing] our Husbands as every Push and Turn, by that means we shall increase, and Multiply, in our undertakings.' The stark shift from

7 *The Belle Alliance, or The Female Reformers of Blackburn* by George Cruikshank.

woman as whore pre-Peterloo to woman as victim post-Peterloo is the result, in part, of the reporting of events in the press. The public was shocked by the descriptions of violence towards women which 'helped to forge new links between radical and moderate reformers', an indication, perhaps, that, through the promulgation of this narrative, widespread support could be achieved.[13]

'The women seemed to be the special object of the rage of these [?] soldiers'. James Wroe's comment in the *Manchester Observer* on 21 August is illustrative of the narrative regarding the treatment of women conveyed in the press.[14] In *The Times* on 19 August, John Tyas describes 'a woman on the ground, insensible, to all outward appearance, and with two large gouts of blood on her left breast.'[15] The plight of women at Peterloo was also addressed on 21 August in the *Leeds Mercury* which states: 'Sex itself could not secure protection; defenceless women and tender children shared in the common overthrow.' The newspaper also reported the death of two year-old William Fildes.[16] Such reporting galvanised the radical press and, it could be argued, began the 'feminisation of suffering', as Ian Haywood describes it, in cultural responses to Peterloo.[17]

'Base brat of reform' 97

8 *Reform Among Females* by J.L. Marks.

On 25 August, the *Black Dwarf* reported the plight of women and children at Peterloo, emphasising the unnaturalness of the yeomanry's actions: 'They *have trampled* on and SABRED WOMEN – children have been bathed in their mother's blood.'[18] Such emotive language is testament to the outrage felt by radicals towards the actions of the state. The reporting of such brutality resulted, in the words of Ashley Cross, in the 'victimised woman' becoming a 'central sign in the struggle to control how Peterloo would be represented.'[19] Such attacks on the mother indicated how corrupt society had become, thus contributing to the portrayal of Peterloo as the epitome of a state at war with its people. By destroying the maternal, the state could also be seen to be destroying itself.

Among the cultural artefacts of Peterloo, printed handkerchiefs and headscarves, a longstanding tradition, were sold to raise money for the injured.[20] One example, designed by John Slack, depicts a yeoman with sabre raised about to strike two fallen women in the bottom right-hand corner of the image.[21] The title declares itself: *A Representation of the Manchester Reform Meeting Dispersed by the Civil and Military Power. August 16, 1819* (see Figure 9).[22] This self-awareness of

9 *A Representation of the Manchester Reform Meeting Dispersed by the Civil and Military Power. August 16, 1819* by John Slack.

artefact as 'representation' extends to the variety of genres and forms within the radical public sphere following Peterloo, as they all share a consciousness of their role in shaping public opinion about the events in Manchester. The 'feminisation of suffering' is also prevalent in graphic satire produced in immediate response to Peterloo, the majority of which contain a central image of a woman.

Another Cruikshank caricature, entitled *Manchester Heroes*, reverses the portrayal of mother protecting her child in another indictment on the unnatural relationship between the state and its people (see Figure 10). Here we see the young boy pleading with the yeoman as his mother falls to the ground: 'Oh pray Sir don't kill Mammy, she only came to see Mr Hunt'. Both Julie Kipp and Stephen Behrendt claim that the portrayal of motherhood and the family in the Romantic period often symbolised the nation, illustrating how, in the words of Behrendt, 'the devastation of the family parallels the inevitable destruction of the state'.[23] It is evident from these examples of graphic satire that the depiction of

10 *Manchester Heroes* by George Cruikshank.

the brutalisation of women and children is making a wider allusion to the future demise of the state, as it was widely hoped by radicals that revolution would ensue.

As well as poems and countless caricatures, other cultural artefacts were produced in response to Peterloo, including commemorative pottery. Although commonly produced to celebrate military, royal or sporting events, it appears that Peterloo was the first time that radicals had used pottery to commemorate a political event. A ceramic jug, one of a collection housed in the Manchester City Art Gallery, bears the familiar image of a woman under attack from a cavalryman with sabre raised (see Figure 11). The falling woman carries a flag declaring 'Liberty or Death'. It would seem that her imminent slaughter suggests she sacrificed her life in the cause of liberty. The inscription on the jug states: 'Murdered on the Plains of Peterloo'. Whereas the caricatures were designed for immediate impact, it appears that artefacts such as this jug were designed for longevity.

These cultural productions, united by both their sentiment and a shared iconography, had a collective role, binding not only audience and artist but also uniting the audience. Although it is not known how many jugs and headscarves were sold, caricatures reached a wide

11 Ceramic jug.

audience both through bookshops and travelling showmen. For those not wealthy enough to purchase one of Cruikshank's prints, they were able to view the images displayed in the windows of printsellers. The repetition of the violation of the maternal in these artefacts strengthens the radical discourse, presenting a unified opposition to the state. Donald notes the prevalence of women and children in the Peterloo caricatures produced in London, suggesting that they had more in common with the 'atrocity imagery' of the sixteenth and seventeenth centuries than with Georgian satire.[24] If indeed that is the case and paintings such as Albrecht Dürer's *Four Horsemen of the Apocalypse* and François Dubois's *St. Bartholomew's Day Massacre* were inspirational to Cruikshank and others, it would suggest their desire to elevate Peterloo above the usual ribald humour of satire to an event of historical significance.

Alongside graphic satire, the poems of the radical press and broadsides contributed to the creation of maternal iconography, again illustrating the way in which both text and image unite in a cultural attack on state brutality. 'The Manchester Yeoman', in parallel with Cruikshank's caricatures, uses satire to ridicule the yeomanry:

> I am d' ye see, a Yeoman,
> All fine from top to toe, man;
> And make my mare to go, man;
> And draw my sword out so, man.

Whilst the caricatures depict the yeomanry as fat, this poem focuses on their stupidity through the simplistic language and style of the poem, in which every line ends in 'man'. The final quatrain intensifies the satire:

> And ride to meet the foe, man,
> And prove that there is no man
> Such 'more than man' can show, man,
> By cutting down – a woman.[25]

The awkward metre in 'woman' where the stress falls on the first syllable highlights the yeoman's idiocy. His false bravado is revealed as cowardice in his slaying of a woman, his stupidity yielding to aggression.

As well as ridicule, satire is used in some of the poems to convey the outrage of the reformers towards the cowardice of the MYC as exemplified by 'The Peterloo Man':

> How brave were the heroes, what muse can relate;
> On the breast of its mother, he bade the babe bleed!
> And the mother herself would in vain shun the fate,
> That awaited her under the hoofs of his steed.[26]

The poet here deploys the religious iconography of mother with a child at her breast, the callous destruction of both presented as an evil, unnatural act. By making reference to 'Waterloo fields' in the first line of the poem, the comparison between Peterloo and its namesake, Waterloo, is inescapable for the reader, whose memories of the famous victory four years earlier would still be fresh. The unfavourable comparisons between the bravery exhibited by soldiers at Waterloo and the cowardice at Peterloo are evident in numerous poems in this anthology. As Mather notes, the treatment of women led to the appropriation of the language of patriotic chivalry by the radical press.[27] In the poems above, this language of chivalry is turned against the perpetrators of violence, depicting them as unchivalrous and unmanly. However, satire is not the only genre used by the radical poets.

In 'The Sword King' by H. Morton the yeoman is no longer a comic character, mocked for his size or stupidity but a hunter, charging down his prey of mother and child away from the chaos of St Peter's field.[28] This somewhat melodramatic ballad narrates the tale of a mother and child fleeing from the eponymous 'sword king with sabre so bloody and bright'. The yeoman sees it as his mission to destroy the next generation of reformers:

> 'Base brat of reform, shall thy cries bar my way,
> To the laurells that bloom for the loyal today?
> Shalt thou live to rear banner, white, emerald, or blue?
> No! this is our yeomanry's own Waterloo.'

The corrupted morality of such actions is again illustrated by the comparison between the murder of a defenceless mother and child and the defeat of Napoleon. The quasi-gothic tone of the poem is evident in the final quatrain:

> The mother she trembled, she doubled her speed,
> But dark on her path swept the black yeoman's steed;
> And ere she arrived at her own cottage door,
> Life throbb'd in her poor baby's bosom no more.

Although this ballad personalises victim and aggressor, moving away from a generalised attack on women to a specific story, it nevertheless allegorises the conflict between a masculine state and a feminine people. As with many of the other representations shown here, the yeoman, with his shining sabre, is seen as a sexually threatening presence, a potential violator of the mother.

This brief exploration of a single trope serves to illustrate the ways in which radical discourse evolved in the weeks and months following 16 August 1819. The widespread use of maternal imagery demonstrates the inter-relatedness of texts across a range of genres and print media, with the commonality of the trope strengthening the radical response to Peterloo. Their longevity is testament to their effectiveness. Together these representations evince a cultural collectivity and an organic evolution of motif into iconography.

1 'The Peterloo Man'[29]

As with many of the poems in this chapter and others, the MYC are depicted as cowardly, primarily due to their violence towards women and children. Published in the *Black Dwarf* on 6 October 1819, the tone of this poem is vitriolic, and the comparison with the battlefield of

Waterloo only serves to highlight the cowardly nature of the yeomen at Peterloo.

> You have heard of the far-renowned Waterloo plains,
> Where the sun, horror-struck at the slaughter declin'd;
> Where courage to frenzy abandoned the reins,
> And liberty fell 'midst the tears of mankind.[30]
>
> But a scene still more dreadful remains to the story,
> Where the blood of the helpless in wild torrents ran;
> When women, and children and grandsires hoary,
> Fell beneath the fierce sword of the *Peterloo Man*.
>
> How brave were the heroes, what muse can relate;
> On the breast of its mother, he bade the babe bleed!
> And the mother herself would in vain shun the fate,
> That awaited her under the hoofs of his steed.[31]
>
> Stained deep with their gore, how he dashed along,
> Of banditti[32] the first, since fell murder began;
> How tremble the feeble among the scared throng,
> When they hear the fierce shout of the Peterloo Man!
>
> What groups there assemble, what ferment prevails!
> 'Tis a nation in search of the savages base;
> And justice demands, in her still even scales,[33]
> To balance the wretches who Britain disgrace.
>
> Whether Yeoman, or Magistrates, forth be they brought,
> Their deeds which a nation indignantly scan,
> Well merit the doom of eternity fraught
> With the vengeance of God on the Peterloo Man.

2 'Peterloo'[34]

BY AN OFFICER OF HIS MAJESTY'S ROYAL NAVY

Through the use of a Waterloo veteran as a poetic persona, this poem focuses on the dishonourable actions of the MYC in stark contrast to the heroism of the British army and navy who fought and defeated 'foreign' enemies in the Napoleonic Wars. Central to the theme of dishonour is the murder of women at Peterloo. Unlike the troops under Wellington's command, who fought to guard the freedom of the British people from Napoleon, the MYC turned their sabres on the very people whom the regular troops had sought to protect. It was printed in the *Manchester Observer* on 13 November 1819.

The heroic muse no more shall boast,
The mighty deeds of Waterloo;
But, this henceforth shall be the toast,
The glorious feats of Peterloo.

Fame, sound thy trump with loud applause,
For men so generous, brave and true,
For men who fought without a cause,
All on the plain of Peterloo.

Tell us no more of Wellington,[35]
Nor of his warlike conquering crew;
How dim the glory of their sun,
Before the blaze of Peterloo.

They madly sought a foreign shore,
And *foreign* armies to subdue,
But these more brave, with *British* gore
Deep ting'd the plains of Peterloo.

To face the brave was the delight
Which former British heroes knew;
To combat those who *could not* fight;
Was all the pride of Peterloo.

Man once was wont to fight with man,
But these would sabre *woman* too,
So high their matchless courage ran,
On the great day of Peterloo.

From clime to clime, let glory tell
Of acts so valiant and so new!
Yea, let her tell, what women fell
On the red plain of Peterloo.

Let these, and future times record,
What unarm'd hosts these warriors slew!
Let all the Earth with one accord,
Cry 'nought was like this Peterloo!'

O woulds't thou Albion,[36] still be free,
And bid to every fear adieu,
Call to thy aid the MYC
They fought so well at Peterloo!

3 'Manchester Yeomanry Valour'[37]

This poem is an example of how the radical press re-printed poems and articles following Peterloo. First published in the *Manchester Observer* on 18 September, it also appeared in *Medusa* on 30 October, aimed at a London rather than Manchester readership. To mark the 150th anniversary of Peterloo, the poem appeared in the *Stockport Advertiser* on 14 August 1969.[38] The unnamed poet begins by directly appealing to St Peter before turning his anger on the cowardly MYC who are described as 'half soldier[s]'.[39] The satirical tone of the poem underlines the cowardliness of those who injured and killed the defenceless. The poem ends with a curse that those responsible for the violence will 'sicken and pine'.

> Sad sixteenth of August! Accursed be the day;
> When thy field, Oh, St. Peter! Was crimson'd with gore;
> When the blue-mantled bullies[40] in hostile array,
> Struck down to the earth the defenceless and poor.
>
> Yes, Yes! It was valour to gash the unarmed,
> To bear down the aged – the cripple – the child;
> It was manly to vanquish the female, unarmed,
> To mangle her bosom was gentle and mild.
>
> Ye cowardly brutes! May the Lancashire fair,
> With merited scorn, your base doings repay;
> May they scoff at the coward, whose half-soldier air
> Serves this counterfeit lion[41] the more to betray.
>
> May the ghosts of the murdered your slumbers infest,
> And may drops of their blood be found in your wine;
> Thus, sinking in heart, and be conscience opprest,
> In remorse, and in tear, may you sicken and pine.

4 'A New Song'[42]

By dedicating this song to the courage of the MYC, the satirical tone is immediately established. Published in *Medusa* on 9 October 1819, no tune is mentioned, although it is evident from both the title and the content of the song, that it was to be sung. The yeomanry's desire for a fight is evident as they charge into the crowd 'on massacre bent'.

> In commemoration of the invincible courage of the Manchester
>   Yeomanry Cavalry, displayed in St. Peter's Field, on 16th August, in
>   the year 1819
> Courage as only seen in great exploits

That virtue WARRANTS and true wisdom guides.
ADDISON[43]

In these times so notorious,
So *happy,* so *glorious,*[44]
What man is there would not rejoice, O?
When for courage renown'd,
And with *laurels*[45] are crown'd
Our Manchester cavalry boys, O!

Tho' thousands appear'd
And their standards they rear'd
Our Yeomanry then show'd no fear, O!
But with sabre so bright,
They burn'd for the fight,
And resolv'd not to let fall a tear, O!

Tho' their fathers or brothers,
Or sisters or mothers,
With innocence all should come arm'd, O!
They had courage enough,
To contend with stuff,
For with that their hearts never were charm'd, O!

So now each on his steed,
Gallop'd off at full speed
While with sabre he wounded the air, O!
And on massacre bent
To Saint Peter's Field went
Nor man, woman, or child would he spare, O!

'Tis true, tho' not armed
Their cause might have charmed
E'en the devil himself to give ear, O!
But these lads of true fire,
Held their characters higher,
And cry'd 'Damn it, what is there to fear, O!'

A woman and child,
In their way ran so wild;
The woman cried –'spare, spare my child, O!'
But these true sons of Mars,[46]
Exclaim'd 'now for the wars,
Our glory must never be spoil'd, O!'

Of courage so vast
In times present or past,
None sure ever heard of the like, O!
For man, woman or child,

Or they frown'd or they smil'd,
These men had the boldness to strike, O!

Of their conduct so bold,
None too oft can be told,
So proverbially always declare, O!
(When of courage you speak,
In the strong or the weak)
'He's as BOLD AS A MANCHESTER HERO!'

5 'The Sword King'[47]

In the 22 September 1819 issue of the *Black Dwarf* in which this poem appeared, the author is stated as 'H. Morton, son of Silas Morton', the reference to the father indicating someone of renown.[48] The woman and child in the poem are fleeing from the yeoman who pursues them as a hunter his prey. By giving voice to the three characters in the poem, Morton personalises the events, emphasising the grotesque actions of the MYC which result, at the end of the poem, in the death of the child.

(No-a-glee.)
He heard with awe
This ruffian stabber fix the law –[49]
* * * *
For Englan's war revered the claim
Of every unprotected name;
And spared amid its fiercest rage
Childhood, and womanhood, and age.[50]
    ROKEBY
Who is it that flies in the tumult so fast
When the yeomanry bugles are mingling their blast?
The mother who folds her dear child to her breast,
And screams, as around her expire the oppress'd;
'Oh! hush my darling! Relinquish they fear,'
'My mother! My mother! The sword king[51] is near!
The sword king with sabre so bloody and bright,
Ah! Shade my young eyes from the horrible sight!'

'Base brat of reform, shall thy cries bar my way,
To the laurels that bloom for the loyal today?
Shalt thou live to rear banner, white, emerald, or blue?
No! this is our yeomanry's own Waterloo.'
'My mother! My mother! And dost thou not hear
What curses the yeomanry shout in thine ear?'
'Oh! hush thee my child, let the murderers come!
There is vengeance in heaven for the base who strike home!'[52]

'A curse on your standards so flaunting and fine,
Surrender or perish! – die rebel – 'tis mine!'
'My mother! My mother! Oh! hold me now fast,
The sword king and steed will o'ertake us at last!'
The mother she trembled, she doubled her speed,
But dark on her path swept the black yeoman's steed;
And ere she arrived at her own cottage door,
Life throbb'd in her poor baby's bosom no more.

6 Peterloo

Both this ballad and the following one were written by John Stafford, a weaver from Ashton-under-Lyne in Lancashire, who appears to have been present at Peterloo.[53] Moreover, this ballad, one of the longest in the anthology, has the detail of an eye-witness. One thing of note here is how Stafford stresses that the murderers were known to their victims; this was, after all, a very local event. The naming of the yeoman by the old woman towards the end of the ballad is a highly poignant reminder of the very personal nature of some of the fighting. According to Palmer, it was to be sung to the tune of 'Green Upon the Cape'.

Palmer notes that 'Green on the Cape' may be another name for 'Plains of Peterloo'.[54] The song 'Green on the Cape' is an Irish song which was published in 1802; however, the use of 'Croppy', a term given to Irish rebels during the 1798 rebellion, indicates it was probably written at this time. The first verse is as follows:

> I'm a lad that's forced in exile from my native land,
> For an oath has pass'd against me, in my country I can't stand
> But while I'm at my liberty, I will make my escape,
> I'm a poor distressed Croppy, for the green on the cape.[55]

Both this song and *Peterloo* have thirteen-syllable lines and, therefore, could be written to the same tune.

> On the sixteenth day of August, it was held at Peterloo,
> A just and lawful meeting we knew it to be true,
> With flags and caps of liberty they did assemble there,
> Both in peace and good order, the reformers did appear.
>
> The stage was erected and reformers stood all around,
> A space was only left between for tyrants and blood hounds,[56]
> The constables and vampires[57] they came to rule the day,
> Stand steady men, stand steady and their truncheons play'd away.
>
> Your flags and caps of liberty we'll entirely take away,
> We'll cut all down before us and show you tyrants play,

'Base brat of reform'   109

For we know you are unarmed, and we'll murder all we can,
Both men, women and children, in spite of 'Rights of man'.[58]

From Smedley[59] cottage to the hustings, it was crowded all the way.
The patriots joined hand in hand, the band did sweetly play,
Not the least thoughts of murder that did commence that day,
Until that cruel action on Peterloo did sway.

The brave champion of reform,[60] when the hustings mounted on,
He fill'd them all with joy, for to see that valiant man,
To see the gallant hero, with courage bold so fair,
He won the heart of every working-man was there.

The patriots agreed that the champion took the chair,
When he saw female reformers, he smil'd at them being there,
But before he had address'd them all, there came that hellish crew
To murder all poor people that were come to Peterloo.

With their glittering swords and carbines[61] to kill unarmed men
They are worse than Algerines,[62] when strangers meet with them
For they've murdered their own neighbours, that striv'd to fill their
    purse,
And now they're half naked must be trampled down with horse.

They form'd themselves four deep, three times over made a charge,
But reformers they stood firm, so they could not play at large
Until a space was opened occupied by their own crew,
For to murder all poor people that were come to Peterloo.

From the outside to the hustings, those ruffians cut sway,
I've a charge against you, Mr Hunt, one of the crew did say,
I am ready now to join you, I'm just at your command,
So they took him to the New Bailey,[63] as before it had been plan'd.

Some flags and caps of liberty, these ruffians did destroy,
But still a valiant female her colour she did fly,
Till she could no longer hold it, amongst that murdering crew
So she fell down amongst the rest on the plains of Peterloo.

A poor woman struggling with an infant in her arms,
One of the crew came riding up for to destroy her charms,
She said spare my little creature but that butcher cut her too,
And left her with her infant bleeding on the Plains of Peterloo.

An old woman hearing this story, and believing it was true,
She went to seek her son that was gone to Peterloo,
And as she went along the street a ruffian did she meet
She knew him from a child, – she had liv'd in the same street.

This old woman spoke right kindly, and she call'd him by his name,
I know you will not hurt me, Thomas Shelberdine,[64] she said,
But to fulfil his orders like the rest of that same crew,
He cut her down that instant as they did at Peterloo.[65]

So now you special constables,[66] I'll give you all your due,
For backing those proceedings that were done at Peterloo,
Both landlords and shopkeepers, your doors I'll pass by,
If you had no swords and carabines,[67] you made your truncheons fly.

So come all you brave patriots wherever that you be,
You must all unite together to gain your liberty,
And not forget those tyrants, but with justice them pursue,
And all such cruel murderers that went to Peterloo.

7 *Another Song Concerning Peterloo*

The second song by John Stafford is written in Lancastrian dialect, which, together with the use of the first person, results in a song rooted in place and time. The old woman in the song exhorts the locals to return to St Peter's Field where the protestors have either been killed or arrested. This version of the song would appear to be incomplete. According to Palmer, it was to be sung to the local tune of 'Joan o' Greenfield'.[68]

The song appears both in dialect form and Standard English and ridicules the naivety of John, who states that he will go to Oldham to fight the French. Frank Kidston's version of the opening verse is as follows:

> Said Jone to his wife one hot summer's day,
> I've resolved that I' Greenfield nae longer I'll stay
> For a'wil go to Owdham as fast as a can,
> So fare-ye-well, Greenfield, and fare-ye-well, Nan.
> For a so-jer a'wll be and fare Owdham a'will see
> And a'll go for a bat-tle wi't' French.[69]

Another version, entitled either 'Joan o' Greenfield and the Bailiffs' or 'Joan o' Greenfield' begins:

> I'm a poor cotton weaver as many one knows
> I've nought to eat in the house and worn out my clothes
> You'd hardly give sixpence for all I've got on
> My clogs are both bursten and stockings I've none[70]

Ewan McColl sang a version of this song entitled 'The Four Loom Weaver' in 1951. Presumably, Stafford chose this tune due to its local connection and familiarity with his audience.

But as soon as we geet'n[71] as far as Blue Pig,[72]
A middle aged woman we met at full trig,[73]
You'd better turn back, unless youn tay[74] your pikes,
For Manchester's fill'd with o' sorts of scrikes.[75]
Yeoman Cavalry are drunken, if they are not aul be sunk'n,
And they're killing folk at every street end.

I said to this woman, you tell a strange tale,
Is that Manchester law! I vow and declare,
Manchester law, mon, and ne'er tall of that,
For justices and constables are all of one mack,[76]
For what they cannot kill fairly, they tane[77] to th' New Bailey,[78]
And th' Infirmary's filled w' lame folk.

8 'To Henry Hunt, Esquire'

Despite this poem being addressed to Henry Hunt, the reference to the murder of women and children warrants its place in this chapter. Written by 'J.F.' on 17 September and printed in the *Manchester Observer* on 25 September 1819, the anti-semitic references make it not only uncomfortable to the modern reader but also unusual in radical poems where such sentiments are rare. The reference to Herod's massacre of young children, as told in the Gospel of Matthew, is used by the poet to underline the barbarity of the actions of the MYC, defining them as 'other' in stark opposition to the 'self' of Hunt and the radical cause. Even compared to the shocking imagery which pervades this anthology, this poem's brutality is harrowing and serves to dehumanise those who committed such acts against their own people.

Hail, glorious Champion of a sacred cause,
Undaunted advocate of freedom's laws!
The voice of slander shall e're long be hush'd,
Ere long the dastardly oppressors crush'd,
Millions, to madness stung, await the day,
When just revenge shall wash their crimes away,
If crimes, like theirs, can ever be forgotten!!!
Ah, no! For when the fiends are dead and rotten,
E'en when a thousand circling years have pass'd,
Their names accurs'd will be with murderers class'd;
Class'd with the refuse of the cut-throat crew,
As having mangled women, CHILDREN too!!
The midnight ruffian, who assaults for prey,
Spares infants, when they come within his way!
In what could slumb'ring innocents offend,
What sin commit to merit such an end?

Who but those demons dire; the ancient Jews,
To shield a helpless female would refuse?
Who but that race, of former days the pest,
Would smite an infant at its mother's breast?[79]
Why British Yeomanry have done the deed,
At which a British SOLDIER's heart would bleed!
Instructed by a mad-brained Magistrate,
Whose duty 'twas to guard the laws and state.
These blood-bath'd bravoes,[80] worse than Israel's band,
Have charged their countrywomen, sword in hand,
Have put their fellow citizens to death,
And sought to ravish e'en of the babes the breath!
Polluted monsters, cowards base and fell!
Too vile to mingle with the dregs of hell,
Where would your Yeoman courage all have been,
Could but a jot of danger have been seen
In this your gallant work? Like morning dew,
The sweat of fear had drench'd them thro' and thro'!
With broomsticks arm'd a dozen palsied hags
Had made you scamper with your warlike nags!
But half a pioneer with half an axe,
Had made ye swoon upon your horses' backs;
And, had a foe dragoon appear'd in sight,
Ye'd all have given up the ghost with fright!!!
Deem not the day of retribution past,
The punishment of murder comes at last!
The daring Champion of unrivall'd fame,
The Patriot HUNT (immortal be his name!)
Has sworn to advocate the suff'rers cause,
And bring to light the spurners of the laws!
But hireling scribblers and their garreteers,[81]
Pursue the dirty work and ribald sneers![82]
But let them not forget the glorious day,
When HENRY HUNT was greeted on the way
But full three hundred thousand CITIZENS;[83]
Nor let the happy truth escape the pens,
That ALL, who form'd his late triumphant train,
Profess his principles, nor think in vain!!!

Notes

1 J. Marlow, *The Peterloo Massacre* (London: Rapp and Whiting, 1969), pp. 150–1; M. Bush, *The Casualties of Peterloo* (Lancaster: Carnegie Publishing, 2005), p. 90.

2 M. Bush, 'The Women at Peterloo: The Impact of Female Reform on

'Base brat of reform'   113

the Manchester Meeting of 16 August 1819', *History* 89:294 (2004), p. 225.
3 Bush, *The Casualties of Peterloo*, p. 31.
4 R. Mather, 'These Lancashire Women are Witches in Politics: Female Reform Societies and the Theatre of Radicalism, 1819–1820', in R. Poole (ed.), *Return to Peterloo. Manchester Region History Review*, 23 (2014), p. 60; R. Poole, 'By the Law and Sword: Peterloo Revisited', *History*, 91:302 (2006), p. 263.
5 I have written elsewhere on this subject. I am grateful to MRHR for enabling me to incorporate some of the essay into this introduction (A. Morgan, 'Starving Mothers and Murdered Children in Cultural Representations of Peterloo', in Poole (ed.), *Return to Peterloo*, pp. 65–78.
6 Bush, 'The Women at Peterloo', p. 210.
7 A. Clark, *The Struggle for the Breeches: Gender and the Making of the British Working Class* (London: Rivers Oram, 1995), p. 159; Mather, 'These Lancashire Women are Witches in Politics', pp. 50, 57.
8 Chapter 4, number 13.
9 Bush, 'The Women at Peterloo', p. 213.
10 Mather, 'These Lancashire Women are Witches in Politics', p. 57.
11 Bush, 'The Women at Peterloo', pp. 211, 232.
12 D. Donald, 'The Power of Print: Graphic Images of Peterloo', in *Peterloo Massacre, MRHR*, pp. 21–30, at p. 26.
13 Mather, 'These Lancashire Women are Witches in Politics', p. 61.
14 *Manchester Observer* (21 August 1819), p. 687.
15 J. Tyas, 'Dispersal of the Reform Meeting at Manchester by a Military Force', *Examiner*, 608 (22 August 1819), p. 2.
16 'Manchester Reform Meeting', *Leeds Mercury*, 2828 (1819), p. 3.
17 I. Haywood, 'Shelley's *Mask of Anarchy* and the Visual Iconography of Female Distress', in P. Connell and N. Leask, eds, *Romanticism and Popular Culture in Britain and Ireland* (Cambridge, 2009), pp. 148–73, at p. 150.
18 *Black Dwarf*, 3:34 (1819), p. 551. Original emphases.
19 A. Cross, '"What a World We Make the Oppressor and the Oppressed": George Cruikshank, Percy Shelley and the Gendering of Revolution in 1819', *Journal of English Literary History*, 71 (2004), pp. 167–207.
20 Donald, 'Power of Print', p. 22.
21 'Peterloo Artefacts', *MRHR*, 3:1 (1989), p. 93.
22 A headscarf with this image is part of the collection of Peterloo artefacts at the Working-Class Movement Library at Salford. The People's History Museum in Manchester has a handkerchief bearing the image.
23 Julie Kipp, *Romanticism, Maternity and the Body Politic* (Cambridge: Cambridge University Press, 2003); Stephen C. Behrendt, '"A Few Harmless Numbers": British Women Poets and the Climate of War, 1793–1825', in P. Shaw (ed.), *Romantic Wars: Studies in Culture and Conflict, 1793–1822* (Hampshire: Ashgate, 2000), p. 14.

24 D. Donald, *The Age of Caricature: Satirical Prints in the Reign of George III* (London: Yale University Press, 1996), p. 192.
25 Chapter 5, number 2.
26 Number 1 below.
27 Mather, 'These Lancashire Women are Witches in Politics', p. 60. The Introduction to Chapter 5 explores the theme and language of chivalry in more detail.
28 Number 5 below.
29 *Black Dwarf*, 3:40 (1819), p. 659.
30 It is interesting to note that the poet does not depict the glory of Waterloo but rather the horror and resulting lack of freedom.
31 The image of a woman being trampled by horse's hooves is the dominant representation of women at Peterloo.
32 A gang of bandits or outlaws.
33 Justice is usually depicted as blindfolded, holding a sword to represent the power of the law, and scales to indicate the balance or objectivity of the law. For more information, see p. 61n.42.
34 *Manchester Observer* (3 November 1819), p. 812.
35 Arthur Wellesley was granted the title of the 1st Duke of Wellington in 1809 following his victory over the French at the Battle of Talavera in Portugal during the Peninsular War. Wellington was feted for his defeat of Napoleon at the Battle of Waterloo in 1815.
36 Albion is the oldest name for the island of Great Britain and is often used in literature to represent England or Britain. See p. 60n.35 for more details.
37 *Manchester Observer* (18 September 1819), p. 718; *Medusa*, 1:37 (1819), p. 296.
38 This newspaper cutting is part of a collection held at the Working-Class Movement Library in Salford (S52).
39 St Peter's field was named after the church which was built there in 1788. It was demolished in 1907.
40 Contemporaneous cartoons, such as Cruikshank's *Massacre at St Peter's*, depict the MYC in blue uniforms.
41 The lion has been a feature of the British royal coat of arms since the reign of Richard I or Lionheart at the end of the twelfth century. In heraldry, the lion symbolises bravery and strength, hence the description of the yeoman as a 'counterfeit lion'.
42 *Medusa*, 1:34 (1819), pp. 271–2.
43 This epigraph varies from the original lines in *Cato* by Joseph Addison: 'True fortitude is seen in great exploits, / That justice warrants, and that wisdom guides.' First performed in 1713, Addison's play tells the story of the eponymous Cato, a Stoic and opponent of Julius Caesar. The play is regarded as an attack on government tyranny, and as a championing of individual liberty, as shown in the Preface to *Cato* written by L. Eusden, who states that the play shows 'how endless joys from freedom spring / How life in bondage is a worthless thing' (Addison, *Cato* (London, 1763), pp. 34, 7).

44 This is a clear allusion to the line in the national anthem, 'Happy and glorious'.
45 In Ancient Rome, laurel wreaths were awarded to men who had been victorious in war. Epstein notes that radicals carried laurel branches or put sprigs in their coats as a libertarian symbol of regeneration (p. 83).
46 Mars is the Roman god of war.
47 *Black Dwarf*, 3:38 (1819), p. 627.
48 No other poem published in the *Black Dwarf* between 1817 and 1824 is accredited to H. Morton.
49 This quotation is from stanza XXII in the first canto of *Rokeby* by Walter Scott, published in 1813. Set in the immediate aftermath of the Parliamentary victory in the Battle of Marston Moor in 1644, the opening of the first canto comprises the villain, Bertram Risingham, narrating to his accomplice, Oswald Wycliffe, how he murdered Philip Mortham during the battle. 'The ruffian stabber' then demands a portion of Mortham's wealth (W. Scott, *Rokeby* (Edinburgh: 1813), p. 31).
50 *Ibid.*, p. 38. Despite the ferocity of the fighting in the English Revolution, this quotation stresses the chivalric code of both the Royalists and Parliamentarians in their sparing of the old, the young and women from the violence. Morton is clearly comparing this with the victimisation of women and children at Peterloo.
51 The naming of the yeoman as the 'sword king' by the child is redolent of folk-tale villains. Indeed, the narrative capitalises on the familiar stories of defenceless women pursued by violent men which feature in countless ballads.
52 'Britons Strike Home' is the subtitle for Cruikshanks's caricature, *Massacre at St. Peter's*.
53 Palmer, *Sound of History*, p. 260. The songs are from Stafford's 1840 book, *Songs Comic and Sentimental* (*Ibid.*, p. 331). John Stafford often sang his song *Peterloo Massacre* at radical dinners and meetings. 'According to the Northern Star (16.11.1839), although Stafford "never had the opportunity of learning either to read or write, [he] has composed songs that would do honour to a Southey"' (J.A. Epstein, *Radical Expression: Political Language, Ritual, and Symbol in England, 1790–1850* (Oxford: Oxford University Press, 1994), p. 154). Epstein goes on to say that Stafford began a column entitled 'National Songs' in the *Manchester Observer* on 23 October 1819 (p. 219). See Chapter 2, number 9.
54 Palmer, *Sound of History*, p. 331.
55 http://ballads.bodleian.ox.ac.uk/static/images/sheets/15000/12464.gif [accessed 19 November 2017].
56 See pp. 12 and 63n.73.
57 Stories of vampires have been published in Britain since the first half of the eighteenth century. However, in April 1819, a short story entitled *The Vampyre* was published, which achieved great popular success and is widely credited with beginning the genre. Written by Dr John Polidori, the

story was begun at Villa Diodati on Lake Geneva in 1816 where Polidori was attending Lord Byron and his visitors, Percy and Mary Shelley and Mary's half-sister, Claire Clairmont. Polidori began the story as part of a competition with the Shelleys and Byron, which also famously produced *Frankenstein*.

58 Paine's *The Rights of Man*, was published in two parts: 1791 and 1792. 200,000 copies were sold in the first two years following publication, suggesting its contents were widely known (D. Wu (ed.), *Romanticism: An Anthology* (Oxford: Blackwell, 2009), p. 27).

59 The area now known as Smedley Dip and Hendham Vale runs alongside the river Irk and is to the north of Manchester city centre in what would have been Lancashire in the early nineteenth century. Joseph Johnson, one of the radicals arrested at Peterloo was from Smedley Cottage.

60 Henry Hunt.

61 A medium-sized gun, in between a pistol and a musket.

62 Algerians. In 1819 Algeria was part of the Ottoman Empire. After the Napoleonic Wars, Algeria was involved in piracy and the enslavement of European Christians, which resulted in the bombardment of Algiers in August 1816 by an Anglo-Dutch fleet after pressure from the Royal Navy to end enslavement and piracy had failed. A treaty was signed in 1816 in which Algeria agreed to abandon piracy and slavery. In this poem, Algerians are used to represent slavers whose desire for money has replaced their humanity.

63 The New Bailey Prison was built in 1787 in Salford next to the River Irwell on what became New Bailey Street. The foundation stone was laid by Thomas Butterworth Bailey, after whom the prison was named. It was closed down in the 1860s following the opening of Strangeways Prison in Manchester. Hunt, along with another eleven people, including two women, was imprisoned in the New Bailey on 16 August. All of the prisoners were released on bail by the end of August after the charges were changed from high treason to conspiracy (D. Read, *Peterloo: The Massacre and its Background* (Manchester: Manchester University Press, 1958), p. 143–4). In 1818, the prison reformer, Elizabeth Fry, visited the prison (Palmer, *A Touch of the Times*, p. 255).

64 Marlow refers to 'Tom Shelmerdine', who was a member of the MYC, and known to his victim: 'An old woman saw Tom Shelmerdine, whom she had nursed as a child, riding down upon her. She cried: "Nay, Tom Shelmerdine, thee wilt not hurt me, I know"' but 'deaf to her supplications he rode her down' (*The Peterloo Massacre*, p. 141). There is no source cited for this evidence but it is strikingly similar to the ballad. Bush outlines the experience of Margaret Goodwin, aged sixty, who was searching for her son and who was 'deliberately ridden down and then cut on the head by Shelmerdine, a man she had known for many years' ('Women at Peterloo', p. 227).

65 Samuel Bamford reports a similar account of an assailant being known to his victim: 'She asked who did it, and Tom [Redford] mentioned a person;

he said he knew him well; and she, sobbing, said she also knew him, and his father and mother before him; and she prayed God not to visit that sin on the head of him who did it, but to change his heart and bring him to repentance' (*Passages in the Life of a Radical*, vol. 1, p. 215).

66 Prior to the establishment of a police force in the 1830s, special constables were law enforcement officers. The constables, under the leadership of Joseph Nadin, were involved in the massacre alongside the MYC.
67 Alternative spelling for 'carbine'.
68 Palmer, *Sound of History*, p. 260. 'Joan o' Greenfield', also known as 'John of Greenfield', 'Jone o Grinfelt' and 'Joan o' Greenfelt' was written by Joseph Lees from Oldham in 1805 and is described by Poole as 'the most successful of all Lancashire songs' R. (Poole, 'The March to Peterloo: Politics and Festivity in Late Georgian England', *Past and Present*, 192 (2006), p. 133). Greenfield is a village in the Saddleworth parish of Oldham.
69 Frank Kidson, *Garland of English Folk-Songs* (London: Ascherberg, Hopwood & Crew, 1926), pp. 94–9.
70 http://ballads.bodleian.ox.ac.uk/static/images/sheets/15000/13935.gif [accessed 19 November 2017].
71 Got.
72 Presumably an inn.
73 Trot.
74 Take.
75 Screams.
76 Make.
77 Taken.
78 See note 63 above.
79 This refers to the Massacre of the Innocents, as narrated in Matthew's Gospel, where King Herod ordered the execution of all young boys in order to protect his throne from the newly born King of the Jews, as the Magi had prophesied: 'Then Herod, when he saw that he was mocked of the wise men, was exceeding wroth, and sent forth, and slew all the children that were in Bethlehem, and in all the coasts thereof, from two years old and under, according to the time which he had diligently inquired of the wise men' (Matthew 2:16). According to Poole, at John Lees' inquest, Robert Lancashire testified to Edward Meagher, the MYC trumpeter, cutting open a woman's breast ('R. Poole, 'What We Don't Know About Peterloo', in R. Poole (ed.), *Return to Peterloo. Manchester Region History Review*, 23 (2014), p. 6).
80 A daring villain or assassin.
81 A literary hack.
82 The poet is accusing certain parts of the press of promoting the government line on Peterloo.
83 See p. 35n.22.

4

'Your memorials shall survive the grave': elegy and remembrance

The ballads and songs within this chapter fall into two camps: elegy and remembrance. Whilst a central feature of elegiac poetry is the way in which it remembers or memorialises the dead, a poem which is one of remembrance is not necessarily an elegy. Several of the songs herein use the date of Peterloo as a temporal marker – with an eye both on the contemporaneous reader or audience and the future reader:

> It was in the year one thousand,
> Eight hundred and nineteen,
> All in the month of August,
> Our Weaver lads was seen.[1]

> The Sixteenth day of August Eighteen Hundred and Nineteen.
> There many thousand people on every road were seen.[2]

In this way these songs are a way of both 'marking and making' history in their attempts to reach an audience beyond Manchester and ensure that the public knew what had happened on 16 August, as well as preserving the event in English vernacular culture.[3] It is also a quest for ownership of the narrative of the day; the speed with which so many of these songs were written and published suggests not only the ferocity of emotions surrounding events but also the need to exert some control over the way in which they were represented. As James Chandler observes:

> The year of Peterloo in British history was exceptional for the recorded volume, value, and topical vicinity of the body of literary work it produced in a range of genres and forms [...] English writing from 1819 is aware of its place in and as history. Much literary work of England in 1819, in other words, seems concerned with its place in England in 1819 – concerned, that is, with a national operation of self-dating, or re-dating, that is meant to count as a national self-making, or re-making.[4]

Much of Chandler's book centres on Shelley's sonnet 'England in 1819' and the way in which Mary Shelley's choice of title locates the poem both in the time in was written and the events it describes; so it is with these Peterloo poems. The detailed depiction of events and use of the collective 'our' in the representational ballads quoted above suggests their writers were directly involved, as participants as opposed to onlookers, thereby enhancing the authority of the narrative. For readers familiar with the events, the ballads validate their stories, strengthening their experience through a shared discourse; for those seeking knowledge of events, the ballads serve as news, recalling the day in an accessible and memorable way.

Although broadside ballads are often regarded as ephemeral, the longevity of oral culture in England and the revival of the ballad in the eighteenth century would have suggested to balladeers that their songs may well endure beyond the immediate aftermath of Peterloo. Indeed, ballads had been written to mark significant events for centuries, such as the Spanish Armada of 1588 and the English Revolution a century later. The ballad *Lord Willoughby* narrates events in the late 1580s when Peregrine Bertie, the thirteenth Baron Willoughby de Eresby fought in alliance with the Dutch Republic against Spain:

> The fifteenth of July, with glist'ring sword and shield,
> A famous fight in Flanders was fought-en in the field.
> The most courageous officers were English captains three,
> But the bravest in the battle was brave Lord Willoughby.[5]

This contemporaneous ballad, although failing to state the year of the battle (probably 1586) begins with the date in order to mark and celebrate Willoughby's heroic efforts. Writing in 1860, W.W. Wilkins notes:

> The popular song is easy, simple and born of the incidents of the day. It is the intellectual personification of the feelings and opinions of a people. It is the delight of the multitude, the joy and solace of the many. It laughs in derision at despotic power, lightens the social burdens of life, and inspires the patriot with hope.[6]

In the seven modes of poetic authority outlined by Maureen McLane, 'ethnographic authority', incorporating a native culture or tradition with the 'poet as informant', aptly describes ballads which mark events.[7] As a means of communication, the broadside ballad was written, printed and disseminated swiftly, hawked around country fairs by ballad singers to be sold and sung. Some were written and sold as a means of raising money for strikers or victims of economic or social hardship. *The Grinders' Hardship* depicts the lives of the Sheffield cutlers at the beginning of the nineteenth century and, according to

Palmer, was probably written by members of the Grinders' Misfortune Society, founded in 1804, in order to raise funds for the men:

> It happened in the year eighteen hundred and five,
> From May-day to Christmas the season was quite dry,
> For all our oldest grinders such a time never knew,
> For there's few who brave the hardships that we poor grinders do.[8]

It is not known whether the songs written to mark Peterloo were written to raise money for the victims but a number of relief committees were established after the massacre and it is reasonable to assume that money raised from the sale of Peterloo memorabilia was forwarded to its victims.

Deriving from the Greek *elegos* meaning 'mournful poem', the *OED* defines elegy as 'a song of lamentation, especially a funeral song or lament for the dead.' David Kennedy defines elegy as: 'men mourning the untimely deaths of other men'; however, unlike the self-memorialisation found in Milton's *Lycidas* and Shelley's *Adonais*, where the poet is of equal importance to the subject, the largely anonymous poems in this chapter are not only funeral laments but also epitaphs, a giving of voice to the silent and disenfranchised.[9] In this sense, the poems themselves are artefacts, monuments to both the dead and living, the lamenting of a lack of memorial to the dead ironically highlighted by the permanence of the text. John Frow remarks that elegy is a genre defined by its content, which, for European cultures, is that of mourning and commemoration.[10] In fact it may be more accurate to define elegy as a mode rather than a genre, as the poems considered here inhabit a range of generic forms, from the lyric to the ballad, and yet the elegiac mood is shared by all. Fuelled by vengeful cries and mournful laments, whether mourning the deaths of one or many, these elegiac poems all demonstrate the ways in which the elegy can be politicised, employing the rhetoric of patriotism to highlight how the actions of the state ran counter to the values and identity of its people with the dead described as 'martyr'd' or 'murder'd' patriots.[11]

Katie Trumpener defines elegy as a 'recording and memorialising activity to effect a compensatory retrieval of national history. [...] it will counter the physical destruction of a national sense of history and a sense of national destiny.'[12] As argued in the introduction to Chapter 2, English radical nationalism is at the heart of many of these poems, the employment of its rhetoric attempting to transform the 'self' of the establishment into the 'other' of the unpatriotic, with the authorities as the 'enemy within'.[13] Elegies as a form of nationalistic collectivity, where mourning serves to unite a people, are commonplace, particularly those commemorating the deaths of kings and military heroes. 'The bold Courage and lamentable Death of King Richard I' exemplifies the qualities of chivalry and patriotism often found in elegies:

> Richard Cordelion in this Land,
> A noble English Name;
> It fills the World with Wonders great,
> With Honour and with Fame.

The unknown author states that the aim of the collection is to preserve 'our old Songs' as 'History, especially our own, as for many Years been too much neglected and the generality of Englishmen are such strangers to ancient Facts and the Customs of their Kingdom, that they are easily misled by any Six-penny Pamphleteer'.[14] As well as ensuring heroes of old were not forgotten, contemporaneous elegies helped to galvanise a nation weary of war. The death of Nelson in 1805 provided such an opportunity:

> Come mourn says Britannia come mourn children dear,
> And for my brave children a monument rear,
> Let it be of polished marble to perpetuate his name,
> And in letters of gold write he dies for England's fame.[15]

The maternal Britannia guides the mourning of her people to the creation of a monument to the fallen hero; the need for a permanent memorial is key to the remembrance of Nelson's patriotic endeavours, in contrast with a number of Peterloo elegies which remark on the lack of a memorial:[16]

> Though on that spot there be no stone,
> The seed of virtue there is sown,
> ......
> Unmark'd with vain distinctions of the day,
> No titles, honours, pomp, proclaim'd you brave,
> Yet your memorials shall survive the grave,[17]

There are echoes of Gray's *Elegy in a Country Churchyard* in 'Elegaic Apostrophe'. Both poems are contemplations on the lives of those whose potentials were unfulfilled, with the poets serving as elegists for the anonymous: 'For thee who, mindful of the unhonoured dead / Dost in these lines their artless tale relate'.[18] Ralph Cohen observes that 'the poem is not about the lives lived or unlived, but about the need or desire for memorialisation'.[19] Just as he provides recognition for the 'unhonoured', so too Gray seeks remembrance and immortality through the permanent memorial of an engraved epitaph upon a gravestone. In an 'Essay Upon Epitaphs', first published in 1810, Wordsworth argues that a written epitaph on a tombstone is needed by believers in the immortality of the soul and also by our desire to be remembered after our death. Wordsworth cites epitaphs as a profoundly democratic form of text: 'An epitaph is not a proud writing shut up for the studious: it is exposed to all – to the wise and the most ignorant' and thus should be short and easily read.[20] Unlike Horatio Nelson's column in Trafalgar Square and Gray's 'frail memorial still erected nigh, / With uncouth rhymes and shapeless sculpture decked,' victims of Peterloo remain unnamed and 'unmark'd'.[21]

Whilst there are examples of elegies or epitaphs in the radical press, it is not a commonly used mode. There are examples of elegies to individuals, usually radicals, such as Joseph Gerrald, member of the SCI and LCS and one of the 'Scottish Martyrs', whose espousal of reform in Scotland resulted in conviction for sedition, and transportation to Australia where he died in 1796, and the Reverend Gilbert Wakefield, a radical writer who died shortly after being released from Dorchester Gaol where he had been sent following conviction for publishing *A Reply to some Parts of the Bishop of Landaff's Address*.[22] However, unlike these examples, the elegies in this chapter do not name their subjects, either through a desire not to single out an individual when there were so many victims or a wariness of naming names in a repressive political climate. Subjects range from the individual 'Patriot' or 'victim' to the collective 'Reformers' and 'Unfortunate Persons', their lack of naming implying that such attacks could happen to anyone.[23] Much of the imagery in these poems is that of the battlefield, and parallels can be drawn with the poetry written about the Napoleonic Wars. 'An Elegy on War', published in *The Protestant Dissenter's Magazine* in 1796, with its images of the bloodstained field and the waste of life is similar to some of the elegies on Peterloo; it combines the individual loss of 'The wife a husband mourns' with the collective:

> See the mad squadrons rush to horrid flight;
> And lavish vengeance fling o'er all the plain:
> Humanity flies far in wild affright
> On some lone surge-beat rock to mourn the slain.[24]

By 1819, Britain had enjoyed a short four years of peace following twenty-two years of war. Many of the protestors and troops at Peterloo were either veterans of the Napoleonic Wars or bereaved families. It is therefore unsurprising that the language of war permeates so many of these poems and songs. The elegy is an apt genre to commemorate not only the dead but also a nation whose military might is turned on its own people.

1 'It is Lovely to Die for Our Country'

This poignant elegy equates the deaths of those at St Peter's Field with soldiers on the battlefield and Christ on the cross. The title reminds the reader of Wilfred Owen's 'Dulce et Decorum Est' written a century later amidst the horror of the First World War, with both poems evoking a bitterness at the waste of life.[25] This elegy mourns the lack of honour and ceremony accorded to the victims but is confident that, spread by a 'holy flame', this death will inspire many. Published in the *White Hat*, it is accredited to T.A.T., who, according to Scrivener, wrote poems for the *Black Dwarf*.[26]

> Should we on cross and scaffold die,
> Or in the field of honour lie,
> Delightful is the patriot's death
> Who for his country yields his breath.
> Freedom his narrow house shall trace,
> And tread with reverence the place.
>
> Though on that spot there be no stone,
> The seed of virtue there is sown,
> From thence a holy flame shall rise,
> Ascend and spread o'er earth and skies,
> Whilst proud of his devoted fate,
> Myriads his fame shall emulate.

2 'The Patriot's Grave'

BY ANTI-YEOMAN

Taking as its focus the death of individuals, this elegy calls on the murderer to imagine the grief caused to a parent by the death of their only child and to a son by the death of his father or mother. The scale of the massacre dealt with by many of the poems is movingly reduced to the grief of a family. Authored by 'Anti-Yeoman' and printed in the *Manchester Observer* on 25 September 1819, the poet curses the yeoman for eternity.[27] This poem has echoes of the opening stanza of 'Arbour Hill', a poem written by the United Irishman, Robert Emmet, as a memorial to those executed for their role in the 1798 uprising in Ireland.

> No rising column marks this spot
> Where many a victim lies,

But oh! the blood which here has streamed,
To heaven for justice lies.[28]

The day is o'er! And many a victim lies
Beneath the hallow'd sod, to Liberty
For ever sacred. The Patriot sleeps in peace;
Oppression's famine, or oppression's sword
Can trouble him no longer. O! Strew
The Laurel[29] there; and let the lily,[30]
In sorrowing silence, bend its humble head
Upon the turf revered. Stranger, tread softly;
For he was Freedom's Friend, when Freedom had but few.
———————————————————To this sad spot!
Who rests below, to moulder here so soon.
Let fancy draw a faithful picture for him!
O! Let him see himself, – the horrid murderer
Of a parent's hope, an offspring's succour!
And let him taste the pang which he has given,
Of poignant grief, of anguish, of remorse.
O! Let the father's sigh, the mother's tear,
Rush on his heart, and to his conscience make
The sad appeal! Be he by turns
The wretched father, looking upon all
That murder left him of his only son, –
His pride, and joy; and let him see
His aged Sire, to whom affection clings,
  A lifeless corpse beneath his aching eye!
Nay, let him see the breast, from which
His earliest nourishment he drew, severed
From off the bosom,* where, in infancy he rested.
Be these keen pangs his portion; and if more
He need; – if more his frame will bear, –
Let more be added. Let him be shunn'd,
Detested and revil'd; – and let the curses
Of the just man rest on his head forever!

* One of the Yeomanry, it is said, boasts of the dexterity with which he cut off one of the breasts of a Female on the [?]. It is a pity the Female in question was not his own Mother.[31]

3 *A Tribute to the Immortal Memory of the Reformers, Who Fell on the 16th of August, 1819*

As with number 11 below, this broadside ballad was printed by Innes of Turner Street, Manchester.[32] The woodcut accompanying the poem depicts six speakers, including a woman on the hustings, led by Henry

Hunt waving a banner in front of a cheering crowd. Soldiers on horseback with sabres raised are charging towards the people. Written in heroic couplets, this sombre elegy provides a memorial for those whose deaths are 'unmark'd' before anticipating a better future when the tyrants are overthrown and liberty triumphs.

> Hail Sons of Freedom who in Britain's cause
> Fell victims to the Usurpers of her Laws;[33]
> The muse shall pay her tribute to your worth,
> And in your cause the nations of the earth,
> Ere long shall join; and Liberty's blest sound,
> Shall thro' each Tyrant's land with joy resound,
> What tho' in poverty's rude grasp ye lay.
> Unmark'd with vain distinctions of the day,
> No titles, honours, pomp, proclaim'd you brave,
> Yet your memorials shall survive the grave,[34]
> Tho' not in conflicts with a foreign foe,
> Ye felt contending death's resistless blow,
> At home ye fell; at home your blood was shed,
> Thrice honour'd few who for your country bled,
> No more cou'd you have done, no more have lost,
> If you in foreign fields had joined the host
> Of warlike heroes in their country's cause,
> And crown'd with laurels gain'd deserv'd applause,
> Lamented Friends, your suffering country mourns
> That her brave sons shou'd meet such base returns,
> But shall Barbarians with a savage hand,
> Destroy the bud of freedom in our land,
> Shall kindred hands be wanton in the blood
> Of her brave Sons, who for their country's good,
> Have advocated Liberty's blest cause.
> Her glorious Rights, her Charter, and her Laws,[35]
> Rest you in Peace, ye much lamented Dead,
> And may your name throughout the land be spread,
> May your example fire the noblest breast,
> Until with Liberty, this Nation's blest,
> Your names shall live whilst truths resistless light,
> Refulgent[36] shall be shed on freedom's night,
> Thus when the Sun of Liberty bursts forth,
> With beaming radiance o'er this joyous earth,
> Then shall Oppression end, then each be free,
> And in the bonds of love united be,
> Weep not ye lonely widows of the Dead,
> Whose brave remains have claim'd their dusty bed,
> Ye yet shall smile in freedom and in peace,

When proud Oppressors and your wrongs shall cease,
And Tyrant's hurl'd from rule by Heaven's command,
And freedom Banner's wave throughout our land,
Your smiling babes shall hail the suspicious reign,
Of Liberty, and ENGLAND'S RIGHTS MAINTAIN.

4 'Elegiac Apostrophe to the Memory of the Unfortunate Persons Who Were Killed at Manchester, on 16th of August'

This poem first appeared in the *Black Dwarf* on 6 October, followed three days later by publication in the *Briton*.[37] The editor of the latter may simply have copied it from the former or the anonymous poet could have sent copies to both periodicals. The attack on the legal system and the church demonstrate, in a manner similar to Shelley in 'England in 1819', how the corruption within the nation spreads beyond the perpetrators of the violence at Peterloo to every cornerstone of the British establishment.

Ye hapless victims of oppression's rage!
Ye frowning spirits of a slaughtered race!
Instil your wrongs in this lamenting page,
To flash confusion in each murderer's face.
By law, by freedom's sacred right upheld,
Ye thoughtless crowded to the fatal plain;
Fearless the savage cowards you beheld,
Who came with base intent your veins to drain.[38]
You, unsuspecting, cheer'd the approaching ill;
You saw your leaders to their mandates yield;
But soon you found it was your tyrant's will,
That death should triumph in this horrid field.
Woman unheeded urg'd her sex's claim;
Friendship unheard for mercy loud impor'd;
Age, infancy, and manhood shared the same,
All dying fell beneath the treacherous sword.
Vainly we seek our country for redress,
While pale corruption bars stern justice out:
And base-born avarice, clad in holy dress,[39]
Applauds those impious deeds with look devout.
Vice, wealth, and power, with clamour for their cue,
The 'small still voice of truth'[40] have almost drown'd;
While law, obsequious, joins the monstrous crew,[41]
And scatter deadly fulminations[42] round.
Yet when that dreaded day of doom arrives,
When these assassins meet God's angry eye,
Then will they vainly curse their hideous lives,

And wish that they, like you, could guiltless die.
And then their sins, all washed by blood away,
Your spirits God will 'mongst his host enrol;
But range those sins in terrible array,
And doubly load each vile assassin's soul.

5 'Stanzas Occasioned by the Manchester Massacre'

Presumably written by an Irish poet, Hibernicus,[43] 'Stanzas' employs the concept of unmasking tyranny which, according to Ian Haywood, is 'a tradition of popular radical poetry' with publications, such as the *Black Dwarf*, in which this poem was published on 25 August,[44] using the trope of the mask as a way of 'decloaking … the repressive state apparatus'.[45] The brutality of the troops at Peterloo and the subsequent support for their actions by both monarchy and state were regarded as revealing the true nature of tyranny.

Oh, weep not for those who are freed
From bondage so frightful as ours!
Let *tyranny* mourn for the deed,
And howl o'er the prey she devours!

The mask for a century worn,
Has fallen from her visage at last;[46]
Of all its sham attributes shorn,
Her reign of delusion is past.

In native deformity now
Behold her, how shatter'd and weak!
With murder impress'd on her brow,
And cowardice blanching her cheek.

With guilt's gloomy terrors bow'd down,
She scowls on the smile of a slave!
She shrinks at the patriot's frown;
She dies in the grasp of the brave.

Then brief be our wail for the dead,
Whose blood has seal'd tyranny's doom;
And the tears that affliction will shed,
Let vengeance, bright flashes illume.

And shame on the passionless thing
Whose soul can now slumber within him!
To slavery still let him cling,
For liberty scorns to win him.

> Her manlier spirits arouse
> At the summons so frightfully given!
> And glory exults in their vows,
> While virtue records them in heaven.

6 'On a Bloody Massacre'

Unusually for this anthology, this poem is without a rhyme-scheme. Written predominantly in iambic pentameter, it reads more like a speech than a poem, with the use of rhetorical questions adding to its oratorical power which culminates in a cry for revenge. The poet pledges to murder those responsible and thus avenge the death of those whom he describes as martyrs. It appeared in *Medusa* on 11 September.[47]

> Who can pourtray the grief, the pangs acute,
> The horrid agony; the bleeding mind,
> Of those who on that fatal day have lost
> Friends, relatives, their dearest hopes in life;
> Or saw them wounded! Lacerated! Torn!
> Beneath the murd'rous arms of Ruffians fell?
> Ruffians by cruel despot arm'd with power,
> For which they would the tyrants thrones cement,
> With E—n's[48] best blood!
> Can any brave free-born Sons endure the sight?
> Oh! No – Perish the heart that does not *wish*,
> That does not thirst for vengeance.
> Rather in one yawning grave,
> In one vast Charnel-house, let all be hurl'd;
> Than to forget *this Deed*,
> We wait the law – If justice flees the court
> Not all the fears of loyal fools, not all
> The whining *cant* of *cowards* shall prevail,
> To keep us from our rights.
> Upon the tomb of immolated innocence,
> Of martyr'd patriots; we will sacrifice
> The murderers! And eager snatch Revenge!

7 'The Peterloo Victim'[49]

It is interesting to note that the word 'victim' appears in the first line of several poems in this chapter. Unlike the poem above, the victim in this poem is dying and is pleading for mercy from his assailant. Written by the unknown 'Latham', and published on 30 October 1819 in the *Manchester Observer*, the initial focus of the poem on an individual victim quickly broadens to encompass those whom the poet blames for the massacre: royalty and the clergy. The final verse alludes to an economic cause of the massacre, thereby suggesting that the involvement of the 'Parsons' was driven by financial greed.

> See on the earth the dying victim lies,
> With eyes upturn'd for mercy loudly cries
> Unto the wretch, who dar'd to aim the blow,
> Which laid at once the guiltless suff'rer low!
>
> The exulting [?] sabre then did wield,
> Soon as the men dropt on the blood stain'd field,
> 'Coward for shame!' a noble Hero* cried,
> Mercy was craved – but mercy was denied.
>
> Convuls'd on earth the expiring victim lay,
> Unable to sustain its tott'ring clay,
> Whilst life flow'd freely through the gaping wound
> And as It streamed, It sank into the ground.
>
> Anon the earth will solemn silence break,
> Then will the blood of murder'd patriots speak;
> For vengeance on the proud assassin's head,
> To satiate justice for the blood he's shed.
>
> Forsooth, the thanks of Royalty came down
> This desperate deed of courage for to crown;
> Which rous'd at once my injur'd country's ire
> To see their friends and liberties expire.
>
> The Parsons countenanc'd the crimson'd crime,
> Who ought to teach us things the most sublime,
> Does not their past and present conduct show,
> 'Tis not the good of souls they have in view.
>
> But to extort by force the Layman's store
> 'Give us our tythes,' cry they, 'we ask no more,'
> Know ye 'that we've large fortunes for to make,
> Give us our dues or other means we'll take.'
> *Salford*, Oct. 26th 1819.

* An Officer in the 15th Hussars.

8 'The Song of the Slaughter, To Commemorate the Horrid Deeds Performed at Manchester on the 16th of August, 1819'[50]

In his autobiography, *Passages in the Life of a Radical*, Samuel Bamford recalls giving his wife one pound of the three pounds he earned from the publication of this poem whilst he was in Lincoln Gaol in August 1820:

> I had, at Hunt's request, written a piece called 'The Song of the Slaughter', which first appeared, I think, in his memoirs, and was afterwards published at the Observer Office, Manchester.[51]

When the poem appeared in Bamford's *Homely Rhymes, Poems and Reminiscences,* published in 1864, it contained only the first four verses, thereby removing any reference both direct and indirect to Peterloo.[52]

The stated tune for the song is the 'Sicilian Mariners' Hymn'. Also known as '*O Sanctissima*', it is a Roman Catholic hymn to the Virgin Mary. According to tradition, it was sung by Sicilian seamen on their boats at the end of the day. It was first published in November 1792 in the *European Magazine and London Review,* with the title 'The Sicilian Mariner's Hymn to the Virgin'.[53] Written in Latin, the first verse is as follows:

> O sanctissima, o piissima
> Dulcis Virgo Maria!
> Mater amata, intemerata,
> Ora, ora pro nobis.
> [O sacred one, tender one
> Sweet Virgin Mary
> Mother beloved, pure
> Pray, pray for us]

> Parent of the wide creation,
> We would counsel ask of thee!
> Look upon a mighty nation,
> Rousing from its slavery!

> If to men our wrongs be stated,
> No redress for us be found;
> All our actions reprobated,
> We are but the faster bound.

> Thou hast made us to inherit
> Strength of body and of mind;
> Shall we rise, and, in thy spirit,
> Tear away the chains that bind?

> Chains, but forged to degrade us,
> O, the base indignity!
> In the name of God, who made us,
> Let us perish, or be free!

Can we e're forget our brothers,
Cold and gory as they lay?
Can we e'er forgive those others,
For their cruel treachery?

Ah! Behold their sabres gleaming,
Never, never known to spare!
See the flood of slaughter streaming!
Hark the cries that rend the air!

Youth and valour nought availed!
Nought availed beauty's prayer!
E'en the lisping infant failed
To arrest the ruin there!

Give the ruffians time to glory!
Theirs is but a waning day:
We have yet another story,
For the page of history.

9 'To The Major of a Certain Regiment'

This elegy, or revenant ballad, is addressed to Major Thomas Trafford, who was the commander of the Manchester and Salford Yeomanry Cavalry (MYC) and the first to receive the order from the magistrates to arrest Hunt and the other radical leaders.[54] Trafford passed on the order to Captain Hugh Birley, who led the charge. Published in the *Manchester Observer* on 11 September and in *Medusa* a week later, the poem is dated 2 September and takes the form of a dramatic monologue, written by a ghost who promises to join the spirits of the murdered to haunt Trafford until his death.[55]

'Tis dead of night, lo! All is dark and drear,
No moon or star the weary night doth cheer;
I for a time forsake my whiten'd shroud,
While I address thee from this sable[56] cloud.
Yea, to expose thee and thy crimson'd deeds,
Whose guilt all other mortals far exceeds;
Who dids't commence the work without delay,
And indiscriminate murder mark'd the way;
The Sun at noon a blazing witness stood,
And saw thee spill thy injur'd country's blood.
O T—FF—D,[57] hear; I speak thus from the shades,
Where silent darkness over all pervades;
Here thy foul deeds are known, thy ruthless pest,
Who only lives, to murder the opprest.

But all the souls who fell upon that day,
In thy retirement, will in dread array,
And straight succession, pass before my eyes,
Whilst in thy ears is heard their piercing cries.
And often in the solemn noon of night,
When wakeful from thy couch thou start'st with fright,
Before thy eyes shall frightful spectres play,
While they remind me of that fatal day.
And I for one, to swell the awful scene,
Clad in my wounds, with all the ghostly train,
Will straight appear and haunt thee until death
Shall seal thine eyes, and stop thy vital breath.
'Twill take ten thousand years for saints to pray,
Before thy sins could half be pray'd away;
When, those are past and gone – as many more
As grains of sand upon the ocean's shore.
Then as a bird, within yon spacious park,
I'll hop from spray to spray soon as 'tis dark,
And there for ages sweetly, yea, and free,
I'll chaunt my notes to thee – O LIBERTY

Churchyard, Sep. 2nd. A GHOST

10 'The Plains of St Peter'

Written to the tune of a Scottish love song, 'Jessie, the Flower o' Dunblane' by the weaver-poet, Robert Tannahill, the unswerving honesty and wrath contained within these three stanzas is at odds with the haunting melody of the original song.[58] Published in the *Manchester Observer* on 6 November 1819, it would appear that the poet was present at Peterloo, with the use of the first person plural giving validity to the abhorrent scenes described.[59]

The poem was first published in March 1808 in *The Scots Magazine and Edinburgh Literary Miscellany*, where the tune was incorrectly stated as 'The Bob o' Dumblane', a reference to a song by Allan Ramsay. Unlike Tannahill's poem and 'The Plains of St Peter', which are written in Alexandrines, Ramsay's song comprises eight-syllable lines:

> Lassie, lend me your braw hemp heckle,
> And I'll lend you my thripling kame,[60]

Tannahill's song also appeared in his collection, *Poems and Songs, Chiefly in the Scottish Dialect*.[61] The opening verse is as follows:

> The sun has gane down o'er the lofty Benlomond,
> And left the red clouds to preside o'er the scene;

While lanely I stray in the calm summer gloamin'
To muse on sweet Jessie, the flow'r o' Dunblane.

The bloody stain'd deeds of the plains of St Peter,
Which disgraced the name of a true Englishman,
Will warm every breast, when the story's repeated,
To revenge, for the blood which so wantonly ran;
Men, women and children, all fell sacrifices
To tyrants and despots, that ruffianly view,
In discussing a right which no law yet denies us,
The day we met on the fam'd Peterloo.

Neither groans of the wounded, nor shrieks of the aged,
Could 'waken compassion, or mercy restore;
But fiends, worse than devils, bright justice outraged,
Till their glittering sabres were clotted with gore;
Still fiercer they rush'd upon heaps of the dying,
Insatiate monsters their rage to renew,
Regardless of infants' sad moans or their sighing,
But ravag'd the plains of the fam'd Peterloo.

Oh! Britons, can you, in the moments of reason,
Sit languid, and see your poor countryman's fate?
Will your blood never warm to resist the foul treason,
But calmly submit to be slaves of the great?
May the time soon arrive, when our country's sad wailing
May vanish away as the sun drives the dew,
And tyrants, in vain, *hire the press* for concealing
The feats which they play'd on the fam'd Peterloo.

11 *Manchester Meeting: A New Song*

Printed by Innes in Manchester, this song is rather vague in its descriptions of Peterloo.[62] Whereas many of the other poems featured in this chapter state the precise date and depict the events in gruesome detail, this poem refers generally to the weavers arriving from the neighbouring towns and villages and fails to mention the violence or Hunt's arrest. It can be concluded from this that the song was written a few days prior to 16 August, an entrepreneurial and probably lucrative venture aimed at providing a souvenir for those attending, just as enterprising balladeers would sell broadsides marking an execution at the event itself.

It was in the year one thousand,
Eight hundred and nineteen,

All in the month of August,
Our Weaver lads was seen,
Each bush and tree was in full bloom,
And Phoebus bright did shine
To be a glorious witness
For our weaver lads to join.
Chorus.
Along with Hunt, &c.[63]

From Stockport town and Ashton,
The weaver lads came in,
Who all behav'd with honour bright,
The Meeting to begin,
Upon the ground they all did meet
Like heroes of renown,
Search all the mannor'd[64] nation,
Our match cannot be found.
The weaver lads from Stockport,
Did all come flocking down,
From Oldham and from Middleton,
And all the country round,
Come let us all rejoice and sing,
And hope for better days,
Through Lancashire and Cumberland,[65]
We'll sing the weavers praise.
Then Sir C. Wolseley[66] in Manchester
Behav'd with honour bright
Squire Hunt spoke up with courage bold
When he appear'd in sight,
With respect unto our weaver lads
He never meant any ill,
And in bright shining pages,
We'll sing his praises still.
Now here's a health to Mr Hunt,
Long may he rule this soil,
And likewise all his gentlemen,
Long may they live and smile,
And let us not forget the day,
That we held up our hands,
We hope to flourish once again,
All in our native land.
Now to conclude and end my song,
I have little more to say,
May our british Manufactures[67]
Flourish more every day,
And our trade shall flourish again,

Through all the British Isle,
Both Lancashire and Cumberland,
And Cheshire likewise.

12 *The Answer to Peter-Loo*[68]

This song was written by the Manchester poet and furniture dealer, Michael Wilson, son of a hand-loom weaver, who wrote numerous political ballads.[69] To mark the 150th anniversary of Peterloo, the poem appeared in the *Stockport Advertiser* on 14 August, 1969.[70] This is one of the few ballads written in support of the 'Gallant' MYC whose actions against the 'Rebelly crew' are glorified. Marlow states that 'one of the only verses that circulated' on the magistrates' side is:

> Blithe Harry Hunt was a slightly man,
> Something 'twixt giant and runt,
> His paunch was a large one, his visage was wan,
> And to hear his long speeches vast multitudes ran,
> O rare Orator Hunt.

She concludes: 'Nobody produced any lines in support of the MYC'.[71]

Using the military theme shared with so many of the radical poems, this example gloats on the defeat inflicted upon the marchers, although falls short of describing the violence that took place, describing only the flight of the 'mob' who left their 'old hats and clogs' behind them. The ballad ends with a toast to the king and a hope that all protests be dealt with in the same way.

> On the sixteenth day of August, eighteen hundred and nineteen,
> All in the town of Manchester the REBELLY[72] CREW were seen,
> They call themselves reformers, and by Hunt the traitor true,
> To attend a treason meeting on the plains of Peter-Loo.
>
> Those hearers at their patron's call came flocking into town,
> Both Male and Female radical, and many a gapeing[73] clown,
> Some came without their breakfast, which made their bellies rue;
> But got a warm baggin[74] on the plains of Peter-Loo.
>
> From Staley-Bridge they did advance with a band of music fine,
> And brought a cap of liberty from Ashton-under-Lyne;
> There was Macclesfield and Stockport lads, and Oldham roughheads too,
> Came to hear the treason sermon preached by Hunt at Peter-Loo.
>
> About the hour of one o'clock this champion took the chair,
> Surrounded by his aid-de-campe, his orders for to hear,

And disperse them through that REBELLY MON,[75] which round his standard drew;
But they got their jackets dusted on the plains of Peter-Loo.

They hoisted up treason caps[76] and flags, as plainly you may see, –
And with loud acclamations shouted Hunt and liberty;
They swore no man should spoil their plan, but well our Yeoman knew;
They assembled in St. James's Square,[77] and marched for Peter-Loo.

The Rochdale band of music, with harmony sublime,
Had placed themselves convenient to amuse Hunt's concubine;[78]
But soon their big drum head was broke, all by our Yeomen true;
They dropped their instruments, and run away from Peter-Loo.

When the Yeoman did advance the mob began to fly,
Some thousands of old hats and clogs behind them there did lie;
They soon pulled down their Treason Flags, and numbers of them flew;
And Hunt they took a prisoner on the plains of Peter-Loo.

Now Hunt is taken prisoner and sent to Lancaster gaol,[79]
With seven of his foremost men,[80] their sorrows to bewail;
His mistress sent to the hospital her face for to renew,
For she got it closely shaven on the plains of Peter-Loo.[81]

Success attend those warlike men, our Yeoman-Volunteers,
And all the Gallant Officers who knows no dread or fears,
Likewise the *Irish Trumpeter*,[82] that loud his trumpet blew,
And took a cap of liberty from them at Peter-Loo.

Now to conclude and make an end, here's a health to GEORGE OUR KING;
And all those Gallant Yeomanry whose praises I loudly sing;
May Magistrates and Constables with zeal their duty do;
And may they prove victorious upon every Peter-Loo.

13 *The Meeting at Peterloo*

The Bodleian Library's Broadside Ballads Collection contains two copies of this ballad, neither of which states the printer. The use of the vernacular in the song lends authenticity to what seems to be an eye witness account of events on the day.[83]

Come lend an ear of pity while I my tale do tell,
It happened at Manchester a place that's known right well,
For to redress our wants and woes reformers took their ways
A lawful Meeting being called upon a certain day.
    So God bless Hunt, etc[84]
The Sixteenth day of August Eighteen Hundred and Nineteen.

There many thousand people on every road were seen,
From Stockport, Oldham, Ashton & other places too,
It was the largest Meeting Reformers ever knew.
Brave Hunt he was appointed that day to take the chair.
At one o'clock he did arrive our shouts did rend the air
Some females fair in white and Green near the hustings stood,
And little still we did expect to see such scenes of blood,
Scarcely had Hunt begun to speak three cheers was all the cry,
What to shout for we little knew but still we did comply
He saw the enemies surround be firm said he my friends
But little still we did expect what would be their ends
Our Enemies so cruel regardless of our woes,
They did agree to force us from the Plain of Peterloo,
But if that we had been prepared or any cause for fear
The regulars might have cleared the ground, and they stood in the rear,
Then to the fatal ground they went, and thousands tumbled down,
And many armless female lay bleeding on the ground,
No time for flight was gave us still every road we fled.
But heaps on heaps were trampled down some wounded and some dead.
Brave Hunt was then arrested and several others too.
Then marched to the New Bailey,[85] believe me it is true,
Numbers there was wounded and many there was slain,
Which makes the friends of those dear souls so loudly to complain.
O God look down upon us for thou art just and true,
And those that can no mercy shew thy vengeance is their due.
Now quit this hateful mournful scene look forward with this hope,
That every Murderer in this land may swing upon a rope
But soon reform shall spread around for sand the time won't stay,
May all the filth that in our land right soon be wash'd away,
And may sweet harmony from hence in this our land be found,
May we be blest with plenty in all the country round.

14 *The Field of Peterloo: An Heroic Poem in Two Cantos to which is Added An Address to Liberty*

Published and printed by the radical shoemaker-turned-publisher William Benbow[86] of The Strand in 1820, this poem states its author as Philo Peter Pindar. Peter Pindar was the pseudonym adopted by John Wolcot, a poet and satirist whose famous *Lyric Odes* published in 1782 are a an irreverent collection of anti-royalist poems which were hugely popular. However, Pindar died in January 1819 and therefore did not write this poem. The use of 'philo' may refer to 'friend of', with another poet 'cashing in' on Pindar's name and reputation. The poem shares its title with a much longer poem on Peterloo, the authorship of which is also contested. Published in 1819, *The Field of Peterloo* states its author as 'Thomas Brown', the pseudonym of the Irish poet, Thomas Moore.[87] In the poem below, the poet takes on the role of the bard, narrating and recording events of 16 August with the detail of an eye-witness.

CANTO I
Oh Muse! Inspire my pen to aid
My mind to clearly shew,
The various facts that happen'd on
The field of Peter-loo.

The morn was fair, the sun's bright beam
Refulgent shown on high,
And ne'er had mortal eyes beheld
A more ethereal sky.

The neighb'ring villagers and swains,
Were summon'd to repair;
That fatal morn, with all their power,
To Manchester's great square.

Th' appointed bands had all agreed
To march upon the ground
In systematical array,
By drum and trumpets' sound.

But here I merely must remark,
They were not met in arms;
Not to disturb the public peace,
Or cause the town alarm.

Th' inhabitants were all prepar'd
To see th' expected corps;
Little they thought o' the miseries
That morning had in store.

The sound of drums announc'd to them
Th' whole would soon appear;
Some look'd afraid, some fled away,
And others 'gan to cheer.

The companies when on the ground
Drew up in many a ring;
And with a general consent
They sang 'God Save the King.'[88]

Another object now appear'd
Attention to engage,

Lo! Hunt, the Bristol orator,[89]
Drew up onto the stage!

He wav'd his hat, and straight began
His speech upon Reform;
It seem'd the subject 'gainst the State
Was desperately warm.

When, lo! His argument was stopt,
(Just rising very high)
For soldiers clos'd the meeting in,
Both Foot and Cavalry.

The word 'advance' was quickly giv'n,
And even with command
The Yeomanry of Manchester
Charg'd onwards, sword in hand.

CANTO II
And now the peaceful air was rent
With dismal cries and moans,
Words of command, the clang of arms,
And dying shrieks and groans.

The ground was soon one scene of woe,
With dying and wounded strew'd,
'Twas then we saw a Briton's sword
In British blood imbru'd.

'Twas vain to sue for mercy then,
Their hearts were steel'd 'gainst good,
These Yeomanry alone desir'd
To end the day with blood.

A mother for her child receiv'd
A dreadful sabre wound,
Which cut her and her offspring down
Unto the very ground.

'Tis needless here that I relate
What havock soon was made;
Th' assembled troops confused fled,
Each Briton was afraid.

The crush was dreadful ev'rywhere,
For in a gen'ral sweep,
No less than sixty thousand men[90]
Retreated in a heap.

Thus those who came intent to hear
A politician's words,
Were clear'd by arbitrary force,
By horses' hoofs and swords.

Then Britons, when this dreadful tale
Is mention'd unto you,
Weep for the souls who fell upon
The field of Peter-loo.

May justice overtake at last,
That persecuting crew,
Who made a seat of massacre
The fields of Peter-loo.

Remember! Britons, not Reform
Can e'er our country bless,
Till we by safe and humble means
Obtain the wish'd redress.

The jealousy of Government
Regards with envious eye,
A numerous corps, lest they should rise
To sudden mutiny.

Let every honest Englishman,
Who for distress doth feel,
Apply, in these most woeful times,
His shoulder to the wheel.

Despair, or rash and forward schemes,
Success will ne'er attend,
But rather ultimately lead
Their authors to the end.

Then may a long and lasting peace
Prove useful to our land,
And yield a fair sufficiency
To every honest hand.

May we no more in Britain have
Presented to our view,
Those cruel acts which stain'd the name
Of bloody Peter-loo!

15 The Peterloo Massacre[91]

This song was written by Michael Wilson and also appears to support the actions of the MYC.[92] The use of Lancashire dialect adds authenticity to the account, as does the knowledge of the MYC, which comprised local businessmen, keen to settle real or imagined disputes with their labouring-class customers. It was to be sung to the tune of 'Gee ho Dobbin'[93] or 'Gee-up Neddy'. The opening line is a commonly used balladic conventions of drawing the listener to the singer before embarking upon the story. A similar opening is found in *The Battle of Trafalgar:*

> Come all you gallant heroes and listen unto me,
> While we relate a battle that has been fought at sea,
> So fierce and hot on every side as plainly it doth appear
> There has not been such a battle fought, not for many years.[94]

> Come, Robin, sit deawn, an' aw'll tell thee a tael,
> But first, – prithee, fill me a dobbin[95] o' ale;
> Aw'm as drey, mon, as soot, an aw'm hurt i' mi crop,
> Havin laft Sam o' Dick's where aw fear he mun stop.

> *For the gentleman cavalry,*
> *Cut 'em down cleverly;*
> *Real Royal yeomanry!*
> *Cavalry brave.*

> Mr Hunt neaw coom forrad an' spoke a few words,
> When the Peterloo cut-my-throats shaken'd there swords,
> Aw thowt sure enoof they wur runni' ther rigs,
> 'Till aw seed moor nor twenty lay bleedin' like pigs.

> Boh lets ta'e a peep o' these Peterloo chaps,
> 'At ma'essich a neyse abeawt cullers an' caps,
> See what they'n composed on, an then we may judge,
> For it runs i' mi moind 'otther loyalty's fudge.

> Theer's the taxman, exciseman, the lawyer, an' bum,
> The pensioner, placeman, an' preycher, that hum:
> The fat-gutted landlord, o' licence in fear,
> Cut the throats o' his neybours who buy his bad beer.

In Standard English, the song reads as follows:

> Come, Robin, sit down, and I'll tell thee a tale,
> But first, – pray you, fill me a quarter-pint of ale;
> I'm as dry, man, as soot, an I'm hurt in my stomach
> Having left Sam at Dick's where I fear he must stop.

For the gentleman cavalry,
Cut them down cleverly;
Real Royal yeomanry!
Cavalry brave.

Mr Hunt now came forward and spoke a few words,
When the Peterloo cut-my-throats shook their swords,
I thought sure enough they were running riot
'Till I saw more than twenty lay bleeding like pigs.

But let's take a peep at these Peterloo chaps,
Who make such a noise about collars and caps,
See what they are composed of, and then we may judge,
For it runs in my mind that their loyalty's nonsense.

There's the taxman, exciseman, the lawyer, and bailiffs
The pensioner, politician, and preacher, that imposter:
The fat-gutted landlord, with a licence in fear,
Cut the throats of his neighbours who buy his bad beer.

16 'The Late Proceedings'

This anti-radical poem appeared in the *Morning Post*[96] on 31 August 1819 and centres around the reading of the Riot Act at Peterloo. The Act was read twice, firstly by Mr Ethelstone out of the window of the house occupied by the magistrates in Mount Street and secondly by Mr Silvester who walked into the crowd; however, the MYC had already advanced through the crowd and many participants claimed never to have heard the reading of the Act.[97] The poem throws scorn on the 'mob' who claimed not to have heard the Riot Act being read. The coverage of Peterloo in the *Morning Post* is unsympathetic to the protestors, describing them repeatedly as 'the mob' and blaming them for the ensuing violence. 'The Riot Act was read, but it did not appear to be much attended by the infatuated crowd, who continued to scowl and laugh at the constables.'[98]

Repeatedly it has been said,
The Riot Act was never read
At Manchester; for several there
Heard nothing of it, they declare.
And if the statement made were true;
If the Act were indeed gone through,
Why then, it needs must be inferred,
That every soul there must have heard.

But Hunt whose word belief commands,
Tells us that all the martial bands

That swelled that morning's grand parade,
Our favourite, 'Rule Britannia' played;
And then, more loyal praise to bring,
They gave the mob 'God Save the King.'
Now we would gladly know the hour
Of this 'essay of Music's power,'
For those sharp eyes and open ears,
(The source of all our recent tears,)
Who saw and heard so much of woe,
And all reported nothing slow;
Who saw the Cavalry that day
Thro' unarmed thousands *hack* their way,
In blood up to their horses;' necks,
And sparing neither age nor sex;
Those who so good a tale could tell
About the two or three that fell,[99]
Would surely, amidst war's alarms,
Have been awake to Music's charms,
And told, when with the pen employed,
How fine a concert they enjoyed.
But not a word of this was told,
'Till Hunt thought proper to unfold
The secret, that in open air
Such tunes had been played then and there.

Since strains so loyal, loud, and cheering,
Escaped by some odd chance a hearing;
Since drums and trumpets on the plain
In concert rolled and roared in vain;
Since all *their* noise, in chaos tossed,
Was in the vast confusion lost,
How marvellous becomes the fact,
That few could hear the Riot Act!

Notes

1 See number 11 below.
2 See number 13 below.
3 J. Chandler, *England in 1819: The Politics of Literary Culture and the Case of Romantic Historicism* (Chicago: Chicago University Press, 1998), p. xvi.
4 *Ibid.*, p. 5.
5 F. Kidson, *Songs of Britain* (Milton Keynes: Read Books, 2008), pp. 22–3.
6 Quoted in R. Palmer (ed.), *A Ballad History of England from 1588 to the Present Day* (London: Batsford, 1979), p. 9.

7 M. McLane, *Balladeering, Minstrelsy and the Making of British Romantic Poetry* (Cambridge: Cambridge University Press, 2008), pp. 191–2.
8 Palmer, *Ballad History*, pp. 90–1.
9 D. Kennedy, *Elegy* (London: Routledge, 2007), p. 10.
10 J. Frow, *Genre* (London: Routledge, 2005), p. 132.
11 See numbers 1, 2, 5 and 7 below.
12 K. Trumpener, *Bardic Nationalism: The Romantic Novel and the British Empire* (Princeton: Princeton University Press, 1997), p. 44.
13 In July 1984, during a speech to the 1922 Committee, Margaret Thatcher notoriously described the miners as 'the enemy within', in an attempt to cast them as the 'other' in the Miners' Strike.
14 *A Collection of Old Ballads* (London, 1725), vol. 3, pp. 11, iii–iv.
15 *Death of Nelson*, Hay Portfolio, 20.
16 Admirers of Nelson had to wait until 1843 before his statue in Trafalgar Square was completed.
17 Numbers 1 and 3 below.
18 T. Gray, *The Poems of Gray, Collins and Goldsmith*, ed. R. Lonsdale (London: Longman, 1969), pp. 135.
19 R. Cohen, 'The Return of the Ode', in J. Sitter (ed.), *The Cambridge Companion to Eighteenth-Century Poetry* (Cambridge: Cambridge University Press, 2001), p. 210.
20 W. Wordsworth, *The Prose Works of William Wordsworth*, eds. W.J.B. Owen and J.W. Smyser (Oxford: Clarendon, 1974), vol. 2, pp. 50, 59.
21 Gray, *The Poems of Gray, Collins and Gold*, p. 135.
22 'A Tribute on an Humble Muse to the Memory of Joseph Gerrald', by M.B. (*Politics for the People*, 2:1 (1794), p. 158); 'To the Memory of the Rev. G. Wakefield', by Lucy Aikin (*Monthly Magazine* (October 1801), p. 220–2); 'Part of an Inscription Designed for a Garden', by J.R. Tutt (*Monthly Magazine* (November 1801), p. 328). In January 1798, Richard Watson, Bishop of Llandaff, published *An Address to the People of Great Britain*, which supported Pitt's proposal for the introduction of income tax. Gilbert's pamphlet opposed this and also blamed the British government for the war with France.
23 Numbers 2, 7, 3 and 4.
24 B. Bennett, *British War Poetry in the Age of Romanticism: 1793–1815* (New York: Garland, 1976), p. 183.
25 Owen describes the Latin motto as 'The old lie: *Dulce et decorum est / Pro patria mori*' (*The Poems of Wilfred Owen*, ed. Edmund Blunden (London: Chatto and Windus, 1968), p. 66, ll. 13–14). It translates as 'It is sweet and fitting to die for one's country.'
26 M. Scrivener (ed.), *Poetry and Reform: Periodical Verse from the English Democratic Press, 1792–1824* (Michigan: Wayne State University Press, 1992), p. 227.
27 *Manchester Observer* (25 September 1819), p. 726.
28 R.R. Madden (ed.), *The Life and Times of Robert Emmet Esq.* (Dublin: James Duffy, 1847), pp. 299–300.

29 In Ancient Rome, laurel wreaths were awarded to men who had been victorious in war.
30 Lilies are often used at funerals as they symbolise an innocence restored after death.
31 There is a reference to a soldier hacking off a woman's breast in 'Saint Ethelstone's Day' in Chapter 5.
32 *Central Library Collection of Ballads*, vol. 2.
33 It is a well-established radical trope that the German monarchy had usurped the ancient laws of Britain.
34 As with this poem, Emmet's 'On Arbour Hill' is a memorial to those buried in unmarked graves.
35 The legal system with its origins in Anglo-Saxon times, the 1215 Magna Carta and the 1689 Bill of Rights are seen by radicals as the cornerstones of the British Constitution.
36 Shining brightly.
37 *Black Dwarf*, 3:40 (1819), p. 659; Keen, *The Popular Radical Press*, vol. 4, p. 320.
38 The poet maintains that the violence was premeditated.
39 Reverend W.R. Hay was Chairman of the Salford Quarter Sessions in 1819. For more information, see p. 86. The writer of 'Elegiac Apostrophe' makes the clear distinction between Christianity and the church by highlighting the corruption of a clergy who sanctioned such violence and the reckoning that awaits the perpetrators after death.
40 This may refer to Kings, Chapter Nineteen, when God speaks to Elijah: 'And after the earthquake a fire; but the LORD was not in the fire: and after the fire a still small voice' (Kings, 19:12).
41 In Book XI of Milton's *Paradise Lost*, Archangel Michael shows the many forms of death to Adam (J. Milton, *The Complete Poems*, ed. J. Leonard (London: Penguin, 2008), p. 377):

> 'Some, as thou saw'st, by violent stroke shall die,
> By fire, flood, famine; by intemperance more
> In meats and drinks, which on the Earth shall bring
> Diseases dire, of which a monstrous crew
> Before thee shall appear, that thou may'st know
> What misery the in abstinence of Eve
> Shall bring on me.'

42 Violent denunciations.
43 Hibernius is also the author of 'To Lord Castlereagh' which appeared in the *Black Dwarf* on 24 February 1819 in which Castlereagh, Sidmouth and Pitt (described as the 'master-fiend') are held to account for their betrayal of the English people (*Black Dwarf*, 3:8 (1819), pp 129–30).
44 The poem was written by 21 August, only five days after Peterloo. (*Black Dwarf* 3:34 (1819), p. 563.)
45 I. Haywood, *The Revolution in Popular Literature: Print, Politics and the*

People, 1796–1860 (Cambridge: Cambridge University Press, 2004), pp. 98, 95.

46 It is unavoidable to make comparisons with Shelley's *Masque of Anarchy* and his depiction of the hated Foreign Secretary: 'I met Murder on the way – / He had a mask like Castlereagh (ll. 5–6). See Appendix for the full text. Jim Clayson states that the description of the falling mask is a 'distinctly Jacobin remark' ('The Poems of Peterloo', in *Peterloo Massacre, MRHR* (1989), 3:1, pp. 31–8, at p. 32).
47 Keen, *The Popular Radical Press*, vol. 4, p. 248.
48 England's.
49 *Manchester Observer* (30 October 1819), p. 796.
50 *Manchester Observer* (5 August 1820), p. 1120. Gardner states that the poem was first published by Henry Hunt in his *Letter to Radical Reformers* dated July 1820. Walmsley notes that the poem was written on 13 July whilst Bamford was in Lincoln Gaol (529). Gardner cites the main influence as Milton's *Paradise Lost* and *Areopagitica* and also notes the similarities to Shelley's *Masque of Anarchy*, which was not published until 1832 (J. Gardner, *Poetry and Popular Protest: Peterloo, Cato Street and the Queen Caroline Controversy* (Hampshire: Palgrave Macmillan, 2011), pp. 30–1; R. Walmsley, *Peterloo: The Case Re-opened* (Manchester: Manchester University Press, 1969), p. 529).

The 2 November 1822 edition of *Wheeler's Manchester Chronicle* reports a court appearance for John Higson, charged with exhibiting a seditious flag. The report goes on to states that, on 16 August 1822, Higson and others sang a seditious song, called 'The Song of the Slaughter' (cited in Walmsley, *Peterloo*, pp. 424–5). Epstein also notes that radicals sang the song in Ashton on the anniversary of Peterloo in 1820 (J.A. Epstein, *Radical Expression: Political Language, Ritual, and Symbol in England, 1790–1850* (Oxford: Oxford University Press, 1994), p. 156).
51 S. Bamford, *Passages in the Life of a Radical*, 3 vols. (Manchester: Heywood, 1842), vol. 2, p. 193.
52 S. Bamford, *Homely Rhymes, Poems and Reminiscences* (London: Simpkin and Marshall, 1864), 67–8. A broadside version of the whole poem, entitled *Song of the Slaughterd*, was printed by J. Wheeler in Manchester between 1827 and 1847. No tune is stated (http://ballads.bodleian.ox.ac.uk/static/images/sheets/15000/13674.gif [accessed 19 November 2017]).
53 22 November, 1792, pp. 385–6.
54 David Fowler defines revenant ballads as those which 'depict otherworld figures or in some way relate to the return of the dead from the grave' (*A Literary History of the Popular Ballad* (Durham N.C.: Duke University Press, 1968), p. 183). *Fair Margaret and Sweet William* or Scott's 'The Daemon Lover' are familiar examples.
55 *Manchester Observer* (11 September 1819), p. 710; Keen, *The Popular Radical Press*, vol. 4, p. 251.
56 Black.

57 Major Thomas Trafford was the son of John Trafford of Crosten Hall near Chorley in Lancashire. The Traffords were a leading Roman Catholic family who traced their ancestry to the Anglo Saxons but who assumed the Norman name of de Trafford in the eleventh century. Thomas inherited his father's estates in 1815 and was appointed commander of the newly formed MYC in 1817.
58 Robert Tannahill wrote numerous poems in the Scottish dialect inspired by Robert Burns and achieved moderate success in his lifetime. 'Jessie, the Flower o' Dunblane' is one of his most famous poems and is alleged to have been written for his sweetheart, Jenny Tennant, whom he believed to be unfaithful. The tune was written by Robert Archibald Smith, 'the most outstanding religious composer of his day' (*DNB*).
59 *Manchester Observer*, 6 November 1819, p. 804.
60 A. Ramsay, *The Poems of Allan Ramsay* (London, 1800), vol. 3, p. 259.
61 R. Tannahill, *Poems and Songs, Chiefly in the Scottish Dialect* (London: Longman, 1817), pp. 137–8. www.scotlandspeople.gov.uk [accessed 4 August 2016].
62 *Central Library Collection of Ballads*, vol. 2.
63 The full chorus was not printed on the original broadside, which suggests that it would have been known to the buyer.
64 Cultivated land.
65 A county in the north-west of England which, since 1974, has formed part of Cumbria.
66 Charles Wolseley. See p. 62n.53.
67 Manufactories.
68 Part of this song appears in Palmer's *Sound of History*, pp. 258–9. It is a ballad without imprint, a copy of which I received from Brian Maidment, as did Palmer (*Ibid.*, p. 331).
69 Palmer, *Sound of History*, pp. 27, 258. Also see number 15 below.
70 This newspaper cutting is part of a collection held at the Working-Class Movement Library in Salford (S52).
71 Marlow, *The Peterloo Massacre*, pp. 175–6.
72 Rebellious.
73 Open-mouthed.
74 Lunch.
75 Man.
76 Caps of liberty.
77 St James' Square is in central Manchester, less than a third of a mile from St Peter's Field. The MYC was actually stationed in Portland Street, nearly a mile away from St James' Square
78 Mary Fildes, President of the Manchester Female Reformers, accompanied Hunt in his carriage to the hustings, although there is no evidence to suggest that she was his mistress (Marlow, *The Peterloo Massacre*, p. 123). Hunt, however, did have a long-term mistress, Mrs Vince, with whom he had lived since around 1800; she does not appear to have been

present at Peterloo (J. Belchem, *Orator Hunt: Henry Hunt and English Working-Class Radicalism* (Oxford: Clarendon, 1985), p. 22). Mrs Fildes 'was invited to jump aboard [Hunt's] open carriage. According to Richard Carlile, she "boldly and immediately acquiesced", sitting on the dickey by the side of the driver and waving a handkerchief in one hand and a small flag in the other. The other members of the committee followed immediately behind the carriage on foot' (Bush, 'The Women at Peterloo', p. 218) Bamford notes: 'On the driving seat of a barouche sat a neatly dressed female, supporting a small flag, on which were some emblematical drawings and an inscription' (*Passages in the Life of a Radical*, vol. 1, p. 205).

79 Along with the other radical leaders, Hunt was transferred from the New Bailey Prison to Lancaster Gaol on 27 August.
80 Eight men and two women were arrested on 16 August; Samuel Bamford was arrested on 26 August. All nine men were transferred to Lancaster Gaol.
81 Mrs Fildes was injured by one of the MYC whilst trying to escape from the hustings (Marlow, *The Peterloo Massacre*, p. 138).
82 Edward Meagher, the MYC trumpeter, who, according to Diana Donald, was a 'pugnacious Irishman'. In J.L. Marks' famous caricature, *The Massacre of Peterloo*, an allusion is made to Meagher by ' a pig-faced trumpeter' who states: 'How Glorious our Ardour to lay down the Lives / Of Defenceless Children, Husbands and Wives. Meagre!!!' (D. Donald, 'The Power of Print: Graphic Images of Peterloo', in *Peterloo Massacre, MRHR*, pp. 21–30, at p. 24). For further information, see p. 117.
83 http://ballads.bodleian.ox.ac.uk/static/images/sheets/10000/09897.gif; http://ballads.bodleian.ox.ac.uk/static/images/sheets/25000/22541.gif [accessed 19 November 2017].
84 As with number 5 above, the fact that the chorus is not printed suggests it would have been well known.
85 For New Bailey, see p. 116n.63.
86 William Benbow (1787–1864) worked first as a shoemaker and then as a radical nonconformist preacher in Manchester. He was sent to London in 1816 by Manchester radicals to work with the Spenceans and also organised the Blanketeers' March in 1817. Following a brief return to Manchester, Benbow joined William Cobbett in the States where he disinterred the bones of Thomas Paine. Benbow returned to Manchester in December 1819 and soon moved to London where he set up a bookshop on The Strand where he published pornography as well as radical texts.
87 T. Brown, *The Field of Peterloo* (London, 1819). Ronan Kelly states that this work was not written by Moore, who remained mysteriously silent on Peterloo (*Bard of Erin: The Life of Thomas Moore* (London: Penguin, 2008), p. 345).
88 According to Epstein, the bands accompanying the marchers played 'God Save the King' (Epstein, *Radical Expression*, p. 83).
89 Hunt spent time working in Bristol, where he established the Bristol

Patriotic and Constitutional Association in 1807. He became known as 'Bristol' Hunt in 1812 when he came to national attention by contesting the seat twice 'in demagogic style' and taking to the streets as the people's candidate (*DNB*).

90 60,000 is the number stated on the red plaque which is on the Radisson Hotel in Manchester (see Figure 4).
91 Palmer, *Sound of History*, pp. 27–8. The song appears in *Songs of the Wilsons*, ed., John Harland (London: 1865), pp. 26–7.
92 See number 12 above.
93 'Gee ho Dobbin' appears to date back to the mid-eighteenth century, when it was also known as 'Laugh and Lay Down' and is to be found in many collections of country dances (W. Chappell, *The Ballad Literature and Popular Music of the Olden Time* (New York: Dover Publications, 1965), pp. 690–1). It was also used for two late eighteenth-century ballads: 'The Kissing Lasses of Yarmouth' and 'General Distress' (Palmer, *Sound of History*, pp. 228–9, 237).
94 *Central Library Collection of Ballads*, vol. 2, p. 20.
95 A gill, which is a quarter of a pint.
96 *Morning Post* (31 August 1819), n. pag.
97 T. Wyke, 'Remembering the Manchester Massacre', in *Return to Peterloo*, ed. R Poole, pp. 142–3; Marlow, *The Peterloo Massacre*, pp. 138–9. Marlow also points out that according to the Riot Act, an hour should be allowed for the dispersal of the crowd; this clearly did not happen at Peterloo.
98 *Morning Post* (19 August 1819), n. pag.
99 The writer is underplaying the scale of the violence.

5

'Those true sons of Mars': chivalry, cowardice and the power of satire

Perhaps unsurprisingly, given its title, this is the longest chapter in the book, comprising seventeen poems, with many in other chapters also warranting a place here. As Scrivener aptly notes:

> Parody, burlesque, and other satirically humorous forms are perhaps the most successful genres of reformist poetry. The implied reader of this comic verse is an already committed reformist, so that the object of such poetry is not to persuade but to delight.[1]

However, many of the poems throughout this collection use satire not only to 'delight' but also as a way of demonstrating defiance and voicing outrage at the actions of the authorities both during and after Peterloo. Cultural representations of Peterloo exemplify the links between visual caricature, literary parody and satire, due, in part, to 'the period's vibrant journalistic sub-culture, which promoted a continuous interchange between the textual and the visual.'[2] Even though satire as a self-consciously literary genre is associated more with the members of the Scriblerian Club in the Augustan Period,[3] Romantic writers, such as Byron, Shelley, Coleridge and, of course, Austen, all employed satire to mock existing social and political norms, with the result that hundreds of satires were written and published during this era.[4] Interestingly, David Fairer considers whether satire 'thrives at a time when a system of values is under threat and new forces are challenging an old cultural hegemony'.[5] Even though Fairer cites 1829 as supporting evidence for his claim, 1819 exemplifies a time in which there was a very real challenge to authority and the reform movement used satire as a form of, what Scrivener, terms, 'cultural defiance'.[6]

The most influential radical satire in the few fervent years after the Napoleonic Wars, according to Marcus Wood, is that of William Hone and George Cruikshank, whose fusion of image and text was commercially successful. Their response to Peterloo, *The Political House that*

Jack Built, published in December 1819, sold more than 100,000 copies in the first few months; a parody of the famous nursery rhyme, *The House that Jack Built*, 'it was the most notorious popular satiric reaction to the Peterloo Massacre'.⁷

> These are the people
> All tatter'd and torn,
> Who curse the day
> Wherein they were born,
> On account of Taxation
> Too great to be borne,
> And pray for relief,
> From night to morn:
> Who, in vain, Petition
> In every form,
> Who, peaceably Meeting to ask for Reform,
> Were sabred by Yeomanry Cavalry.⁸

The accompanying image depicts ragged men in the foreground, whilst, in the background, defenceless women are hacked down by soldiers with sabres held aloft. The 'vicious illustrations' provide a perfect visual accompaniment to the bitterness of the poetry.⁹ William Hogarth had pioneered print satire in the first half of the eighteenth century, with works such as *A Rake's Progress* (1733) and *Gin Lane* (1751) satirising the immorality of the time. James Gillray and George Cruikshank, among others, soon followed, transforming Hogarth's social satire into a political weapon. Despite the fact that graphic satire was largely the weapon of loyalists during the Napoleonic Wars, radicals were inspired by the acerbity of works by Gillray. Coupled with the difficulty in prosecuting such images, the power of caricatures was harnessed by radicals and reformers after 1815.

Inspired by the effective and extensive use of propaganda by the politician John Wilkes in the 1760s, radical writers Thomas Spence and Daniel Isaac Eaton employed similar tactics to promote their own brands of radicalism and attack the government. Advertising, religious parodies and coins were used as forms of popular satire during the 1790s.¹⁰ Even the titles of radical periodicals, such as *Pigs' Meat* and *Hog's Wash*¹¹ were satirical, lampooning Burke's famous description of the people as the 'swinish multitude'. Citing these titles together with Hone's rewriting of liturgies and nursery rhymes, Dyer claims that 'parody was the dominant technique of populist radicalism' in the Romantic period.¹² The epistolary poem, 'Paddy Bull's Epistle to his Brother John', continues Spence's parodic trope with Paddy describing the authorities as a 'swinish herd' before cautioning his cousin:

> Thou'rt a hog and if grunting and grumbling thou goes,
> Thy masters must put some cold steel in thy nose;
> And this bit of cold metal when fix'd in thy snout,
> Will keep thee from poking and muzzling about;
> And by way of restraint, in thy nose let me tell ye,
> Is far better by far than if thrust in thy belly.[13]

The warning that limits on freedom are preferable to death, coupled with the animal imagery, reveal the dehumanised lives being led by so many. The sharing of a satirical motif between the 1790s and 1819 strengthens the radical discourse, thereby highlighting the lack of political progress in the intervening years. Irreverence, contempt for authority and the Rabelasian carnivalesque abound in radical texts and images of the 1790s and 1810s, with the sharing of humour at the expense of those with power a means of asserting ownership and authority in times of fear.

That the Manchester and Salford Yeomanry Cavalry (MYC) is a main object of the satire is, again, unsurprising, due to the contempt in which it was held from its establishment. Commanding 120 men, it was 'formed in 1817 as a law-and-order instrument, and comprising local volunteers who were sufficiently wealthy to buy the necessary horse, they were held up to ridicule by reformers as "feather-bed soldiers" or "the church and guts mob"'.[14] Variously described as 'bloodhounds', 'butchers' and 'assassins', many of the poems focus on the cowardice of the 'flush'd and drunk' MYC:[15]

> When first your slumb'ring weapons active grown,
> Weapons whose force no foreign foe has known.
> Distress'd, defenceless Britons, hack'd and hew'd.
> And dy'd their maiden blades in women's blood;[16]

The pointed alliterative statement in the second line highlighting the lack of active service seen by the men is followed by the stark image of the first blood on these weapons being that of women, thereby underscoring the cowardice of such actions.

Some poems employ the first person as a means of ridiculing the MYC; however, the use of the first person in the first poem in this chapter creates a more sinister character:

> By Richardson's best grinding skill,
> Our blades were set with right good will,
> That we these Rogues might bleed or kill,
> And 'give them of Reform their fill,'
>   And what d'ye think of that?

The premeditated act of having its sabres sharpened suggests a force intent on maiming and killing, its incompetence masking a thirst for blood, the description of the MYC as 'the local business mafia on horseback', seemingly apt.[17] Poole observes that 'one local magistrate let slip that "the yeomanry cavalry had previously petitioned to have the honour of making the first charge"', perhaps due to the pronounced 'class polarisation (and hatred) found in Manchester', as suggested by John Belchem.[18]

Another theme evident in this chapter is that of chivalry; whether satirically or otherwise, chivalric language is often used in relation to the MYC, illustrated by the refrain of 'Peter Loo Field':[19]

> I'll weave a gay garland with vict'ry entwining,
> With murderous valor pot-valiant combining;
> I'll weave a gay garland with vict'ry entwining,
> To crown the brave Yeomen of Peter Loo Field.

The comparison of the 'brave Yeomen' with the victorious military heroes of classical times, for whom laurel wreaths were woven, exemplifies the invective levelled at the MYC in so many of these poems and songs.

Chivalry as a facet of English national identity was a contentious issue during the eighteenth century, with its revival by conservatives such as Burke fuelling a radical counter-revival focused on a new age of political chivalry. It was regarded both as a support for the monarchy and aristocratic ideals and a yearning for a society in which honour and justice predominated. As a consequence, the language and symbolism of chivalry were adopted by both conservatives and radicals in support of their cause. Burke famously bemoans the treatment of Marie Antoinette at the hands of the revolutionaries:

> Little did I dream that I should have lived to see such disasters fallen upon her in a nation of gallant men, in a nation of men of honour and of cavaliers. I thought ten thousand swords must have leaped from their scabbards to avenge even a look that threatened her with insult. – But the age of chivalry is gone.[20]

Burke's rather florid lament was met with force by William Godwin: 'Indeed; "the age of chivalry is" not "gone"! The feudal spirit still survives, that reduced the great mass of mankind to the rank of slaves and cattle for the service of the few.'[21]

Despite Godwin's view, detailed both in *Political Justice* and *Caleb Williams*, that chivalry is inseparable from the feudal society from which it originated, many radicals saw that a new age of chivalry had arrived and seized on the notions of honour and a strict moral code. Many writers were inspired by Richard Hurd's *Letters on Chivalry and Romance*, published in 1762, which champions Gothic chivalry as central to English literature, particularly through the genre of the romance. Scott's medieval romances helped bring chivalry back into fashion, aided by Byron's 'Romaunt', *Childe Harold's Pilgrimage*, which succeeded in simultaneously reviving the genre and subverting it.[22]

Robert Shorter's poem, 'The Bloody Field of Peterloo!', satirises the actions of the Yeomanry through the employment of chivalric language:[23]

> You shall live in deathless fame,
> For chivalry you there did show;
> Children shall lisp the Yeoman's name,
> And Heroes all of Peterloo!
> How on that memorable day,
> Ye did with martial ardour glow;
> And such heroic zeal display,
> All on the plains of Peterloo!

Here Shorter is appropriating the language and values of chivalry through language such as 'martial' and 'heroic zeal', thereby implicitly accusing the yeomanry of cowardice. Linda Colley comments that, as well as presenting a stylised image of war as opposed to reality, chivalry 'reaffirms the paramount importance of custom, hierarchy and inherited rank'.[24] Shorter skilfully uses the chivalric code to illustrate the ways in which the MYC transgressed it. Similarly, the repeated reference to the striking of women signifies the lack of honour. Hurd's claim that 'love of God and of the ladies went hand in hand in the duties and ritual of chivalry' is in stark contrast to the presentation of the actions of the MYC:[25]

> Whose chivalry, let *female wounds* attest,
> Whose mercy, suppliant woman's bleeding breast,
> Sought from the things in vain; (I ask again,
> Would you call those who could deny it, *men*?)[26]

Subversion of chivalric codes of honour are deemed unnatural, with the Yeomen no more than 'licens'd butchers'.[27] It is the writers of these poems who have seized the chivalric narrative, using it both to shame and ridicule the cowardly actions of the 'Noble Minded Yeoman Cavaliers'.[28]

Northrop Frye defines satire as one of the four mythoi in his taxonomy of literary modes which permeates many genres.[29] Dyer concurs, maintaining that such 'sophisticated discursive assault' can be found in a variety of genres and forms.[30] Evidence to support this is evident throughout this chapter from the burlesque aria in the first poem to the epistolary poems found towards the end. Humour is ribald and dark, employed by the writers of the time to mock and excoriate and, despite the centrality of context and time to the success of satire, the power to shock and amuse is undimmed.

1 *The Renowned Atchievements of Peter-Loo on the Glorious Sixteenth Day of August, 1819*[31]

Described by Marlow as a 'schoolboy parod[y]', this broadside ballad, part of the Manchester Central Library Collection, states its author as Sir Hugo Burlo Furosio di Mulo Spinissimo, BART, M.Y.C. and A.S.S.[32] 'The music composed by the celebrated Dr Horsefood;[33] to be had at the Cat and Bagpipes, St Mary's Gate, Manchester'.[34] The use of cod Italian in the song, along with musical terminology, both satirises classical music as being the cultural domain of the ruling classes and demonstrates through parody the writer's knowledge of that culture.

RECITATIVO
When fell sedition's stalking through the land,
It then behoves each patriotic band
Of NOBLE MINDED YEOMAN CAVALIERS;
To sally forth and rush upon the mob,
And execute the MAGESTERIAL JOB
Of cutting off the Ragamuffin's ears.

ARIA BRAVURA[35]

(*Forte*)[36]
How valiantly we met that crew
Of infants, men and women too,
Upon the Plains of Peterloo,
And gloriously did hack and hew (a)[37]
The d—d[38] reforming gang;
Our swords were sharp you may suppose,
Some lost their ears – some just a nose,
Our horses trod upon their toes
    E're they could run t' escape our blows,
    With shrieks the welkin[39] rang.

(*Andante*)[40]
So keen were we to rout these swine,[41]
Whole shoals of constables in line,
We gallop'd o'er stile so fine,
By orders of the SAPIENT[42] NINE.[43]
    First friends – then foes – laid flat;
By Richardson's best grinding skill,[44]
Our blades were set with right good will,

                    That we these Rogues might bleed or kill,
                    And 'give them of Reform their fill,'
                        And what d'ye think of that?

(Piano)[45]   They swear, for work they're not half paid,
                    By th' tyrants of the weaving trade,
                    Who lives like Kings (b)[46] by th' toil they've made–
                    These lies of us are daily said
                        By this ragg'd hungry swarm.
                    No reason have they thus in prate,
                    While we've recourse to th' Parish rate,[47]
                    We'll send them there for hours to wait
                    The diff'rence to receive we 'bate
                        Of wage – and where's the harm?

(Sotto voce)[48]   These rag-tag, bob-tail herds of brutes,
                    Are not content with noble roots (c)[49]
                    But think therewith that beef well suits,
                    Their chops, e'en water for rare fruits,
                        The lousy growling dogs;
                    They think forsooth, that they should dine
                    Like gentlefolks, and drink their wine
                    Or guzzle ale, or eat pig's chine,[50]
                    For game and fish they even whine,
                        Rank treason 'mongst these hogs!!

(Pianissima-mente)[51]   And then those Owls[52] who think, because
                    They've filch'd the Pow'r to make our laws,
                    They'll raise their rents thro' th people's maws,[53]
                    We'll gull by thunders of applause
                        For doubling th' price of corn.[54]
                    We'll curse and fight through 'thick and thin,'[55]
                    All those who make a dev'lish din
                    About dear bread – for there's no sin
                    In taking thus the great folks in
                        For th' RATES by th' LAND are borne.

(Con Baldanza)[56] With 'ell-wide jaws'(d)[57] we'll roar and sing,
                    We'll bravely fight for Church and King;
                    Those who no arms with them shall bring,
                    And may each vile Reformer swing
                        That we miss cutting down.
                    To our good things we'll stick like wax,
                    And throw the laws upon their backs;
                    These bare-bone herds we'll make our hacks,
                    Then nobly gobble Tythe and Tax,
                        And *thus* support the Crown.

2 'The Manchester Yeoman'

This was only one of two poems on Peterloo to be printed in the *Examiner*,[58] where it appeared on 5 September 1819.[59] The repetition of 'man' at the end of every line accentuates the stupidity of the eponymous Yeoman, whose cartoon-like buffoonery is humorous until the final line reconnects the reader with the reality of the situation.

> I am d'ye see, a Yeoman,
> All fine from top to toe, man;
> And make my mare to go, man;
> And draw my sword out so, man;
> And frown, and fume, and blow, man;
> And mutter Pshaw! And Poh! man;
> And to the rich bow low, man;
> And say to the poor Ho! Ho! man;
> And should they saucy grow, man,
> And meet to pick a crow, man,
> With CASTLEREAGH[60] and Co., man,
> And things *in status quo*, man,
> I make the goblet flow, man,
> And beef and port I stow, man,
> And then like any Roman,
> Within my bow-window, man,
> Power *ex-officio*,[61] man,
> I take on me, I trow,[62] man,
> And ride to meet the foe, man,
> And prove that there is no man
> Such 'more than man' can show, man,
> By cutting down – a woman.

3 'Verses for the Boys of Manchester'

The poet J.B.[63] makes an interesting comparison between the Gunpowder Plot of 1605 and Peterloo, arguing that the events of 16 August are of such great significance that the name of Guy Fawkes will be overshadowed. He contends that the bloodshed in Manchester is a greater attack on English democracy than Fawkes' attempt to blow up the Houses of Parliament. The poem was published in the *Black Dwarf* on 20 October 1819, only two weeks prior to Bonfire Night.[64]

> Never remember the fifth of November,
> Gunpowder, treason and plot.
> Bloodshed and murther carried much further,
> Will make Guy's name forgot.[65]

Blue bloodhounds[66] worse than Guy,
In many a company,
With big-wigs did contrive,
To cut up the people alive.
Unhappy the man, accursed the day,
That saw these monsters go to their prey,
Arm'd cowards on the throng,
Charged with horse and sword along.
The laws we need not fear,
The Doctor keeps all clear,
The swinish people's blood,[67]
Will form his choicest food:
Highest thanks will be our meed,[68]
Then forward 'urge the steed.'
As I was flying over the ground,
I saw the devil with a blue blood hound,
He grinn'd and look'd so like the other,
You'd say he was his own twin brother.
His brains were made of lead,
No shame his heart had fear of,
His valiant hand with a bloody sword,
Cut an old woman's ear off.
A twopenny loaf to feed such an oaf,
A nine-tailed cat[69] to bring him,
Exciseable slop,[70] he shan't have a drop,
But a good strong drop to hang him.
Hollo boys! Hollo boys! God save the king.
Hollo boys! Hollo boys! Let the bells ring.

4 'PETER LOO FIELD'

'PETER LOO FIELD' was subtitled 'Parody on the Waterloo Song' when it appeared in the *Manchester Observer* on 11 September 1819 under the authorship of 'T.W.'[71] The comparison between the ungallant MYC and the heroes of Waterloo is implicit in this song, unlike others in this chapter. It was to be sung to the tune of 'The Garland of Love', the choice of tune adding another layer to the parody. 'The Garland of Love' was written by Theodore Edward and was a popular ballad in the nineteenth century. Also known as 'The Lad that I Love' and 'I'll Weave Him a Garland', the song itself is undated, although one of the prints in the Bodleian is by J. Pitts of London and dated between 1802 and 1819, which indicates both its familiarity and availability at the time of Peterloo. The chorus is as follows:

Then I'll weave him a garland,
A fresh blowing garland,
With lilies and roses,
And sweet blooming posies,
A garland I'll give to a lad that I love.[72]

Oh, great were your heroes of ancient Shudehill fight,[73]
When women and children to soldiers did yield;
And mighty great were thine, fam'd St. George's kill night,
But greater, far greater, thine, Peter Loo Field.

CHORUS. – I'll weave a gay garland with vict'ry entwining,
With murderous valor pot-valiant[74] combining;
I'll weave a gay garland with vict'ry entwining,
To crown the brave Yeomen of Peter Loo Field.

Our transcendent Magistrates scheme was unfurled,
When soldiers and constables weapons did wield;
Then Yeomen grim death on the Reformers hurled,
And spilled their blood upon Peter Loo Field.
    CHORUS. – I'll weave &c. &c.

Bold Hunt,[75] spite of Devils, again will address you,
The New Bailey Dungeon[76] his mouth hath not seal'd;
While thraldom[77] alone, with her fetters caress you,
Upheld by the Yeomen of Peter Loo Field.
    CHORUS. – I'll weave &c. &c.

Will Manchester still these foul Yeomanry nourish?
Must asses, and monkeys, dominion still wield?
Or fools, with their truncheons, o'er Englishmen flourish
Who strove against freedom on Peter Loo Field.
    CHORUS. – I'll weave &c. &c.

Yet their laurels[78] are mingled with cypress and willow,[79]
Kill'd, wounded, and starving Reformers all yield;
And conscience the Yeoman disturbs on his pillow,
For shedding of blood upon Peter Loo Field.
    CHORUS. – I'll weave &c. &c.

Our Town Legislators some medals should order,
The Yeomen to wear them their safety to shield;
And on them inscribed, 'A Son of Disorder,
Who butcher's Reformers on Peter Loo Field.'
    CHORUS. – I'll weave &c. &c.

                                          T.W.

Manchester, 2nd September, 1819

5 'The Bloody Field of Peterloo! A New Song'

Described by Jim Clayson as 'a rollicking ten verse ballad',[80] this song was written by the editor of the *Theological and Political Comet*, Robert Shorter,[81] and published therein on 6 November 1819.[82] Chivalric discourse is employed to satirical effect, further heightened by Shorter's role as a bard, custodian of national culture, who, rather than celebrating military victories, is regaling the world of the '*glorious deeds*' of the MYC.[83] Shorter successfully melds the traditional ballad verse form with elements of the Pindaric ode, resulting in a song which combines vernacular and self-conscious literary cultures.

> Hero[e]s of Manchester, all hail!
> Your fame the astonish'd world shall know;
> Th' immortalizing bard can't fail,
> To sing the *deeds* of Peterloo!
>
> The Muse shall soar on daring wing,
> And her ecstatic numbers flow;
> But Pindar's[84] muse wou'd fail to sing
> Your *glorious deeds* at Peterloo![85]
>
> How on that memorable day,
> Ye did with martial ardour glow;
> And such heroic zeal display,
> All on the plains of Peterloo!
>
> How swell'd your breasts with rapture high,
> To meet the *well arm'd* banner'd foe;
> What courage teem'd in yeoman's eye,
> When dashing on to Peterloo!
>
> Methinks I see the mettled[86] steed,
> Trampling the mangled corses[87] low,
> Whilst charging round, in furious speed,
> The *bloody field* of Peterloo!!
>
> Methinks I hear the cries, the groans,
> (And view their fatal overthrow)
> Heart-rending sighs, and piteous moans,
> Rise from the field of Peterloo!
>
> Methinks I see the crimson flood,
> And mark the well aim'd fatal blow,
> The Yeoman's sabre dy'd in blood,
> Reeking on far fam'd Peterloo!

But Yeomen's hearts are form'd of steel,
Ardent to fields of blood they go;
Their gallant souls disdain to feel,
Whilst dealing death at Peterloo!

My muse the truth shall ne'er deny;
The good, the wise, the just, we know,
Think you deserve promotion high,
In *iron case*[88] on Peterloo!!

6 'To the Gentlemen Yeomanry of Manchester'

This short verse was published in the *Black Dwarf* on 15 September 1819.[89] Addressed to the MYC, it 'congratulates' them on the nature of their crimes, which has elevated them above the petty criminals to the level of 'extraordinary villains'.

Sweet sirs, you've done a very charming feat
All history must sink abashed before ye;
Not e'en the Newgate Calendar[90] can treat
With such a dashing deed our love of glory
Small rogues are they who filch pounds, pence and shillings,
Murderers are extraordinary villains.[91]

7 'The Butcher and Hog: In imitation of a scene on St. Peter's Field, Manchester'

This short poem, written by G.R. and published in the *Manchester Observer* on 2 October 1819, employs the trope of yeoman as butcher, seen in a number of Peterloo poems.[92] The use of hog as a metaphor for one of the victims is a well-used radical appropriation of the term which dates back to Edmund Burke's famous description of the people as 'the swinish multitude'.[93] The black humour of the poem is undercut by the final line in which the dehumanisation of the people leads to the questioning of their rights.

Thus spake the Butcher, in his hand the blade,
The Hog upon the tressel screaming laid:
'I wish my hat were in your gullet ramm'd!
'Lie still, and have your throat cut and be d——d,
'You're but a Hog – sure, by the coil you keep,
'You think yourself as good as any *Sheep*!
'Bleed quietly, and cease that frightful bawl;
''Tis faction and sedition makes you squall;
'Shall Hogs pretend to any *rights* at all?'

8 'Tribute to Certain Military Heroes Occasioned by the Recent Horrors of Manchester'

This poem begins by describing the oppression of Greece by its Ottoman conquerors before comparing such barbarians with the Manchester murderers. Combined with the Latin epigraph, the style and content of the opening stanza suggest a well-educated poet who locates Peterloo in an international context. Written by the unknown 'W.H.D', it was published in the *Black Dwarf* on 1 December 1819 but is dated 20 August, a mere four days after Peterloo.[94]

> '*Quid facient hostes capta crudelius urbe?*' – CATULLUS[95]
> What in a captured town could foes more savage do?
>
> Thus Greece beholds on her degraded shore,[96]
> Where valour fights and freedom breathes no more
> Barbarian cowards lord it over the land
> Who at the sight of Russia's hardy son,[97]
> Or when Albania[98] leads her warriors on,
> With shameful haste ere yet the foe is nigh
> Retire, arm'd, not to combat but to fly
> Yet these, the scandal of a soldier's name
> Alive to nought but danger, dead to fame
> With what unshaken nerve their valour braves
> The abject crowd of *unprotected slaves*!
> On them their wanton cruelty they wreak,
> And flash their weapons on each helpless Greek!
>
> And are not these fit rivals of your worth,
> Ye English Janizeries[99] of the north[100]
> Ye licens'd butchers in your dread array,
> Who, unappall'd can force your vengeful way,
> Where *unarm'd hosts* alone you might oppose,
> *Defenceless victims, not determined foes.*
> When your first essay in the fields of fight,
> Could make reforming thousands turn to flight;
> When first your slumb'ring weapons active grown,
> Weapons whose force no foreign foe has known.[101]
> Distress'd, defenceless Britons, hack'd and hew'd.
> And dy'd their maiden blades in women's blood;
> Amid that scene, which you unmov'd could see,
> Remorseless and cold blooded butchery.
> Not your's the hands to hold, or hearts to share,
> Fell blood hounds![102] When you 'rous'd you from your lair,
> And gnash'd your fangs, as eager as the prey.' (a)[103]

And void of love, or pity cut your way.
Still, in your souls the watchword and the cry,
'Away to heav'n respective lenity' (b)[104]
'Lay on 'curse him, the first cries hold' enough' (c)[105]
Could human hearts be made of sterner stuff?
Was it for this, your country's erring laws,
Allowed *you arms*, to guard her *hallow'd cause*?
That you should use the sacred gift she gave,
Not to protect her children, but enslave.
To revel in the slaughter of her sons
Unchain'd oppressions ruthless myrmidons?[106]
Delight in deeds, to savage hordes unknown,
Which lawless bandit tribes might blush to own.
How did you dare to veil your acts of shame,
Usurp the British soldiers' honour'd name;
Gods! Shall such foul associates strive to brand,
The brave defenders of our native land?
And their unsullied scutcheon[107] dare to spot,
With this most infamous, eternal blot?
Would that the things (and may I ne'er again
Call them by that gross misnomer, men)
Were, for the meed[108] of their unhallow'd deeds,
Bade, where true valour nobly dares and bleeds,
Their nerveless arms, and skilless swords, oppose,
When man with man in equal fight must close;
When arduous deeds must win the doubtful day,
When dangers throng, though glory points the way.
How soon would then the cloven foot[109] disclose,
And in base root their coward souls expose,
Ye matchless warriors, who in martial pride,
Yet lack'd the needful skill your steeds to guide;
Which could not e'en a peaceful hustings storm,
Till your disorder'd ranks had time to form;
Whose valiant daring was to be declar'd,
By your snug ambush in a carrier's yard;
So dear was Falstaff's maxim to each heart,
'Discretion still is valour's better part,[110]
Who, as in action bold, in counsel wise,
Most sagely trampled down *your own allies*;
Whose temp'rate sabres show'd, to all which saw,
The lamb's own bosom with the lion's paw;
Whose chivalry, let *female wounds* attest,
Whose mercy, suppliant woman's bleeding breast,
Sought from the things in vain; (I ask again,
Would you call those who could deny it, *men*?)

Henceforth lay by your arms, or cease, for shame,
To wield them in your injur'd country's name;
Who ne'er in utmost need, would stoop to sue,
The useless aid of miscreants, such as you.
God serve the bigot autocrat of Spain,[111]
Support his tottering throne, and tyrant reign;
Go! And in realms beyond the Atlantic waves,
Follow the standard, fight the cause of slaves.
There find a field to such deservings due,
You worthy of your Prince, and he of you!

August 20th, 1819

9 'A Prayer'

Of the M——r Y——y C——y[112] before they took the field by Jones

Written from the perspective of the MYC, this poem takes the form of a pagan prayer. By depicting the MYC as 'heathens', the poet highlights the lack of Christian values in their actions on the day. Together with their invocation to Jove to make them like Turkish warriors, the MYC are portrayed as the 'other', un-Christian and un-British, a feature shared with the previous poem. 'A Prayer' was published in the *Manchester Observer* on 30 October 1819.[113]

Great Jove to whom all heathens pray'd
Whene'er in martial pomp array'd;
We Heathen Yeomen would demand,
Thy succour in a *Christian* land.
And when we've shown ourselves expert,
Do thou convey us off unhurt:
If in our heart some feeling lurks,
Rout out and give us hearts of Turks.[114]
Let all unarm'd before us stand,
And soon the blood shall stain the land,
That we may show our valiant tricks,
Keep from them cudgels, stones and bricks.
You know great Jove we're not a crew,
Who deign'd to fight at Waterloo;
We never like to take the plain,
When men presume to fight again.
We're wiser than the gang who ran,
In danger's face with Wellington;[115]
Let such in fields resign their breath,
But keep us from the arms of death.
Let *dantes*[116] [?] who seldom deal in blows,

And men as harmless be our foes,
Our courage all on *ale* depend,[117]
Do then such gallant troops defend.

10 'To the Livery'd Assassins'

This poem is laden with supernatural imagery, aimed at dehumanising the MYC. As seen in many other poems in this anthology, the unnatural acts of the Yeomanry are in stark contrast with the regular forces bound by loyalty to the crown and military codes of conduct. With its blend of Christian and Pagan imagery, it is an example of a revenant ballad, defined by David Fowler as one which depicts 'otherworld figures or in some way relate to the return of the dead from the grave.'[118] Here the MYC are described as 'the fiends of hell' led by Beelzebub to slay the innocent. Written on 9 September in Preston by 'a poor weaver', the poem appeared in the 2 October issue of the *Manchester Observer*.[119]

Dark deeds of horror, tell it not, oh, shame!
Nor say to whom attach'd the impious blame;
Nor say it did originate in shades
Where rank envenom'd[120] malice still pervades;
Say not, away the thought, it was with men!
Eternal infamy sure must condemn;
Men could not, would not act the hellish part;
Tho' base and blind, and villainous his heart.

Who did it then? What fiends of hell sprung up
To mount aloft, and pour th' invenomed cup
Of bitterest gall, of rage and fume[121] and spite,
That ever stigmatiz'd the sons of night?
Did Beelzebub himself, with all his crew,
Appear on earth in arms, what more could do
The hellish legion, lost and ever curst,
If on the sons of men their rage should burst?

Say, was it soldiers, men of high renown?
Dress'd up and set apart under the crown,
Support its dignity, act within the law,
Sustain the virtuous, keep the base in awe.
And if their country's good should be at stake,
In time of danger in it would partake;
Would act like men – be number'd with the brave;
And soldier-like, their country help to save?
Soldiers, I say! Oh, name it not; oh, fie!
Soldiers, I say! The name you know sounds high;
Soldiers in battle still would fight for fame,

And scorn the act producing sense of shame;
Soldiers, when call'd on, like the brave would bleed;
Soldiers would proudly march in time of need;
Soldiers would not toll the dark hidden knell,
Then act the cowardly part, like fiends of hell.

Who did the business then, who led the van?[122]
Who meditated the infernal plan?
Who brought these elves into the sanguine[123] field
Of Peterloo, the bravo's sword to wield?
To kill and slay, and bathe in human gore
The innocent, defenceless, now no more;
Murdered in cold blood by those puff'd[124] empty imps,
Of menial sycophants and courtly pimps.[125]

Oh! M———r,[126] dire and black was the day,
When manufacturing outangs[127] got the sway;
To govern thee, and serve corruption's cause,
Laid by humanity and virtue's laws;
Usurp'd the power and base despotic sway,
And sound the loud alarm, go kill and slay;
Go forth to murder all who dare to live;
Men, women, children, none shall have reprieve.

Now mounted, flush'd and drunk,[128] the mushroom[129] band
Dash'd forward with their murderous swords in hand;
Each mighty hero, high set on his nag,
Hath stood a long campaign at Brobdinnag;[130]
And, oh! What mighty deeds they now perform;
Break on the people like a thunder storm;
Fly now ye women, fly ye children, fly,
The Brobdinnags have doom'd you all to die.

Hermaphrodite[131] and mushroom things we see;
Oh! Fate, how strange sometimes thy stern decree:
The lion sometimes hurt with pricks of thorn,[132]
Tho' he would look o'er tigers, wolves, with scorn
Like him, the people mighty on that day,
They by the Brobdinnags were drove away;
But Lion-like, they'll start and rise again,
Reverget [?][133] he's good of those so basely slain.

Oh! Truth perverted, black has turned white,
The noon-day sun is visible midnight;
Vice is virtue, virtue vice has turn'd,
And truth and justice with contempt are spurn'd;
The powers that be, the best of men condemn,

'Those true sons of Mars' 167

The worst are prais'd, caress'd and thank'd by them;
Witness their boast, and how they make their brags,
And thank the Major[134] and his Brobdinnags.

Yet, notwithstanding truth the base defies,
Retorts and puts to flight attested lies,
And shines resplendent, drives the gloom away,
Whose sullen darkness hides the glorious day;
Thus, liberty, tho' clouded now in shades,
Glows in the bosom, ev'ry pore pervades,
And will shine forth a great and glorious day,
And strike perdition's sons with dire dismay.

No more, ye monsters, till the judgement day,
No more to you at present shall I say;
Horror awaits you, dreadful is your doom,
Blasphemous guilt in black shall be your tomb;
Fiends from the shades shall hover round your bier,
And mortally shall form a rank entire;
And lastly this, your epitaph shall be,
'Beneath lies SCORN, REPROACH and INFAMY!'
                                    A POOR WEAVER
Preston, Sept. 9, 1819

11 'The Norwich Declaration'

Immediately preceding the poem in the *White Hat* on 16 October 1819 is a letter to the editor signed 'A Friend to the Constitution' and dated 9 October.[135] The letter outlines recent events in Norwich which began with a public meeting, at which the Mayor, Mr Bolinbroke, and the local MP Mr Gurney, heard representations from local people concerned with events in Manchester. The 13 October issue of the radical newspaper the *London Alfred* details the resolutions made at this meeting which opposed the actions of the authorities and which were passed; these include:

> It is impossible for us, as Englishmen, to contemplate this disgraceful scene, without feeling for its authors and actors the strongest emotions of shame and indignation; and viewing it as a direct and deliberate violation of the chartered rights and privileges of a free-born People, we denounce it at once to the execration of our contemporaries and posterity.[136]

Subsequently, a number of local dignitaries, including aldermen and clergymen, met to issue a declaration in which they stated that they fully supported the actions of the MYC. Described in the *White Hat* as 'the sons of corruption', they obtained, by fair means and foul, more than twelve hundred signatures on the declaration. The letter in the *White Hat* concludes:

> We insert a versification of the Norwich declaration, which exhibits its sentiments very fairly, and may serve as a model for the sapient gentry of other places who are not yet provided with one. It is extracted from the *Norwich Courier* of Saturday last.[137]

> We, the loyal of this most seditious of times,
> Who think blaming great folks of the greatest of crimes,
> Do hereby declare our abhorrence of those
> Who've expressed their aversion to murder and blows.
>   Derry Down, & c.[138]

> What though we most prudently shrunk from the call
> Which summoned us lately to meet at the Hall,[139]
> Yet now that we've distanced the orators there,
> Our opinions (on paper) we'll freely declare.

> Here, safe from all dangers, we right royal elves,
> Can boldly descant on our own noble selves,
> And tho' not behind columns St. Andrew's that grace,[140]
> In Stephenson's columns we're sure of a place.[141]

> The late 'Resolutions' we vote are a shame,
> 'A proceeding so harsh and ill timed we disclaim;'
> In our nature so peaceful, so dove like, and mild,
> We scorn to resent e'en the death of a child.

> We moreover declare that the thing's premature,
> For though a few lives have been lost to be sure,
> Yet for decency's sake we must always deplore,
> That their haste could not wait for a few hundreds more.

> We object to no plan for a small Reformation,
> But Radicals hold in great abomination,
> And think that what scores may in fairness demand,
> Is in *thousands* high treason so we understand.

> As friends of humanity, deep we deplore
> The blood that is laid to [the] Manchester Corps,
> Yet it is to our minds source of great consolation,
> They had proper advice on this *trying* occasion.

> Bold Yeomen! Our thanks to your valour is due,
> We're panting to share in such glory with you;
> But alas! The folks *here* are such sticklers for law,
> If they meet ne'er so oft, not a sword must we draw.

12 'The Devils that Stirred up the Storm: A New Song by the R-G—T'S Ministers and the M——R MAG——TES'[142]

Even though no tune is stated for this poem, which appeared in the *Manchester Observer* on 16 October and the *Cap of Liberty* four days later, it is evident from both the form and the content that it was intended to be sung.[143] The poet satirises the politicians Castlereagh and Canning, along with the magistrates and the Prince Regent, as devils. Castlereagh is identified as the ring leader or 'chief Devil' who orchestrated the response of the authorities and subsequent support of the magistrates following Peterloo.

> Come join me all ye who to murder are foes,
> Come join me ye friends of Reform;
> We've beings unsung yet in verse or in prose,
> The Devils that stirred up the storm.
>
> Then sing C——agh,[144] skilled in blowing up strife,[145]
> 'Twixt tempers else made to conform;
> Each brother he armeth against his brother's life,
> Chief Devil in raising the Storm.
>
> Sing Deputy R-g—t a praying old wight,[146]
> Whose circulars reeking and warm,
> With blood from the victims dispatched to black night,
> New horrors shed over the Storm.
>
> Sing *Nullius filius*,[147] a jester most keen,
> Whose tongue could e'en beauty deform;
> He'll laugh at our misery, and banter, I ween,[148]
> While fearfully rages the Storm.
>
> Our M-g—trates sing with heads warm & hearts cool,
> Fit things direful deeds to perform;
> †*Sir* Knave and *Sir* Fool[149] so dazzled each tool,
> That they willingly stirr'd up the Storm.

13 'Four Wise Heads Together'

This thinly veiled attack on four senior members of Liverpool's government was published anonymously in the *Black Dwarf* on 12 January 1820.[150] The poet is unsparing in his criticism, which includes allegations of corruption and the misappropriation of public monies, thereby exposing the perverse loyalty within the establishment where the politicians offer their support to the Manchester Magistrates "Cause they supported us.'

Now Cas, and Can, and Sid, and Van,[151]
Those worthy co-partakers,
In Council sweet, their noses meet;
O, the profound wiseacres![152]

For there had been a great ado-
A bustle in the North;
And Fame's loud trumpet through the land
Had blown the tidings forth.

So, as I said, friends Cas and Can,
Sagacious Sid, and little Van,
In conclave met to peep about,
To find, forsooth! the falsehood out.

And first Hibernian Cas[153] arose,
And with a smile begun;
'Whate'er we now intend to do,
Let's mind dear number one.

'For (other things apart) I swear,
Judge you, if I'm an Ass;
No country dearer is to me,
Than well-beloved Cas.

'Such patriots too, I know you are;
Each loves his own dear self;
Each in his time has deeply dipp'd
His finger in the pelf.[154]

'For this the busy lifelong day,
And sleepless night we've pass'd;
No other end in view than this,
To hold our places fast.

''tis hard, co-partners to resign;
The thought we can't endure;
So then, whate'er be our resolve,
Let's make our places sure.'

Then up got Van, as well he might,
With look of glad portent;
'Egad! He thought his noble friend
Had been right eloquent.

'This he could say with all his heart,
That for the special weal,
He always had, and always should
Continue still to feel.

'"Twas true that taxes griped and ground,
And why was that the worse?
For much ne'er reached the public fund,
But slipp'd into their purse.'[155]

Sagacious Sid, arose and said,
'Friend Van had been of service;
For true it was, that as to cash,
Naught else so well could serve us.

'Friend Cas's rule he much admired,
Self was the top of all,
The noble thought his bosom fired,
Conquer we must – or fall.

'And now, my friends, a word or two;
The order of the day;-
As to those worthy magistrates
What part have we to play?

'"Tis true they've cut, and maimed, and killed,
Sabred, and trodden down;
The fatal slaughter may have been
Illegal too, I own.

'Legal or not – that's not the light
In which we view the fuss;
We will support the magistrates,
'Cause they supported us.

'Therefore I move, – a vote of thanks;
These butchers have – that done –
My friends our pudding we will eat,
But let us hold our tongue.

Time serving Can – the slippery soul –
Well knew what game to play,
Which ever side the currant turned,
Turned he the self same way.

Or good or bad, the same to him;
People or King, the same;
Give him the pudding – that's enough –
He plays the winning game.'

So up he got with bought grimace,
And – The pudding still in view –
And thus the sneerer spoke, 'My friends,
Whate'er you say is true.

'The rascal Radicals deserved
No sparing mercy – none –
And for the loyal magistrates
Naught wrongful had they done.

'The vote of thanks he well approved,
And – pudding – still in view
No recompence too great for those,
Who loyal were, and true.'

The vote was passed with hand and heart;
And up the conclave broke, –
Well pleased that each had played his part,
Towards his dearest hope.

Now long live noble Cas, and Can,
Sagacious Sid, and little Van;
And may each lover dear of pelf.
Continue still t' adore himself.

14 'From Mr Batty, Clerk to – Milne, Esq. Coroner,[156] to his Friend in London'

This epistolary poem, one of the longest in the collection, appeared in the *Black Dwarf* on 15 September 1819.[157] The letter is written from the perspective of Mr Batty, who was not in fact clerk to Mr Milne but was the deputy coroner to Mr Farren in Oldham, where the inquest of John Lees, a Waterloo veteran, was to be heard, the only sustained inquest to be held in relation to those killed at Peterloo.[158] The *Examiner* reports that when Coroner Milne arrived at Oldham from Manchester to lead the inquest, he refused to proceed, due to the fact that Oldham was not in his district and, as a consequence, insisted that the inquest was adjourned for two weeks until the local Mr Farren returned. The poem satirises the hapless Batty who is more concerned with missing his dinner than conducting the inquest.

> You'll see by the Papers, the context I've had,
> With Harmer, the lawyer, I think the man's mad,
> What business had he, to trouble his head,
> Respecting John Lees, when the fellow was dead![159]
> How the Inquest would turn, or what might be said.
> But this vile Democrat with his queries and law,
> Had a mind to perplex me, and find out a flaw,
> But I learnt of the Quorum[160] with prudence profound,
> When Hunt with his wit, tried their sense to confound.

The best way was the short one, of Trafford[161] and others
(I mean by this term his magistrates brother's)
Whenever a question too closely should cut,
By silence each purpose completely rebut.
You remember the case, the Reformists were tried,[162]
When the magistrates sat, and the judge in his pride:
When Radical Hunt, the bold and the free,
A dangerous fellow ('tis feared he will be)
Appeared at the bar, holding law at defiance,
In himself and his cause, having every reliance;
But the case was not heard, for the bench to a man,
Had all predetermined their notable plan,
Had resolved if impertinent queries were made,
As to 'where a man lived,' or 'what was his trade.'
To bear him clear off, upon their *ipsi dixit*,[163]
And take all the power from the pris'ner to fix it.
In the instance with me, what had Harmer to do,
My dinner was spoilt, and ruined my stew:
Sure the dead man[164] could wait until dinner was over,
Against Harmer I'll have an action at trover.[165]
What a fuss is there made about wounded and dead,
I wish they would mind their own business instead;
If the sword had not laid so many in dust,
Oppression, affliction, and misery must.
This lawyer was anxious that men must depose
How Lees met his death by unmerciful blows,
But I was alarmed, and altered my mind,
How would I proceed until I had dined.
Harmer urged the request of prompt deposition,
But I (Batty) most firmly refused his petition:
Resolved not to act 'till the Coroner came,'[166]
For the fish would be spoilt, and ruined my game.
Besides on the subject, I would not define,
And I said nothing more, than 'I must and would dine.'
Still that troublesome Harmer continued his dinner here,
But the inquest could wait 'while I went to my dinner.'
I wish you Reformers were all at the D—l.[167]
If they'd let me alone, I'd be quiet and civil.
They may rail and declaim, let them write from the press,
Of the 'nation's decay' and the 'R——'s[168] excess;'
Can we fear Reform while the P****e[169] keeps in pay,
Cold Liverpool, Sidmouth, and proud Castlereagh,[170]
And the Dutchman[171] who thrives, while John Bull is his tool –
They may scoff at his 'NUMBERS' he's more knave than fool.
And as to our troops what have they to do, –

But to meet the Reformers and 'kill off a few,'
Each gallant can cleverly handle a lance,
It was known in Poland, we had it from France;[172]
But nothing beyond this imported should be, –
France now owns no despots THAT NATION IS FREE
Her people no longer oppression can feel,
They've no letter de-cachet since they burnt the Bastille.[173]
I wish we had both, and we come very near it,
Let Hunt look to this, would that Burdett[174] could fear it!!!
I don't think the people would be much appalled,
By the regulars[175] which they all chuse to be called;
Tho' bravely they conquered, and freely they bled,
They will ne'er aim a blow at a countryman's head.
Our Yeomen (and many can speak to their cost),
Who weep a loved friend, or relative lost,
They alone, are the men to slay, cut, and maim,
Were they called out again, they would still do the same,
But your soldiers – they vaunt of their pleasure to save,
Say that 'mercy's the boast of the valiant and brave';
And for women – they love, they adore the dear race,
Could they wound their fair forms, if they looked in their face;
No, our Manchester Yeomen alone could do this,
For to cherish weak women they ne'er knew the bliss.

15 'Paddy Bull's Epistle to his Brother John'

This epistolary poem, written in rhyming anapestic couplets, is from the Irish Paddy Bull to his brother, John. A well-established symbol of Britishness, John Bull featured in numerous caricatures and cartoons from the 1790s and represented the middle-class British man, respectable and loyal, if not hugely intelligent.[176] In this poem, however, John is silent and it is the voice of the Irish Paddy that we hear, providing an outsider's view of events in England; moreover, the contemporaneous reader would have been familiar with recent events in Ireland which colour Paddy's narrative. Presumably a Catholic, given his name, the poem resonates with religious discourse peppered with references to his own involvement in radical activity at home.[177] The poem ends with a pledge for unity between the English and the Irish to defeat the oppressors. It was printed in *Medusa* on 18 December 1819.[178]

> Brother Johnny, my darling! Faith, what is the matter,
> Why the deuce[179] dost keep up such a bother and clatter,
> Here's the big Whigs complaining they can't keep thee quiet,
> And say thou'rt inclined for to kick up a Riot;

By thy pranks thou hast put 'em in such a sad fright
That the hair of their wigs is all standing upright;
By my soul they are making most woeful long faces
And are chatt'ring like monkey's with monstrous grimaces;
They are fearing lest thou, getting addled and crazy,
Should's knock the dust out of each well powder'd jazey,[180]
But I've known thee, my jewel, a good natur'd fellow.
Yet, I own, rather humoursome when thou art mellow;
Tho' I have known thee full oft take a frolicksome part,
I never yet knew thee have malice at heart.
But Johnny, they say thou dost jeer at thy betters,
Art grown quite impatient and weary of fetters;
That of passure[181] obedience thou mak'st a meer scoff,
And has said that thy shackles htou soon wilt knock of[f];
That thou hast in thy noddle[182] a monstrous queer plan,
About Liberty, Freedom, and 'Paine's Rights of Man.'[183]
Absurdly asserting how'er they treat
Thou'st a soul, and hast feeling as well as the great.
Has said, howe'er humble and Lordly thy station,
That thou art the nerve and the soul of the Nation;
That Lords, Dukes and Descendants, and Princes and Kings,
Are vicious, expensive and troublesome things;
Men baubles at best, but that often we find
The[y]'re the scourges, the curses, and pest of mankind –
That the[y]'re great carcase Butchers slaughtering in blood,
That the world but for them would be happy and good;
Hast a habit of swearing and say'st thou 'lt be d—d.
If by their vile tricks thou wilt longer be sham'd.
But Johnny my darling do take my advice,
Thou shalt have it quite cheap, without money or price;
Oh! My dear, dont make use of one grain of thy reason,
Or, my honey, they'll hang thee – they call it rank treason;
Dont bother thy nob with affairs of the state,
But leave thou the whole swinish herd[184] to their fate;
Is'n better they all should in misery pine,
Shame Prince! Leave off gaming, and whoring, and wine,[185]
Oh! Then, brother Johnny, my jewel, my honey,
Be easy, my love, now and give 'em your money,
Or how can your Lords, Duke, and Princes by scores
Keep Pavilions,[186] Parks, Palaces, Panders,[187] and Whores;
Then give thyself up to thy rulers discretion,
Be patient and humble, don't call it oppression,
Don't grumble what burthens[188] soever you bears
Let Sidmouth and Castlereagh mind my affairs;
Nor dare those presume their merits to scan,

They'll govern thee, John, on a wonderous plan,
Of Castlereagh's kindness full well dost thou know –
I'd some very strong proofs but a short time ago.[189]
Thou'rt a hog and if grunting and grumbling thou goes,
Thy masters must put some cold steel in thy nose;
And this bit of cold metal when fix'd in thy snout,
Will keep thee from poking and muzzling about;
And by way of restraint, in thy nose let me tell ye,
Is far better by far than if thrust in thy belly.[190]
Here's Sam Straw, Harry Hobnail, Ben Buckskin, and more,[191]
To quiet thee joins in a Yeomanry corps;
And like Manchester heroes, with right and left buts,
If thou open'st thy mouth they will rip out thy guts;
Then an honest sensation I trow[192] thou would feel,
To see thy guts dangling about at thy heel;
They say too, not having God's fear in thine eyes,
The Clergy so pure thou dost always depise –
Hast said they love hunting, and whoring, and drinking,
Much more than their books and the trouble of thinking.
That the story they tell thee is all a mere trick,
Just to keep off thine eyes while thy pockets they pick;
That unless thy guineas most freely are prid,[193]
There is no Pater Noster[194] for thee to be said;
And altho' of their zeal they now make such a boast,
For just so much money there's so much Holy Ghost;
That unless they're well paid, for the story they tell,
They'd not preach a sermon to save thee from Hell.
That Mammon[195] they worship like Judas of old,
And give 'em the money their God's to be sold,
That titles, and hnours and places, and pensions,
And to flatter rich rogues take up all their attention.
Now Johnny once more prythee take my advice,
About telling a thumper[196] be not over nice,
Say thy Princes are virtuous, lovely, and kind,
And that malice itself not a blemish can find; –
That they all live in comfort at home with their wives,
And ne'er did commit a *faux pas* in their lives –
That they ne'er run in debt, head and ears, and then pray
For their whoring and gaming the nation would pay –
Say thy Statesman are honest, and careful, and good,
And thy welfare and happiness well understood:
Say old England is flourishing, prosp'rous, and free,
And no nation on earth is so happy as we;
Say thy judges are learned, and wise, and upright,
And never judge any in malice or spite,

Say thy laws are impartial and free of expence,
That the rich and the poor get strict justice from thence;
Say the Parsons thou pays such large sums for to preach,
To the full always practice the doctrines they teach;
And no persecutors but hnmble and lowly,
Despising the world, self-denying, and holy;
All this my dear Johnny by thee may be said,
Then of losing thy head, thou needs not be afraid;
There's Reform and Reason, two things thou must shun,
Or thou'lt have thy *quietus*[197] with sword or with gun,
'Till some better times come, and together we pull,
I'm sincerely thy Brother and friend – PADDY BULL.

16 'An Humble Address; 1.TO THE MAG–ST—TES 2. TO THE M—T—Y; AND 3. TO THE SP-C—L CONS—BLES'[198]

Engaged in the glorious work of Monday last.

Written only two days after the massacre and printed on 21 August in the *Manchester Observer*, this is the earliest dated poem in this anthology and possibly the first Peterloo poem to be published.[199] Its author, 'P.N', in the persona of an inexperienced bard, addresses a stanza each to the three audiences outlined in the title: the magistrates, the military and the special constables. Galvanised by the events of 16 August, the poet sees it as his duty to report the events, as well as calling for the perpetrators to be hanged. The level of detail in the poem suggests the poet was present at St Peter's Field.

I.
Oh! Ye dread Sirs, who bear the name
    Of Mag–st—tes, – once sacred, now despised, –
'Tis fit some bard should spread the fame
    Of deeds, which cannot be too highly prized.
    But shall I dare attempt it? I am weak –
    As yet my muse has only learn'd to squeak
In lowly accents; – never heed,
I'll try – I will indeed.
    'Tis not of acts long past that I shall sing

Although *for those* you well deserve to *swing*
    Aloft: – your doings for a day,
    Even for Monday last,[200] men say,
Are such as ought to make Old England ring,
Of these I'll tell: First how you sent about
    Full many a scout,

To see if folk's were preparing
Themselves for an airing, –
And (as you chose to say) to make a stir
At Manchester.
Appalling as the news they brought
Of countless numbers moving on –
Appalling as it might be thought,
Yet still you lived, your breath was not quite gone!
'And are they arm'd?' you ask'd. Oh no!
'Then we shall do.
'Now send to th' Cavalry, and tell them that,
('As the reformers will not make a riot,)
'They must, when all is peaceable and quiet,
'Prance in among the People, – lay them flat, –
'Help Constables to take the leaders, –
'Those cursed *peaceful* meeting breeders; –
'And bid them then disperse the mob,
'By hundreds down to mow them;
('They'll like the job,)
'And dead upon the field to strew them.
'As for ourselves, – we'll creep into some houses;
'Though to some eyes, the sight be frightful,
'Yet thence, *serve* as any louse,
'To look at it will be delightful.'
All this you did: – your bidding done,
You ventured out, to lead your pris'ners on.

II.

And you, ye gentle *military squires!**
Ye gratify'd a part of your desires – ;
But why proceed no further – ?
'Tis true, ye kill'd perhaps a score;
And cut, and crush'd, and trampled hundreds more;
But this was hardly *genteel, wholesome murther!*[201]
Methinks I see you galloping between
And over, *quiet half-starv'd* men and women;
(They were unarm'd, – for, had they not, I ween
Ye would have got a very pretty trimming).
How did ye trample o'er them,
And gash and gore them!
Oh! Ye were mounted quite sublime,
On steeds whose speed outskipp'd old time!
How ye exulted in your actions,
Though hardly done to the satisfactions
Of those, at whose commanding nod,
Ye kill your neighbours, – would abjure your God!

Well, well, you did your best, – for which I praise ye,
        And wish that ye may be
        Exalted on a tree,
With each, about your necks, a rope to raise ye.

        III.

Can I forget you *Sp–c—ls*? In the plan,
        The peace-disturbing plan, ye had a place;
'Tis not a foremost one, – not in the van;[202] –
        The rear ye occupy'd with signal grace.
And, when by horse and foot well guarded,
        Ye *did duty* so prime,
        That I long for the time,
When you shall, as you ought, be rewarded.

        IV.

Too much, the muse has sung in playful tone,
Of deeds, the doers' lives can ne'er atone.
Of deeds of horror; – deeds of sin and shame; –
Deeds for which MURDER is too mild a name.
'He that doth shed man's blood,' it hath been said
By God, 'tis just that man his blood should shed.'[203]
Ye smile! – infernals![204] – ye may smile away;
Your smiles will turn to tears of blood. – The day
The day of reck'ning surely will arrive;[205]
Till then against your fellows ye may strive.
I know ye're now beyond the reach of justice;
Yet that shall fail wherein your hope and trust is:
I mean usurped power, – sustained by fraud,
And robbery, and rapine,[206] and the hord
Of hireling scribes, – who for a little pelf[207]
Would, each one, see his country, conscience, self;
Who hail, and glory in the oppressive sway
That shuts their patriot-countrymen from day,
In loathsome dungeons; – loading them with chains,
And racking all their bones with direful pains![208]
Hasten the time, O freedom's God! When all
Tyrants, – and those who succour therein shall fall; –
Wrong from its lofty throne o'er man, be hurl'd;
And UNIVERSAL RIGHT SHALL RULE THE WORLD.
August 18, 1819

*I would be understood here to address myself PARTICULARLY to the Yeomanry. They are Volunteers in the work of butchery and blood. Let this never be forgotten.

17 'Saint Ethelstone's Day'

This poem, 'one of the best and most graphic squibs in the "canon"', 'belong[ing] to the robust strain of political stanzas and satirical choric songs of the vivid years of the 1790s'[209] is a coruscating attack on Reverend Charles Wicksted Ethelstone (1767–1830), an Anglican clergyman and leading Manchester Magistrate. Written by the Spencean shoemaker-poet, Allen Davenport,[210] and set to the tune of 'Gee-up, Dobbin',[211] it appeared in the *Theological and Political Comet* on 6 November 1819. A letter, signed 'A.D', accompanied the poem, stating:

> The following little song is from the last, new, deep and affecting tragedy, called, 'The *Peterloo Massacre*,' or, 'SAINT ETHELSTONE'S DAY,' 1819, with unbounded applause; and, it is conjectured, from the high patronage which this tragedy has met, that it will be repeated during the present season! Indeed, some are so sanguine in their expectations, that they think it probable, it may have a run during the Christmas holidays, instead of 'George Barnwell'!![212] But, be that as it may, I here present you with the song, which is to the Prince's favourite tune of – 'Gee-up Dobbin.'[213]

Davenport highlights in the poem, not only the hypocrisy of Ethelstone, whose Christianity did not get in the way of his bloodlust, but also his desire for fame and renown.[214]

> A Manchester parson, to church and king staunch,
> Much fam'd in the pulpit, but more on the bench,[215]
> Resolv'd to be sainted without more delay;
> And the SIXTEENTH OF AUGUST was fixed for the day.
>
> To contrive the best means, all his genius was bent,
> How to celebrate such an auspicious event;
> When he saw the Reformers in marching array,
> Move on to the field on SAINT ETHELSTONE'S DAY.
>
> Then, the oath of his office, inform'd him, 'twas good,
> That the vest of a saint should be sprinkl'd with blood;
> When his Counsellors whisper'd, ''Twill be the best way,
> 'The Reformers to crush on SAINT ETHELSTONE'S DAY.'
>
> He took the advice, and, to make all things sure,
> Read the riots act o'er, on the step of his door;[216]
> When the yeomanry Butchers, all gallop'd away,
> To do some great exploit on SAINT ETHELSTONE'S DAY.
>
> They hack'd off the breasts of the women,[217] and then,
> They cut off the ears and the noses of men;[218]

In every direction they slaughter'd away,
'Till drunken with blood on SAINT ETHELSTONE'S DAY.

Cut away, my brave fellows, you see how they faint,
'They are BLACKGUARD REFORMERS!' exclaimed the new *Saint*,
'Send them to the Devil, my lads, your own way,
And no doubt, they'll remember SAINT ETHELSTONE'S DAY.

Notes

1 M. Scrivener (ed.), *Poetry and Reform: Periodical Verse from the English Democratic Press, 1792–1824* (Michigan: Wayne State University Press, 1992), p. 25.
2 D. Duff, *Romanticism and the Uses of Genre* (Oxford: Oxford University Press, 2009), p. 4.
3 The group was founded c. 1713 and members included Jonathan Swift, John Gay and Alexander Pope. Writing under the pseudonym Martin Scriblerus, the group ridiculed what they considered to be the lack of taste in learning (*DNB*).
4 G. Dyer, *British Satire and the Politics of Style, 1789–1832* (Cambridge: Cambridge University Press, 1997), p. 8.
5 D. Fairer, *English Poetry of the Eighteenth Century: 1700–1789* (Harlow: Longman, 2003), pp. 23, 25.
6 Scrivener, *Poetry and Reform*, p. 25.
7 M. Wood, *Radical Satire and Print culture: 1790–1822* (Oxford: Clarendon, 1994), p. 215.
8 W. Hone and G. Cruikshank, *The Political Showman at Home* (London: Hone, 1821).
9 R. Holmes, *Shelley: The Pursuit* (New York: New York Review Book, 1994), p. 539.
10 Spence produced many coins as a parody of the fashion for commemorative currency and also its utilisation as propaganda during the French Revolution and subsequent wars (Wood, *Radical Satire and Print culture*, pp. 67–71).
11 *Politics for the People* was named *Hog's Wash* when it was first published in 1793. For more information on Spence and Eaton, see the Introduction.
12 G. Dyer, *British Satire and the Politics of Style, 1789–1832* (Cambridge: Cambridge University Press, 1997), p. 75.
13 Number 15 below.
14 M. Bush, 'The Women at Peterloo: The Impact of Female Reform on the Manchester Meeting of 16 August 1819', *History* 89:294 (2004), p. 228.
15 Number 10 below.
16 Number 8 below.
17 M. Krantz, *'Rise Like Lions': The History and Lessons of the Peterloo Massacre of 1819* (London: Bookmark Publications, 2011), p. 12.

18 R. Poole, 'By the Law and Sword: Peterloo Revisited', *History*, 91:302 (2006), p. 263; J. Belchem, *Orator Hunt: Henry Hunt and English Working-Class Radicalism* (Oxford: Clarendon, 1985), p. 107.
19 Number 4 below.
20 Burke, *Reflections on the Revolution in France* (Oxford, Oxford University Press, 1993), p. 76.
21 W. Godwin, *Enquiry Concerning Political Justice* (London: Penguin, 1976), p. 91.
22 Duff explores the chivalric revival and its political manifestations in *Romance and Revolution: Shelley and the Politics of a Genre* (Cambridge: Cambridge University Press, 1994), pp. 117–52.
23 Number 5 below.
24 L. Colley, *Britons: Forging the Nation 1707–1837* (New Haven: Yale University Press, 1992), p. 147.
25 R. Hurd, *Letters on Chivalry and Romance*, ed. Hoyt Trowbridge (Los Angeles: University of California Press, 1963), p. 19.
26 Number 8 below.
27 *Ibid.*
28 Number 1 below.
29 N. Frye, *Anatomy of Criticism: Four Essays* (Princeton: Princeton University Press), 1957.
30 Dyer, *British Satire and the Politics of Style, 1789–1832*, p. 10.
31 Manchester Central Library Broadside Collection (1819/2/B). When the song was exhibited as part of the 2009 Peterloo exhibition at Manchester Central Library, it was accompanied by a manuscript note by Isabella Banks, author of *The Manchester Man*, stating that the song was written jointly by her grandfather, James Varley, a republican who was in France at the time of the fall of the Bastille, and his son James. I am grateful to Robert Poole for supplying me with a copy of his notes from the exhibition.
32 J. Marlow, *The Peterloo Massacre* (London: Rapp and Whiting, 1969), p. 173. The author's purported name refers to Hugh Birley, who commanded the MYC at Peterloo, with 'furioso' as a reference to Birley's anger. 'Mulo Spinissimo' refers to the spinning mule, invented by Samuel Crompton in the 1770s, which was used widely in the cotton factories of Manchester and is an allusion to Birley's textile factory on Oxford Road.
33 This could be a reference to Reverend William Robert Hay, the Chairman of the Salford Quarter Sessions. For more information, see p. 86n.56.
34 St Mary's Gate is in central Manchester, a little over a hundred metres from the Royal Exchange Theatre. It appears that the Cat and Bagpipes is a fictional tavern.
35 A musical work demanding brilliant execution.
36 Loudly. The Italian words and phrases in this poem are a mixture of the authentic and invented.
37 The four lettered footnotes in this poem are in the original broadside. Such paratext adds to the quasi-educated tenor of the poem.

'(a) HEW – Destruction by cutting.
Then to the BEST his wrathful hand he bends,
Of whom he makes such havoc and such HEW,
That swarms of damned souls to hell he sends.
                    Spencer's *Fairy Queen* VI. VIII. 49'

38 Damned.
39 Sky or heaven.
40 Slowly.
41 See p. 16.
42 Wise. A reference to the Manchester Magistrates who ordered the charge.
43 According to Read, eighteen magistrates were in post in Manchester in 1819; McKeiver lists twelve (D. Read, *Peterloo: The Massacre and its Background* (Manchester: Manchester University Press, 1958), p. 76; P. McKeiver, *Peterloo Massacre 1819* (Manchester: Advance Press, 2009), p. 61).
44 At the inquest into the death of John Lees, the cutler, Daniel Kennedy claimed that he was in the employment of James Richardson and that he sharpened sixty-three swords for the MYC in July 1819 (*Coroner's Inquest into John Lees* (London: Hone, 1820), p. 161).
45 Softly.
46 '(b) One of whom declared, he ONLY got thirteen hundred pounds per week, or sixty-seven thousand six hundred pounds a year – See reports of Cases at the New Bailey, for 1818. This income arising out of a Cotton Factory, forms a much greater amount than the whole estate and emoluments of the great Lord Burleigh, Prime Minister, in the days of Queen Elizabeth for his care of the whole nation; and his present Majesty HAS ONLY THE APPROPRIATION of sixty thousand pounds a year out of the Civil List.'
47 Poor relief dates back to the sixteenth century, when legislation was introduced to place responsibility on the Church of England for the support of the poor. Due to the reduction of wages for spinners and weavers following the end of the Napoleonic Wars, workers were forced to beg for money from the church to support their meagre wages (E.P. Thompson, *The Making of the English Working Class* (Middlesex: Penguin, 1980), pp. 224–7).
48 With lowered voice.
49 '(c) "Potatoes, not vegetables." Wright N.B.M. and one of the nine.' Archibald Prentice names one of the Manchester Magistrates as R. Wright (*Historical Sketches and Personal Recollections of Manchester* (London: Gilpin, 1851), p. 155).
50 A cut of meat from the back of an animal, known as the saddle: one of the more expensive cuts of meat.
51 This phrase does not appear to be Italian. *Pianissimo* means 'very softly' and 'mente' means 'of the mind'.

52 'A person likened to an owl [...] in looking solemn or wise (freq. with implication of attendant dullness or underlying stupidity' (*OED*). The poet is clearly making reference to politicians, lawyers and other establishment figures.
53 Stomachs.
54 A reference to the Corn Laws of 1815, which placed restrictions on imported grain, resulting in very high prices in England.
55 The *OED* dates this phrase to Old English c. 1000 AD.
56 With confidence.
57 '(d) "Spreading their ell-wide Lanthorn Jaws abroad." – Peter Pindar'. Peter Pindar was a poet and satirist. For more information, see pp. 137–8.
58 The other poem is 'Lines Written During Confinement in Lancaster Castle' by Samuel Bamford, which was published on 3 October, having previously appeared in the *Manchester Observer*. See Chapter 6, number 6.
59 *Examiner*, 610 (1819), p. 567.
60 See pp. 169, 189n.145 and 192n.189.
61 In discharge of one's duty.
62 Trust.
63 A poet using the initials 'J.B.' in *The Watchman* in 1796 has been identified as James Bisset (B. Bennett, *British War Poetry in the Age of Romanticism: 1793–1815* (New York: Garland, 1976), p. 174).
64 *Black Dwarf*, 3:42 (1819), p. 691.
65 The original rhyme which dates back to the seventeenth century is as follows:

> Remember, remember the fifth of November
> Gunpowder, treason and plot
> I see no reason why gunpowder, treason
> Should ever be forgot.

66 See pp. 12 and 63n.73. Blue refers to the colour of the uniforms of the MYC.
67 See p. 16.
68 Reward.
69 A cat o' nine tails was a whip with nine knotted lashes and was widely used in this period as a punishment in the armed forces and in prisons.
70 Alcohol subject to duty.
71 *Manchester Observer* (11 September 1819), p. 710.
72 http://ballads.bodleian.ox.ac.uk/static/images/sheets/10000/07429.gif [accessed 19 November 2017].
73 Shudehill or Shude Hill is in central Manchester between Manchester Victoria Station and the Northern Quarter. In 1782, the inventor and industrialist Richard Arkwright built a steam-powered textile mill here, which was Manchester's first textile mill. 'Shudehill fight' refers to the food riots of 1757, in which special constables, under orders from the sheriff of Lancashire, opened fire on the rioters, killing three of them (S. Hylton, *A History of Manchester* (Andover: Phillimore, 2010), p. 49). It

is of interest to note that one undated version of 'The Garland of Love' was printed by J. Kiernan of Garden Street, Shude Hill (http://ballads.bodleian.ox.ac.uk/search/advanced/?q_RoudNumbers=&q_TitleElements=the+garland+of+love&q_TextBodyElements=&q_Subjects=&q_Themes=&q_ImprintElements=&q_TuneNameElements=&q_Printers=&q_Authors=&q_Notes=&q_References=&searchany=on [accessed 19 November 2017]). On 16 August, Bamford led the Middleton marchers through Shudehill on their way to St Peter's Field (R. Poole, 'What We Don't Know About Peterloo', in R. Poole (ed.), *Return to Peterloo. Manchester Region History Review*, 23 (2014), p. 160)
74 Made brave through the consumption of alcohol.
75 Henry Hunt.
76 Along with the others arrested at Peterloo, Hunt was initially imprisoned in the New Bailey Prison in Salford.
77 State of servitude.
78 In Ancient Rome, laurel wreaths were awarded to men who had been victorious in war.
79 The cypress and willow trees are symbols of mourning.
80 In his 1989 essay, Clayson identifies thirty original Peterloo poems in the radical journals of the time ('The Poems of Peterloo', pp. 34, 32). More than seventy appear in this anthology.
81 For more information on Shorter, see the Introduction, pp. 22–3.
82 Keen, *The Popular Radical Press*, vol. 6, pp. 91–2.
83 Scrivener comments that the song is written 'with contemptuous sarcasm, embodied in the very folkloric designation for the Manchester massacre, sustained and elaborated in its mock heroism of the soldiers who are "celebrated" for attacking an unarmed crowd of working class families' (M. Scrivener (ed.), *Poetry and Reform: Periodical Verse from the English Democratic Press, 1792–1824* (Michigan: Wayne State University Press, 1992), p. 219).
84 Pindar was a first-century BC Greek poet, famed for his odes celebrating achievements at the Olympic Games. The Pindaric ode was used widely by British poets as a form of public address or celebration, notably by William Collins and Thomas Gray in the mid-eighteenth century. Shelley's 'Ode to Liberty', written in 1820, also uses the form of a Pindaric ode. Shorter may well be alluding to the classical poet and Peter Pindar, the contemporaneous poet and satirist. See pp. 137–8.
85 In 'Progress of Poesy' Gray uses the term 'Theban eagle' to refer to Pindar who, according to Gray's accompanying commentary, 'compares himself to that bird, and his enemies to ravens that croak and clamour in vain below, while it pursues its flight, regardless of the noise' (T. Gray, *The Poems of Gray, Collins and Goldsmith*, ed. R. Lonsdale (London: Longman, 1969), p. 176). The metaphor of a poet as a bird is evident in this stanza.
86 Spirited or lively.
87 Corpses.

88 Could refer to shackles: 'Scotch boot n. now *hist.* an instrument of torture formerly used in Scotland, consisting of a tight-fitting iron case in which a person's leg is enclosed, iron wedges being then driven between the case and the leg' (*OED*).
89 *Black Dwarf*, 3:37 (1819), p. 611.
90 This was a very popular publication in the eighteenth and nineteenth centuries, which contained details of crimes, trials and executions; it was originally written by the keeper of Newgate Prison in London.
91 This form of six-line stanza is known as a *Venus and Adonis* stanza after the poem by Shakespeare.
92 *Manchester Observer* (2 October 1819), p. 731. Examples include 'Manchester Heroes' in Chapter 2 and 'Peterloo' in Chapter 5.
93 See p. 16.
94 *Black Dwarf*, 3:48 (1819), pp. 787–8.
95 The quotation is from *Poem 62* by Catullus, an epithalamium or marriage poem. The line compares the cruelty of taking a daughter away from her mother with that wrought by soldiers on a captured town.
96 Greece was part of the Ottoman Empire from the fifteenth century until the Greek War of Independence in 1821.
97 Russia was almost constantly at war in the seventeenth and eighteenth centuries with the Ottoman Empire over territory in what is now Eastern Europe. It is not clear to whom or what this phrase alludes.
98 Albania was also part of the Ottoman Empire until it gained independence in 1912.
99 Janizary – a guard of the Turkish King (S. Johnson, *A Dictionary of the English Language* (London: 1794), p. 442).
100 The employment of heroic couplets throughout the poem is in ironic opposition to the unheroic deeds of the MYC.
101 The poet is making the point that, unlike the Fifteenth Hussars, the MYC had not seen active service in the Napoleonic Wars.
102 See pp. 12 and 63n.73.
103 Notes a, b and c feature in the original text. '(a) Lord Byron's Child Harold. The line, from fortieth stanza of the first Canto, reads: "What gallant warhounds rouse them from their lair, / And gnash their fangs, loud yelling for the prey!"' In this part of the Canto, Byron describes the horrors of the Peninsular Campaign of 1807–14, which drew in part upon his visit to the battlefields of Talavera in the summer of 1809. The poet is making a direct comparison between the barbarism of the MYC and Napoleon's army.
104 '(b) Shakespeare's *Romeo and Juliet*'. The line is from act three, scene one, line 85 and is spoken by Romeo following Tybalt's entrance shortly after the killing of Mercutio.
105 '(c) Shakespeare's Macbeth'. The line, from act five, scene eight, lines 33–4, reads, 'Lay on, Macduff / And damned be him that first cries, "Hold, enough!"'. It is taken from the final scene of the play and contains Macbeth's last words before he is slain by Macduff. As with the quotation

from Catullus in the epigraph, the quotations from Shakespeare and Byron indicate an educated and well-read poet.
106 In Homer's *Iliad*, a Myrmidon is 'a member of a warlike people inhabiting ancient Thessaly, whom Achilles led to the siege of Troy.' It also refers to a bodyguard or loyal follower (*OED*).
107 Escutcheon: a shield on which coats of arms are painted.
108 Wages or payment.
109 An allusion to the Devil.
110 A misquotation from Falstaff in the first part of *Henry IV*: 'The better part of valour is discretion, in the which better part I have saved my life.' (Act Five, scene four, lines 120–1).
111 Following the allied successes in Spain, Ferdinand VII was restored to the throne in 1813 until his death in 1833. He re-established an absolute monarchy and led a repressive regime, which included harsh restrictions on the press, which may explain the reference here.
112 Manchester Yeomanry Cavalry.
113 *Manchester Observer* (30 October 1819), p. 796.
114 Even though the Ottoman Empire was in decline in the early nineteenth century, the Turks had a reputation as fierce warriors. Due to their Muslim beliefs, the reference here also carries connotations of the barbaric 'other'.
115 Arthur Wellesley, Duke of Wellington, was the commander of the forces who defeated Napoleon at Waterloo in 1815.
116 A wild beast with a hard skin.
117 According to Marlow, many members of the MYC were drunk when they charged into St Peter's Field (*The Peterloo Massacre*, p. 135). She quotes a witness as saying of one of the MYC, 'He could hardly sit on his horse, he was drunk; he sat like a monkey' ('The Day of Peterloo', in *Peterloo Massacre*, p. 4).
118 D. Fowler, *A Literary History of the Popular Ballad* (Durham N.C.: Duke University Press, 1968), p. 183. The traditional ballad *Fair Margaret and Sweet William* is an example of a revenant ballad.
119 *Manchester Observer* (2 October 1819), p. 731.
120 Poisoned.
121 A fit of anger.
122 The foremost division or detachment of a military or naval force when advancing.
123 Bloody.
124 Swollen with pride, pompous.
125 Rather than the usual meaning of one who takes a proportion of earnings from a prostitute, 'pimp' could mean a despicable person or an informer.
126 Manchester.
127 A shortened form of 'orang-utans'.
128 See note 117 above.
129 Something which has sprung up or grown rapidly, an upstart.
130 This probably alludes to 'Brobdingnag', a fictional land occupied by giants

188   *Ballads and songs of Peterloo*

  in *Gulliver's Travels* by Jonathan Swift, published in 1726. The term refers to anything of enormous size. The poet is using the term to highlight the unnatural nature of events at Peterloo.
131 Combining two opposite qualities or attributes.
132 In the classic tale of *Androcles and the Lion*, Androcles is a runaway slave who takes shelter in a lion's cave and removes a thorn from a lion's paw, which is then tamed and is loyal to Androcles.
133 This may be a misspelling of '*Resurgat*' meaning 'to rise again'.
134 Major Thomas Trafford was the commander of the MYC. See p. 147n.57.
135 *White Hat*, 1:1 (1819), p. 16.
136 Keen, *The Popular Radical Press*, vol. 6, p. 202.
137 *Ibid.*
138 According to Claude M. Simpson, 'Derry Down' was one of the most popular tunes in the eighteenth century and is also known as 'The Abbot of Canterbury', 'The King and Lord Abbot', 'Lord John and the Abbot of Canterbury' and 'A Cobbler There Was' (C.M. Simpson, *The British Broadside Ballad and its Music* (New Jersey: Rutgers University Press, 1966), p. 100). Versions of the song can be found in Ritson's *Ancient Songs and Ballads* and Percy's *Reliques* (J. Ritson, *Ancient Songs and Ballads* (London, 1829), vol. 2, p. 183; T. Percy, *The Reliques of Ancient English Poetry* (1765), vol. 2, p. 314). William Chappell dates it to at least 1563–64 when the tune was used to the ballad 'A Defence of Mylkemaydes against the Terme of Mawken'. It was subsequently used for many songs and ballads during the English Revolution; however, its most famous incarnation is in Air 56 in *The Beggar's Opera* (London: 1769), n. pag. 'Derry Down' had also been used for radical songs, notably *The Miseries of the Framework Knitters*, a Nottingham broadside, written during the Luddite uprisings of 1811–12 (R. Palmer, *A Touch of the Times* (Middlesex: Penguin, 1974), pp. 204–5). In *This is the House that Jack Built*, a satirical poem written in 1819 by William Hone and illustrated by George Cruikshank, Lord Castlereagh was referred to as Derry Down, due to his Irish heritage and title of Viscount of Londonderry (n. pag).
139 According to the letter writer, they met at the Common-hall in Norwich.
140 St Andrew's Hall in Norwich dates back to the fifteenth century, when it was the nave of the friary, designed as a preaching hall for the residents of Norwich. Since the mid-sixteenth century it has been used for civic occasions. (www.standrewshall.co.uk [accessed 17 August 2015]). According to the *London Alfred*, the original meeting of the Mayor and MP was held in St Andrew's Hall on 16 September (P. Keen (ed.), *The Popular Radical Press in Britain 1817–21*. 6 vols. (London: Pickering and Chatto, 2003), vol. 6, p. 200).
141 The 'Friend to the Constitution' states that 'afraid to meet their fellow citizen in the open field of combat [...] the sons of corruption assembled to the amount of a dozen, in some tavern' (Keen, *The Popular Radical Press*, vol. 6, p. 267).

142 'A New Song by the REGENT'S Ministers and the MANCHESTER MAGISTRATES'.
143 *Manchester Observer* (16 October 1819), p. 780; *Cap of Liberty*, 1:7 (1819), p. 112.
144 Castlereagh.
145 As acting Chief Secretary for Ireland in 1798, Castlereagh played an instrumental role in crushing the Irish Rebellion. His cruelty to the rebels made him a hate figure amongst English radicals.
146 A supernatural or unearthly being.
147 '* Geo. Canning, son to Nobody; ergo, an honour to Nobody.' George Canning was President of the Board of Control in 1819 with responsibility for the British East India Company. He had held a series of cabinet positions since the 1790s and was also one of the founders of the *Anti Jacobin*, a newspaper opposed to reform. Canning wrote satirical anti-reformist poetry for the *Anti Jacobin*, which may explain the reference to him in the poem as a 'jester'. In speeches in Lancashire and the House of Commons, Canning voiced his support for the Manchester magistrates. The description of him as 'son of a nobody' may allude to his modest background. Born in London to Irish parents, his mother took to the stage in order to support herself and her children following the death of Canning's father.
148 Believe.
149 '† Who knows, but some of our M——r M——tes may have St. or Kt. At least tagged to their names.'
150 *Black Dwarf*, 4:1 (1820), p. 34.
151 Castlereagh, Canning, Sidmouth and Vansittart. For information on Castlereagh, see pp. 169, 189n.145 and 192n.189. For Sidmouth, see pp. 3, 7 and 10. For more information on George Canning, see note 147 above. Nicholas Vansittart was the Chancellor of the Exchequer between 1812 and 1822 and was a close political ally of Castlereagh, often representing him in the House of Commons.
152 One who thinks himself, or wishes to be thought, wise; a pretender to wisdom; a foolish person with an air or affectation of wisdom.
153 Robert Stewart, Lord Castlereagh, was also the Marquis of Londonderry and was Irish by birth, hence the description of him as 'Hibernian'.
154 Stolen goods.
155 An article preceding the poem, entitled 'The State of the Revenue' reports the current state of the government's finances, released on 5 January. According to the unnamed author (possibly Wooler), the government had predicted a revenue of six million pounds to go towards a sinking fund aimed at repaying the national debt. However, despite raising three million pounds in new taxes, the fund was almost one million pounds in debt, with plans to raise taxes further. The writer calls for opposition to new taxes, commenting that 'the higher orders themselves prefer prating about their loyalty to paying for it' (*Black Dwarf*, 4:1 (1820), pp. 31–4).

156 According to an article in the *Examiner* on 19 September, when Mr Harmer, a radical lawyer at the inquest, objected to the decision to adjourn, citing the ill-health of many of the witnesses as reason to continue, Mr Milne replied: 'I will not take the inquest, and shall advise Mr Batty not to proceed to it. I do not choose to enter into any further explanations' (*Examiner*, 612 (1819), p. 596). Harmer was also one of the lawyers representing the radicals arrested at Peterloo (S. Bamford, *Passages in the Life of a Radical*, 3 vols. (Manchester: Heywood, 1842), vol. 2, p. 117).

157 *Black Dwarf*, 3:37 (1819), p. 610.

158 Poole, 'What We Don't Know About Peterloo', p. 6.

159 John Lees died on 7 September from the injuries he sustained at Peterloo and it was the inquest into his death that was to take place in Oldham. Mr Milne claimed not to have seen the body and believed it had been buried, whereupon Mr Harmer assured him that Mr Farren had not seen it either, although Mr Batty had. Radicals were determined that the actions of the magistrates were deemed illegal at Lees' inquest, hence the involvement of two sympathetic lawyers, Harmer and Dennison, who were working on the case *pro bono*. The inquest finally began on 25 September with Farren as coroner. Proceedings were repeatedly adjourned and were declared null and void when it was discovered that the coroner and the jury had not seen the body together. An outcry in radical and liberal circles across the country ensued (Read, *Peterloo*, pp. 147–9).

160 Justices of the Peace.

161 Major Thomas Trafford was the commander of the MYC. See p. 147n.57.

162 As Hunt's trial did not begin until March 1820, this may refer to the trial of Dr James Watson for his part in the Spa Fields Rising of 1816. Hunt testified as a witness for the defence at Watson's trial for high treason in 1817.

163 Translated as: 'He himself said it.'

164 John Lees.

165 'The act of finding and assuming possession of any personal property; hence (in full, action of trover), an action at law to recover the value of personal property illegally converted by another to his own use' (*OED*).

166 The poet claims it is Batty rather than Milne who refused to conduct the inquest into John Lees' death.

167 Devil.

168 Regent's.

169 Prince.

170 For information on Liverpool, see pp. 2–3. For Sidmouth, see pp. 3, 7 and 10. For Castlereagh, see pp. 169, 189n.145, 192n.189.

171 This is a reference to Nicholas Vansittart, the Chancellor of the Exchequer, whose family were of Dutch origin. For more information, see note 151 above.

172 Polish troops fought with Napoleon. Under the terms of the Congress of Vienna in 1815, Russia gained much of Poland.

173 In pre-revolutionary France a *lettre de cachet* was a letter which was signed by the king and counter-signed by one of his ministers and was often used under the *ancien regime* to authorise someone's imprisonment in a state gaol, such as the Bastille, which was stormed on 14 July 1789 at the beginning of the French Revolution. *Lettres de cachet* were abolished by the Constituent Assembly in 1790 (www.oxfordreference.com/view/10.1093/oi/authority.20110803100101600 [accessed 19 November 2017]).
174 Sir Francis Burdett, Radical MP. For more information, see pp. 4 and 12.
175 The Fifteenth Hussars, regular army troops.
176 The character of John Bull dates back to 1712 when he appeared in a satire by John Arbuthnot entitled *Law is a Bottomless Pit; or the History of John Bull*. Tamara Hunt maintains that the symbol of the bull shows not only how the British people are treated with brutality but also how there is an underlying threat of them fighting back; yet the bull also shows its lack of intelligence and needs to be governed firmly but fairly, which explains why the symbol was used by both radicals and conservatives (T. Hunt, *Defining John Bull: Political Caricature and National Identity in Late Georgian England* (Hampshire: Ashgate, 2003), p. 145). By the end of the Napoleonic Wars, John Bull was identified with the newly emerging middle classes as honest and hardworking (p. 169). He was usually depicted at this time as rather fat and wearing a blue jacket with beige breeches, as in George Cruikshank's 1814 caricature entitled *Peace and Plenty or Good News for John Bull*. Clayson observes that the poem is a 'parody of the "Bull" pamphlets issued by the Loyal Associations from 1792' ('The Poems of Peterloo', in *Peterloo Massacre, MRHR* (1989), 3:1, pp. 31–8, at p. 37).
177 Scrivener maintains that 'there was not a great deal of emphasis in the radical culture of the commonality of the Irish and the English (*Poetry and Reform*, p. 249). Alan Booth states that there were 40,000 Irishmen in London in the 1790s and approximately 10,000 in Manchester by 1800 ('Irish Exiles, Revolution and Writing in England in the 1790s', in P. Hyland and N. Sammells (eds), *Irish Writing: Exile and Subversion* (Hampshire: Macmillan, 1991), pp. 64–81, at p. 68). His essay outlines the involvement of the Irish in the English radical movement. See Chapter 4, number 5 for an example of a radical poem written by an Irishman.
178 Keen, *The Popular Radical Press*, vol. 5, pp. 335–6.
179 Scrivener notes: 'The large number of misspellings and grammatical errors indicates an attempt to represent an unlettered Irishman, although the gesture is not consistent, as the persona uses and spells correctly *faux pas* and *quietus*' (*Poetry and Reform*, p. 249). However, it is not uncommon for misspellings and typographical errors to be found in radical journals, as evidenced in this collection. The errors may be an indication of the speed with which the publications were compiled.
180 A worsted wig (*Poetry and Reform*, p. 249).
181 Presumably 'passive'.
182 Head.

183 *Rights of Man* by Thomas Paine was published in two parts: 1791 and 1792.
184 See number 7 in this chapter.
185 The Prince Regent was notorious for his love of women, wine and gambling, as captured in many cartoons by Cruikshank.
186 A reference to the Royal Pavilion at Brighton, an Oriental-inspired palace designed by John Nash for the Prince Regent. The re-design of the smaller Marine Pavilion took eight years from 1815–23.
187 A go-between in clandestine love affairs, a pimp.
188 Burdens.
189 Castlereagh's involvement in quashing the Irish Uprising in 1798 understandably resulted in him becoming a hate figure for the Irish. This suggests that Paddy was a member of the United Irishmen.
190 See number 7 in this chapter.
191 These fictitious names indicate that the MYC were ordinary men.
192 Think or believe.
193 Paid.
194 'Our Father' or 'The Lord's Prayer', another allusion to Paddy's Catholicism.
195 An inordinate desire for wealth or possessions, personified as a devil or demonic agent. It also features in the Gospels of Matthew and Luke: 'No man can serve two masters: for either he will hate the one, and love the other; or else he will hold to the one, and despise the other. Ye cannot serve God and mammon' (Matthew, 6:24).
196 A lie.
197 An acquittal or discharge granted on payment of a debt; a receipt.
198 Magistrates, Military and Special Constables.
199 *Manchester Observer* (21 August 1819), p. 686.
200 16 August 1819 was indeed a Monday.
201 Murderer or assassin; however, its use here is 'murder'.
202 Vanguard.
203 This is taken from Genesis, 9:6: 'Whoso sheddeth man's blood, by man shall his blood be shed; for in the image of God made he man'.
204 Fiends or devils.
205 This refers to judgement day, as outlined in The Gospel According to St Matthew, 25:14–30.
206 Plunder or pillage.
207 Stolen goods, booty.
208 Torture in England was abolished around 1640, although judges had declared the use of the rack to be contrary to English law in 1628 when the Privy Council applied to use the rack on John Felton who was accused of murdering George Villiers, the first Duke of Buckingham (Jardine, *A Reading on the Use of Torture in the Criminal Law of England* (London: Baldwin and Craddock, 1837), pp. 10–12).
209 Clayson, 'The Poems of Peterloo', p. 36; A. Janowitz, *Lyric and Labour in the Romantic Tradition* (Cambridge: Cambridge University Press, 1998), p. 125.

210 Allen Davenport was a shoemaker poet, journalist and Spencean. He had poems published in *Sherwin's Weekly Political Register* and *Medusa*. He also published a number of works in in his own right, including an anthology of poems, *Kings, or, Legitimacy Unmasked* (1819), and a drama, *Claremont* (1820), inspired by the Queen Caroline Affair. He became an active Chartist. Clayson claims that his satirical poems are 'among the best productions of the genre' ('The Poems of Peterloo', p. 36).

211 'Gee-up, Dobbin' is also the stated tune of *The Peterloo Massacre* by Michael Wilson. See p. 149.

212 The ballad of 'George Barnwell' appears in the third volume of Thomas Percy's *Reliques*. George Barnwell was apprenticed to a London merchant but was lured by a whore called Sarah into spending his master's money upon her. Once this had gone, George robbed and murdered his wealthy uncle and then managed to escape to sea. He wrote his confession and Sarah was arrested, tried and hanged whilst George was imprisoned in chains. The play was very successful in the eighteenth century and, following two performances on 27 December 1731, which was a holiday for apprentices, a tradition was established which lasted into the nineteenth century (*DNB*).

213 Keen, *The Popular Radical Press*, vol. 6, p. 131.

214 According to Read, he employed a wide network of spies and, 'in spite of his cloth he showed little Christian charity towards the Radical Reformers' (*Peterloo*, p. 77).

215 Janowitz notes that, in his poems, 'Davenport enlists the heroic couplet of the eighteenth century to mark his place within print culture' (*Lyric and Labour in the Romantic Tradition*, p. 117).

216 Prentice claims it was Ethelstone who read the Riot Act on 16 August, 'which nobody ever heard' (A. Prentice, *Historical Sketches and Personal Recollections of Manchester* (London: Gilpin, 1851), p. 169).

217 There is a reference to a soldier hacking off a woman's breast in 'The Patriot's Grave' in Chapter 4.

218 The description of the violence is similar to that in numbers 1 and 8 above.

6

'Freeman stand, or freeman die': liberty and slavery

The words 'liberty' or 'freedom' feature in forty-three poems in this collection, indicative of the centrality of this theme to the radical discourse of the day. Banners declaring 'Liberty or Death' and sticks adorned with caps of liberty were held high by marchers on 16 August whilst they sang 'God Save the King' and 'Rule Britannia'.[1] Since the Glorious Revolution of 1688, when a Catholic monarch was replaced by Protestant one without blood being shed, Britain had regarded itself as a 'bastion of liberty and justice'; however, following the end of the Napoleonic Wars, oppression became the order of the day and radicals called on patriots to free England from its slavery:

> Liberty is banished from our shores, and we move and breathe in the open air, at the mercy of Lord Castlereagh, and his brother secretaries of state.[2]

In an era of almost unprecedented repression and curtailment of rights, working people wished to rid themselves of their chains and reclaim their lost liberties. The introduction to Chapter 2 outlines the links between radical English nationalism and the yearning for the restoration of ancient Anglo-Saxon rights, which are also evident in some of the poems and songs in this chapter. The broadside ballad, *Peterloo*, is illustrative of this in its predictions, 'Soon shall fair freedom's sons their rights regain,' before exhorting:

> Britons be firm, assert your rights, be bold
> Perish like heroes, not like slaves be sold.[3]

Epstein argues that this need for radicals 'to arm themselves with the borrowed language of the past', with references to Anglo-Saxon rights and the constitution, was a way of proving an Englishman's right to liberty.[4] The poems and songs below celebrate both the forthcoming return of liberty, presented as a goddess, and Henry Hunt as liberty's human representative.

The restoration of liberty as an end to slavery is a common trope within English radical discourse, and poems often depict the radical patriot endeavouring to rescue his country from an imposed and unnatural tyranny and return it to its true state of liberty; however, this trope predates the era of revolution when such rhetoric was common currency. John Lucas observes that, 'in the early years of the eighteenth century, liberty and Englishness become synonymous concepts and virtually interchangeable terms, and it is in response to this that the construction of a national literature was and would continue to be so important'.[5] Eighteenth-century poems such as William Collins' 'Ode to Liberty' and Thomas Gray's 'Progress of Poesy', champion both liberty and English national identity, with the fusion of public and private, celebratory and discursive. These progress poems depict liberty and poetry as dwelling within the English national consciousness. To both Collins and Gray the role of the modern poet is akin to that of the ancient bard: a voice of freedom championing ancient national rights and a protest against tyranny. Central to this exploration of nation is the locating of England as the rightful home for liberty and poetry, a concept evident in James Thomson's *Liberty* written in 1735–36 and further developed by Collins and Gray.[6] Just as the poems below were inspired by the Peterloo Massacre, Lucas maintains that Collins' 'Ode to Liberty' was a response to the massacre of the Scots at Culloden in 1745 and, according to William Levine, 'redefines the poet's role as spokesman for the English national conscience.'[7]

Collins' opening is a call to rouse the troops in the defence of the goddess Liberty:

> Who shall awake the Spartan fife,
> And call in solemn sounds to life
> The youths,[8]

Despite the ancient location of Sparta for the opening stanza, clear allusions are made to the need for armies to fight for freedom in the eighteenth century, a fact rendered more pertinent given the backdrop of the Jacobite Rebellion. Collins locates poetry at the very heart of Anglo-Saxon culture:

> The chiefs who fill our Albion's story,
> In warlike weeds, retired in glory,
> Hear their consorted Druids sing
> Their triumphs to the immortal string.[9]

By locating liberty and poetry within an ancient England, Collins highlights the role of poetry to promote both liberty and national culture, and therefore communicates such traditions to a new audience.

The centrality of liberty to the discourse surrounding the French Revolution is evident in the poems and songs of this period. 'An Ode Addressed to the Friends of liberty', published in *Politics for the People* in 1794, can be regarded as a companion piece to Collins' ode both through the use of genre and understanding of the role liberty played in the nation's history. It begins:

> Liberty once was England's boast,
> But now, alas! That treasure's lost,
> And all our boats are vain.
> Therefore let us with zeal unite
> To claim the just, the long lost right,
> And Liberty regain.[10]

The poem mourns the severing of the link between England and Liberty whilst acknowledging that the time is now right to regain lost rights; moreover, the use of the first-person plural pronouns 'us' and 'our' is indicative of the poem's role as a communal form. The poet sees war and imminent slavery as 'quench[ing] the flame of Liberty', citing the French as 'determin'd to be free' and calling on British patriots to follow suit.[11]

After the failure of the French Revolution, and more than twenty years of war, a resurgent Liberty had been superseded by an altogether different depiction. Cruikshank's 1817 caricature, *Liberty Suspended! – With the Bulwark of the Constitution*, depicts Liberty as a young woman hanged and gagged holding a placard upon which the words 'Magna Charta, Bill of Rights and Habeas Corpus' are written (see Figure 12). Cruikshank is satirising the harsh government measures such as the suspension of Habeas Corpus that followed the Spa Fields riot in 1816 in which a handful of Spenceans seized arms and began to march towards the Tower.[12] However, the hope that change was imminent in the days and weeks after Peterloo is manifested in many of the poems written at the time. Several of the poems below resurrect Liberty as a goddess, heralding her arrival with a fervent hope which has echoes of Collins. 'Address to Liberty' employs the metre of 'God Save the King' in its hymn to the goddess:

> Yes, yes, dear Goddess! Now
> We feel thy sacred glow
> Our bosoms fire!
> We will our rights again,
> Them stedfastly maintain,

12 *Liberty Suspended! – With the Bulwark of the Constitution* by George Cruikshank.

Or on th' ensanguin'd plain
With thee expire!¹³

The adoption of religious language in this devotional address parodies the original anthem. The collective 'we' allied with the unequivocal 'will' is further emphasised by the metre, with the stresses falling on 'will' and 'rights' in the fourth line above. Although the reference to the 'ensanguin'd plain' makes the link with Peterloo a definite one, the lack of specificity has resulted in a poem for all time. For liberty's supplicants, the options of liberty or death are the only ones available.

Whereas 'liberty' or 'freedom' appears in more than half the poems within this collection, 'slavery' only appears in about a fifth. Often presented as the current state of Englishmen, from which liberty would free them, what is noteworthy is that only one poem makes direct reference to the transatlantic slave trade. Although this was abolished in 1807, it was not until 1833 that the slave trade in the British Empire was outlawed. As a dominating force in the transatlantic slave trade, Britain played a key role in the transportation of men, women and children from Africa to the Americas and Europe. It is estimated that more than twelve million Africans were taken as slaves between 1500 and 1867. The Society for Effecting the Abolition of the Slave Trade was established in 1787 with the MP William Wilberforce as one of its leading lights. Described as 'the great moral question of the age', Debbie Lee questions why slavery is not represented in Romantic poetry. She argues that the rise of the abolition movement coincided with the rise in print culture. The resulting saturation of print culture with works on slavery led the Romantic poets to approach it in a more oblique way and that, even though references to the language of slavery through words such as 'freedom', 'oppression' and 'tyranny' are commonly found in poetry of this period, their pertinence to transatlantic slavery cannot be ignored.[14] Whilst it is true that poems written during this period cannot be read without the context of slavery, it is noteworthy that direct comparisons between groups of enslaved workers of this time are all but absent. I have found no references to the transatlantic slave trade in the *Black Dwarf* or the *Examiner*, and very few in *Pigs' Meat* or in broadside ballads; however, a seminal anti-slavery poem and 'highly popular abolitionist broadsheet' is *The Negro's Complaint* by William Cowper. Written on behalf of the Committee for the Abolition of the Slave Trade in 1788, the ballad was sold on the streets and sung to music. It was even edited for children and printed with accompanying woodcuts.[15]

> Men from England bought and sold me,
> Paid my price in paltry gold;
> But, though slave they have enrolled me,
> Minds are never to be sold.
>
> Still in thought as free as ever,
> What are England's rights, I ask,
> Me from my delights to sever,
> Me to torture, me to task?

The reference to 'England's rights' neatly reminds readers of the slaves' romantic yearning for the rights of old, whilst simultaneously linking England with the promulgation of such barbarism.

It would appear that the only radical poet in the years following Waterloo to routinely make reference to transatlantic slavery is Robert Wedderburn, the mixed-race Spencean preacher and son of a slave.[16] In poems such as 'The Negro Boy Sold for a Watch', Wedderburn's 'sentimental pathos' in the portrayal of the boy's plight is fuelled by rage at such treatment by those considering themselves religious:

> In isles that deck the western waves,
> The unhappy youth was doom'd to dwell,

> A poor forlorn insulted slave
> A beast that Christians buy and sell.[17]

Wedderburn's ballads stress the humanity of the slaves and their sense of lost freedom, homeland and identity. Whilst they are sentimental, the fact that Wedderburn was himself a product of the slave trade increases the poignancy of his writings.

As the only poem in this collection which draws parallels between the slavery of Britons and Africans, 'Address to the Rabble' questions the enslaved English:

> Can you, like Afric's injured sons,
> Whose blood 'neath tyrant's lashes runs,
> Live in perpetual pain?[18]

The poet urges the 'English warriors' to 'rescue all from slavery', employing the comparison with African slaves as a means of warning the English of the realities of slavery embedded within the social and economic structure of a country.

Many of the poems and songs below are celebratory; some welcome an anticipated end to oppression and the return to an England of Anglo-Saxon laws where liberty and poetry co-exist, as envisaged by Collins, whereas others convey that hope in the form of Henry Hunt, the erstwhile 'Champion' and 'conquering hero', his white hat symbolising the caps of liberty hoisted at Peterloo.[19]

1 *Peterloo*

This song appears to be one of the most re-printed in this collection. It was printed both as a broadside and in *Medusa* on 25 September where it is entitled 'The Triumph of Liberty', although it is not known which version was written first.[20] Many copies of the song are extant and are evidence of its continued popularity in the latter half of the nineteenth century.[21] The song optimistically prophesies the coming of liberty as a direct result of the 'fell corruption' of Peterloo, with England leading the way for the emancipation of Europe. In *Medusa*, the tune is stated as 'See the Conquering Hero Comes', also used for 'National Songs – No. 1' in Chapter 2.[22]

> See! See! Where Freedom's noblest champion stands,
> Shout! Shout! Illustrious patriot band.
> Here grateful millions their generous tribute bring,
> And shouts for freedom make the welkin[23] ring,
> While fell corruption and her hellish crew,

The blood stained trophies gain'd at Peterloo.
Soon shall fair freedom's sons their rights regain,

Soon shall all Europe join the hallowed strain.[24]
Of Liberty and Freedom, Equal Rights and Laws,
Heaven's choicest blessing crown this glorious cause,
While meanly, tyrants, crawling minions too,
Tremble at their feats performed at Peterloo.

Britons be firm, assert your rights, be bold
Perish like heroes, not like slaves be sold,
Firm and unite, bid millions be free,
Will to your children glorious liberty,
While cowards – despots, long may keep in view
And silent contemplate, the deeds on Peterloo.

2 'Address to Liberty'

Published in *Medusa* on 27 November, this song was to be sung to the tune of 'God Save the King', with the Goddess Liberty replacing the monarch as the subject of the anthem.[25] Radical appropriations of the national anthem had been common in the 1790s, with one of the most well known, 'God Save the Rights of Man', being published under the authorship of both Robert Thomson and Philip Freneau in 1793.[26] As with 'Address to Liberty', radical versions sought to re-appropriate the national anthem, subverting its original purpose of a celebration of monarchy to provide an alternative national identity. In the months following Peterloo, Shelley also wrote his own anthem, which is addressed to Liberty. The unnamed author of 'Address to Liberty' uses religious discourse to give hymn-like qualities to the song.

O! Sacred Liberty,
We will thy vot'ries[27] be,
Espouse thy cause;
That we may Patriots prove,
And fearless rise above
Corruption's Laws.

O! Liberty arise!
Before our anxious eyes
The banner wave:
Assembling at thy call,
Nought can our hearts appal;
We will, in spite of all,
Our country save.

United, firm and true,
Thee may we keep in view
With stedfast eye;
Bid ev'ry fear retire,
With courage us inspire
T'obtain our hearts desire –
O hear our cry!

Yes, yes, dear Goddess! Now
We feel thy sacred glow
Our bosoms fire!
We will our rights again,
Them stedfastly maintain,
Or on th' ensanguin'd plain[28]
With thee expire!

3 'Song of Liberty'

One of the first Peterloo songs to be published, this appeared in *Medusa* on 28 August where it stated that it was to be sung to the tune of 'The Sweet Lass of Richmond Hill.'[29] Also known as 'The Lass of Richmond Hill', the tune was written by The Irish barrister and playwright Leonard Macnally for his wife, Frances, shortly after their marriage in 1787.[30] Frances came from Richmond in Yorkshire, hence the title of the song. It became a very popular tune and many broadsides of the song were published throughout the nineteenth century. The Vaughan Williams Memorial Library contains numerous versions of the song; the earliest, which was printed by J. Roach in a chapbook entitled *The Whim of the Day*, dates to 1790.[31] It states that it was sung by Mr Incledon and composed by Mr Hook. James Hook was an organist and composer who performed at one of the leading venues for entertainment in London, Vauxhall Gardens, from 1774 until 1820, which is where he met the singer, Charles Incledon, who began singing at the gardens in 1786.[32] The song is number 1246 in the Roud Broadside Index and begins:

On Richmond Hill there lives a lass,
More bright than May-day morn,
Whose charms all other maids surpass,
A rose without a thorn.

As with the previous song, Liberty is described as a goddess with origins in a feudal Britain.

Let pension'd minions[33] sing in praise
Of rank and dignity;

A Briton born, I chant my lays[34]
In praise of Liberty.
I hail with joy
That ne'er can cloy,
The Goddess Liberty!

Her presence cheers the toiling swain,[35]
And noblest feeling gives;
Devoid of care, he tills the plain,
And ever happy lives.
In peaceful state,
With heart elate,
He sings of Liberty!

Her charms can deepest grief assuage,
And fortify the mind;
Her power can still Oppression's rage,
And fiercest tyrants bind.
Then firm and true
I'll keep in view
The Goddess Liberty.

How blest the man of her possesst,
What joys to him are known;
What calm contentment fills his breast,
When it is Freedom's Throne.
O happy he
Must surely be
That's blest with Liberty.

4 'Acrostic to Liberty'

Appearing in the same 11 September issue of *Medusa* as 'On a Bloody Massacre', this acrostic describes the lamentations of the recently buried and calls on the reader to avenge the dead and unite under the flag of liberty.[36]

L ist! 'tis the coronach[37] borne on the breeze,
I t strikes on the ear, with its sad notes of sorrow;
B lood must the manes[38] of the murdered appease;
E re freedom's blest cause can a ray or hope borrow,
R ouse, then, the soul of each Patriot; and throng
T o the standard; and wreak on the Tyrants each wrong
Y e have felt, and recover the *Theme* of my song!

5 'Downfall of Despotism'

Capturing the optimism felt amongst many radicals in the ensuing months after Peterloo, this poem, published in *Medusa* on 11 December 1819, employs the traditional motif of light as a signifier of hope together with religious discourse as a metaphor for political enlightenment.[39] The song was also published in 1833 in a chapbook entitled *Harp of Liberty*, evidence that some of the Peterloo songs had a longevity beyond the periodicals in which they first appeared.[40]

> Exulting, I see the first dawnings of light
> Through the dark clouds of prejudice shine;
> Dispersing the shadows, dispelling the night.
> By the beamings of knowledge divine.
>
> Above the horizon already 'tis risen,
> Its radiance illumines the skies;
> Before it dense fog of error is driven-
> Before it fell ignorance flies.
>
> Still, rising resplendent, thy glories display,
> Let each human heart catch the glow;
> Till Liberty, Justice, and Reason's bright ray,
> Shall through the wide universe flow.
>
> Then hail it, ye Britons! With rapture O hail!
> Those beamings of light from above;
> Its power o'er Oppression and fraud shall prevail,
> And all mortals its blessings shall prove.

6 'Lines Written During Confinement in Lancaster Castle By S. Bamford, author of the "Weaver Boy"'[41]

First published in The *Manchester Observer* on 18 September 1819, this poem is one of only two with direct relevance to Peterloo to be published in the *Examiner*, where it appeared on 3 October 1819, having been written by Bamford in gaol on 6 September.[42] Samuel Bamford was present at Peterloo, although he was not arrested until 26 August and was subsequently incarcerated in Lancaster Castle along with the others who had been arrested, including Hunt. In his autobiography, *Passages in the Life of a Radical*, Bamford tells of his arrest early in the morning of 26 August:

> I now perceived that my visitors were a strong posse of police, some soldiers of the 32nd Regiment; Mr. Nadin, the deputy-constable of Manchester; and several officers of infantry and hussars. These seemed

interested by the proceedings, and were attentive observers of what took place. The military force consisted of a company of Foot, and as I afterwards learned, a troop of hussars. The officers were no doubt surprised that such a parade should have been deemed requisite for the apprehension of a poor weaver in his cellar.[43]

They were released on bail on 17 September, after Sir Charles Wolseley and Thomas Chapman became sureties for the accused, although Bamford was later sentenced to one year's imprisonment in Lincoln Gaol. In the poem, despite his incarceration, Bamford focuses on his unbowed determination to continue the fight against the 'bloody tyrants'.[44]

> O! here is no repining,
> Every heart is true and steady.
> Here is no declining,
> Still for England's service ready.
> Here is not a tear shed,
> Such a weakness, we disdain it;
> Here is not a bow'd head,
> Sign of sorrow, we refrain it.
> The more the bloody tyrants bind us,
> The more united they shall find us.
>
> The Patriot on his cell-bed
> Can sleep an undisturbed sleep,
> The Pander[45] on his hell-bed
> May curse and groan and madly weep.
> When daylight dimly breaketh
> In stony cell, through bars so high,
> And innocence awaketh,
> It looketh with a thankful eye.
> Though justice dash her scales away,
> Shall MURDER, fearless, front the day?
>   Sept. 6, 1819

7 'TO THE YEO—N-Y, SP–C—L CON—BL–S, &c ON PETER'S FIELD'

This poem begins in a familiar way, with an attack on the Manchester and Salford Yeomanry Cavalry (MYC) and others who, acting on behalf of tyrants, attacked the marchers on St Peter's Field. However, as the poem continues, the tone becomes a little more conciliatory as the poet appeals to their humanity and encourages them to read the work of Major John Cartwright, a moderate radical. The poem ends with an optimistic prediction that, once the MYC and special constables have seen the light, they will join together with the radicals in freedom's cause. Written by James Willan, the poem was published in the *Manchester Observer* on 28 August 1819, making it one of the first Peterloo poems.[46]

> As fiends in arms, with fury dauntless,
> When destroying naked men;
> Your dreadful deeds, your hate relentless,
> The page of history will stain.
>
> Inflamed by the ardent spirit,
> Produce of enslaved woe;
> To spread the mis'ry is your merit,
> To freedom you have been a foe!
>
> I ask, what object is your ardour
> Thus excited to procure?
> Peace! Oh, no! – by useless murder,
> Slavery's chain to make secure.
>
> What blessings for yourselves await you,
> While, for tyrants, you disgrace
> The name of man, a sacred duty
> To enslave the rising race!
>
> And while with plenty you are blessed,
> Think of hunger's cruel pain,
> By children's cries, parents harassed,
> Of their suffering must complain.
>
> Now robb'd of freedom, and its blessings,
> Alas! By tyrants we are tax'd;
> And to extend their vile oppressings,
> The law itself is oft relax'd.
>
> We say, give us the Constitution,[47]
> Give us but our native right;
> Then want and woe, and base delusion,
> Will vanish quickly from our sight.
>
> And who are they, not interested
> In this just and glorious cause?
> The borough-dealers,[48] and Tax-eaters;
> With * * * * * above the laws.
>
> But can the state you now rejoice in,
> Continue to oppress the land?
> Since you have dar'd to sound the tocsin,[49]
> 'Gainst reform to make a stand.

No! – its foundation truth and reason,
And by peace it will succeed;
It prospers 'midst the stormy season;
Its foes destroy the noxious weed.

Of groundless fears, and stark forebodings,
And give it renewed pow'rs;
Divested of all sad corrodings,
The world will smile 'neath freedom's show'rs.

And should your league, unholy, prosper,
Will its effects ne'er reach to you?
Yes, tyrants have no friendly feeling;
Self – self is all they have in view.

The honest workmen, why despise them?
Why oppress the poor and weak?
You know, by nature, all are freemen;
Let justice and let conscience speak.

And should our birth-right, by your efforts,
Be ever torn from our hands;
No more you'll rank with freedom's cohorts,
You'd satraps[50] be to ruffian bands.

Then ponder well what you are gaining
By your present mad career!
Reformers, from outrage refraining,
Prove they are freedom's friends sincere.

And as you wish to be enrolled
Friends to freedom and to man;
By passion cease to be controlled,
Impartial read th' old Major's[51] plan.

And there you'll find a view so clear
Of Briton's boasted noblest rights,
That advocates you'll be sincere,
Nor 'gainst them will you longer fight.[52]

Excuse the warmth of the first sentence,
Ignorance did lead you on;
But knowledge will bring true repentance,
And make our hearts, as int'rests, one.

To serve your country's your intention,
Mine's the same while this I warn;
Then let us drop all vain contention,
And strive to gain a just Reform.

8 'A Soliloquy of Lord Ch———,[53] on beholding a Vision of the Goddess of Liberty as he rose from his dinner, to proceed to the H—e of C——s,[54] with his new Bills[55] against the remaining liberties of Englishmen'

Written by the unknown 'T.H.',[56] this poem is a parody of Macbeth's famous soliloquy from the third act of the Shakespearean tragedy, in which he considers whether to murder the king, Duncan, in order to fulfil the prophecy of the three witches that Macbeth 'shalt be king'.[57] Published in the *Black Dwarf* on 2 February 1820, the poem cleverly mirrors the original with the ambitious Lord Castlereagh in the role of Macbeth, contemplating the destruction of the Goddess Liberty.[58] This speech from *Macbeth* is also parodied in an article in *Medusa* on 7 January 1820. The article, 'Observations from the Exeter Alfred on the Pretended Plots' maintains that the government creates imagined threats 'and terror spreads like wildfire over the land.' In particular, the author focuses on reports of an alleged planned meeting in Manchester on 13 December, which was banned by the authorities through the use of old laws against witchcraft; this forms the basis of the parody:

> My stars, in the air there's a *knife*,
> I'm sure it cannot be a *hum*.
> I'll catch at the handle, odds life,
> And then I shall not *cut my thumb*.
> I've got him! No! At him again,
> Come, come, I'm *not fond of these jokes*,
> There must be some blade of the brain,
> Those *witches* ———————
> (meaning, thereby, *Lancashire* witches)
> ————— are given to *hoax*,
> Ah! No, 'twas a dagger of *straw*;
> Give me blinkers to save me from starting,
> The *knife*, that *I thought that I saw*,
> Was nought but my eye, Betty Martin.[59]

> Is this the Goddess that I see before me,
> Her back turn'd on herself? Soft, let me stab her.
> I've done it not, and yet I struck with force;
> Art thou not, hateful vision, sensible
> To feeling, as to sight? Or art thou but
> Th' effect of indigestion, a false creation
> Proceeding from this overloaded stomach?
> I see thee yet, in form as palpable,
> As these six Bills[60] I hold-
> Thou marshals't me the way that I was going;

And such majority I was to have –
Mine eyes are made the fools o' th' other senses,
Or else worth all the rest – I see thee still;
And on thy snow-white garment gouts of blood,
Which was not so before. –There's no such thing. –
It is the deeds at Manchester, which inform
Thus to mine eyes. –Now o'er one half of the world,
Tyranny has sway, and plumed troops[61] invade
The People's peace; now Princes celebrate
Th' Alliance Holy;[62] and starving Radicals,
(Rous'd into action by the sense of right,
And pangs of want) thus with their murd'rous Pikes,
In dead array, tow'rds their foul design
Move like a troop of ghosts. –Ye Reformers,
Hear not the lies of A and B, for fear
Ye should unfold the secret of my plot;
And take the present horror from the *saints*,
Which now suits with them. – Whilst I threat, ye live –
I *move* and it is done; the hour invites me.
Britons, hear not my speech, for 'tis a breath
That gives ye Liberty, or me her death.
[Exit with a genteel flourish of the body and much self complacency.]
Horsleydown, Southwark, Jan 31 1820[63]

9 'Hunt and Liberty'

This poem appeared alongside 'The Triumph of Liberty' in *Medusa* on 25 September.[64] Like so many poems and songs in this collection, it calls upon the English to arise and assert their long-held freedoms, with Henry Hunt as the figurehead for this regaining of ancient rights and assertion of freedom. According to John Tyas' report in *The Times* on 19 August, reformers from Rochdale and Middleton carried two green banners 'bearing the inscription, "Hunt and Liberty"'.[65]

While mad oppression tills the land,
Arise and claim your charter[66]
Nor even lend[?] a willing hand
Your liberties to barter
United who shall dare oppose,
A cause so great and glorious,
Exert your voice, o'erwhelm your foes,
Till Britons are victorious
And every patriot's song shall be
In praise of Hunt and liberty.

Swift thro' the land the echoes fly,
Form north to west resounding,
Tremendous shouts of liberty,
From every tongue resounding.
The vaulted sky with songs of praise,
The melody so glorious,
Re-echo back the pleasing lays,[67]
Britons must be victorious.
And every patriot's song shall be
In praise of Hunt and liberty.

Let Sidmouth[68] yelp aloud his thanks,
To men of blood and plunder,
And send them thro' his marshall'd ranks,
In peals of rattling thunder.
The brave undaunted fearless stand,
His country's cause is glorious,
His voice shall echo thro' the land
Till Britons are victorious.
And every patriot's song shall be,
In praise of Hunt and liberty.

10 *A New Song*

This broadside ballad focuses on Hunt's triumphant entry into London on 15 September, in between his arrest at St Peter's Field and his trial at York in March 1820. In London, he was greeted by cheering crowds, among whom was John Keats, who wrote to his brother, George: 'It would take me a whole day and a quire of paper to give you anything like detail. The whole distance from the Angel at Islington to the Crown and Anchor was lined with multitudes'.[69] The ballad stresses Hunt's popularity with the people and assures him of an equal welcome when he returns to Lancashire.

Draw near me sons of freedom and listen to my song,[70]
It is but a few verses and will not keep you long,
'Tis of Hunt that champion bold the father of the poor,
His praises now come let us sing till time shall be no more.

When he arrived in London the air with shouts did ring
With banners of sweet liberty they led this champion in
The bands did play and flags did fly and with loud beat of drums
The tune they play'd with loud huzzas the conquering hero comes.[71]

The carriages and coaches in vast numbers they did come
The numbers of spectators they were without a sum

To have seen the glorious joyful scene would cause despair to smile
The shouts that hail'd our conqueror they reached five English mile.

All ages, sex, ranks and degrees our hero they did hail
With true hearts and tongues cried our darling will not fail
The poor men cry he will not fail to make us happy homes
And all the while the music plays our conquering hero comes.

It is not the dark dungeons that can such virtue keep
Nor is it loathsome Peterloo will make our darling weep
Since friends unnumber'd legions have left their native homes
When three hundred thousand voices they will cry 'the conquering hero comes'.

So fare you well our darling Hunt farewell for a while,
May your next visitation cause slavery's sons to smile,
And when you come to Lancashire we'll leave our native homes,
We'll welcome you with loud huzzas the conquering hero comes.

11 *With Henry Hunt We'll Go*

Despite extensive research in the late nineteenth century by the folk song collector, Frank Kidson, he was unable to recover more than a single verse and chorus of this song, even though he 'met with several people who remember the song being sung'.[72] The choice of 'The Battle of Waterloo' for the tune is a deliberate irony on the part of the writer; the comparisons between Waterloo and Peterloo are numerous at this time. The broadside ballad, *The Battle of Waterloo*, has the following chorus:

> So with Wellington we'll go
> So with Wellington we'll go
> For Wellington commanded us
> On the Plains of Waterloo

The similarity with the chorus of *With Henry Hunt We'll Go* suggests a shared tune.[73]

Another song on Hunt, seemingly sung to the same tune, entitled 'A Radical Hunting Song' by Hafiz[74] was published in the *Morning Post* on 16 November 1819. In more recent times, the song has been recorded by folk musicians.[75]

> Chorus
> With Henry Hunt we'll go, my boys,
> With Henry Hunt we'll go;
> We'll mount the cap of liberty
> In spite of Nadin Joe.[76]

'Twas on the sixteenth day of August,
Eighteen hundred and nineteen,
A meeting held in Peter Street
Was glorious to be seen;
Joe Nadin and his big bull-dogs,[77]
Which you might plainly see,
And on the other side
Stood the bloody cavalry.

12 *An Acrostic*

This acrostic appeared on the same broadside as *A Tribute to the Immortal Memory of the Reformers, Who Fell on the 16th of August, 1819*.[78] Printed by Lanes in Manchester, the woodcut on the broadside depicts Hunt and the others on the hustings looking on helplessly as the MYC and Hussars attacked the crowd with sabres.

H ail all noble Champion of thy Country's cause,
U nlike the base corrupters of her Laws,
N one dare like thee their sinking country save,
T hou Son of Liberty both renowned and brave.

Notes

1 M. Roberts, 'Radical Banners from Peterloo to Chartism', in R. Poole (ed.), *Return to Peterloo. Manchester Region History Review*, 23 (2014), pp. 93–109, at p. 97; J.A. Epstein, *Radical Expression: Political Language, Ritual, and Symbol in England, 1790–1850* (Oxford: Oxford University Press, 1994), p. 83.
2 B. Bennett, *British War Poetry in the Age of Romanticism: 1793–1815* (New York: Garland, 1976), p. 24; *Black Dwarf*, 1:10 (1817), pp. 145–6.
3 See number 1 below.
4 Epstein, *Radical Expression*, p. 4.
5 J. Lucas, *England and Englishness: Ideas of Nationhood in English Poetry 1688–1900* (London: The Hogarth Press, 1990), p. 12.
6 Thomson describes Liberty thus: 'Her bright temples bound with British oak' (*Thomson's Poetical Works* (Edinburgh: Nichol, 1853), p. 170, l. 29). William Levine compares Thomson's *Liberty* with Collins' 'Ode to Liberty', claiming that Collins 'borrows and transforms' much of Thomson's poem ('Collins, Thomson, and the Whig Progress of Liberty', *Studies in English Literature 1500–1900*, 34:3 (1994), pp. 553–77, at p. 553).
7 Lucas, *England and Englishness*, p. 44; Levine, 'Collins, Thomson, and the Whig Progress of Liberty', p. 553.
8 W. Collins, *The Poems of Gray, Collins and Goldsmith*, ed. R. Lonsdale (London: Longman, 1969), p. 443, ll. 1–3.

9 *Ibid.*, ll. 109–12.
10 *Politics for the People*, 2:12 (1794), p. 12. For more information, see pp. 16–17.
11 *Ibid.*, p. 13.
12 D. Worrall, *Radical Culture: Discourse, Resistance and Surveillance, 1790–1820* (Hertfordshire: Harvester, 1992), pp. 97–104.
13 See number 2 below.
14 D. Lee, *Slavery and the Romantic Imagination* (Philadelphia: University of Pennsylvania Press, 2002), pp. 1, 26, 29.
15 *Ibid.*, p. 180. www.bl.uk/learning/citizenship/campaign/myh/photographs/gallery2/image4/cowperpoem.html [accessed 19 November 2017].
16 See pp. 69–70 for further information.
17 The poem was published in the radical journal, *Axe Laid to the Root* in 1817 (Scrivener, *Poetry and Reform*, p. 196).
18 Chapter 2, number 2.
19 See number 10 below.
20 *Medusa*, 1:32 (1819), p. 355.
21 Copies can be found in Preston Harris Library (Harkness Collection, vol. B); Manchester Central Library Collection (1819/2/W) and Madden Collection, University of Cambridge (no. 203). The imprints by Harkness from Church Street, Preston are dated between 1840 and 1866. The song can also be found in *Curiosities of Street Literature*, a collection of broadsides published anonymously in 1871 (Anon. (London: Reeves and Turner, 1871, p. 98), evidence of its continued popularity. Two of the imprints by Harkness have a wood cut of a soldier on a horse and a soldier with sword raised about to attack a prone victim.
22 For more information on the tune, see Chapter 2, number 9.
23 Sky or heaven.
24 Progeny.
25 P. Keen (ed.), *The Popular Radical Press in Britain 1817–21*. 6 vols. (London: Pickering and Chatto, 2003), vol. 5, p. 331.
26 I have written elsewhere on radical versions of the national anthem. See '"God Save Our Queen!" Percy Bysshe Shelley and Radical Appropriations of the British National Anthem' (*Romanticism* 20:1 (2014), pp. 60–72). The original of the tune and words to 'God Save the King' is not known. However, early versions of the song date back to Jacobite drinking songs of the late eighteenth century, which were written in support of the exiled Stuart monarch, James II. The song gained popularity in England in 1745 when a new arrangement by Thomas Arne was played at Drury Lane Theatre in support of George II following the defeat of the British by the Jacobites, led by Bonnie Prince Charlie, at Prestonpans (*Ibid.*, pp. 60–72).
27 People devoted to a religious life.
28 Blood-soaked field – a direct reference to Peterloo.
29 Keen, *The Popular Radical Press*, vol. 5, p. 355.
30 Macnally, a Catholic, was a member of the United Irishmen and actively

involved in events leading up to the 1798 uprising. In more recent years, it has been discovered that he was in fact a government informer who betrayed, among others, Robert Emmet, who was hanged for his part in the failed 1803 uprising (*DNB*).

31 Anon. (London: Roach, 1790), p. 35.
32 *DNB*.
33 Government officers who enjoyed generous pensions and sinecures in return for loyalty to crown and state.
34 Songs.
35 Servants or, more generally, the labouring classes.
36 Keen, *The Popular Radical Press*, vol. 5, p. 243.
37 A funeral song or lamentation in the Highlands of Scotland and in Ireland; a dirge.
38 The spirits of the dead.
39 Keen, *The Popular Radical Press*, vol. 5, p. 344.
40 'Patriotic Song' in Chapter 1 also features in the same chapbook, which can be found in the Working-Class Movement Library in Salford (AG-Songs).
41 Bamford published *The Weaver Boy, or, Miscellaneous Poetry*, his first published collection of poems, in 1819.
42 *Manchester Observer* (18 September 1819), p. 718; *Examiner*, 614 (1819), p. 635.
43 S. Bamford, *Passages in the Life of a Radical*, 3 vols. (Manchester: Heywood, 1842), vol. 1, p. 228.
44 The first stanza of this poem is included in *Passages in the Life of a Radical*: 'On some nights, when my cough was rather merciful, I found amusement in composing, as at Coldbath Fields, bits of rude verse […] This verse pleased my companions exceedingly, and it afterwards became of some celebrity amongst the reformers. (p. 207).
45 A person who assists the immoral urges or evil designs of others.
46 *Manchester Observer* (28 August 1819), p. 694.
47 The English Constitution has never existed as a document. Magna Carta and The Bill of Rights are often cited as part of the constitution; however, belief in an Anglo-Saxon constitution was a major tenet of the radical movement. Epstein states: 'The appeal of the Anglo-Saxon Constitution, while historical in form, was often a simultaneous appeal to some notion of natural law – the assumption being that the lost liberties of Anglo-Saxon England had embodied notions of original right' (*Radical Expression*, p. 21). Indeed the utilisation of a historical precedent, combined with the theory of natural rights, strengthened the radical movement providing it with gravitas and authority. However, this was not a view shared by everyone in the radical movement. In the first part of the *Rights of Man* written in 1791, Thomas Paine asserts: 'No such thing as a constitution exists' in response to its appropriation by Edmund Burke's *Reflections on the Revolution in France* (p. 123).
48 As with 'borough-monger', one who trades in parliamentary seats for boroughs.

49 An alarm, usually sounded by a bell.
50 A subordinate ruler; often suggesting an imputation of tyranny or ostentatious splendour.
51 Major John Cartwright. For more information, see p. 15.
52 One of Cartwright's key works is a pamphlet published in 1776, *Take Your Choice*, in which he outlines his case for annual parliaments, universal male suffrage, the payment of MPs and secret ballots (E.P. Thompson, *The Making of the English Working Class* (Middlesex: Penguin, 1980), p. 91).
53 Castlereagh.
54 House of Commons.
55 The six bills (later known as the Six Acts) were passed in November 1819 in order to strengthen state power over dissent. The acts were as follows: 1 The Training Prevention Act; 2 Seizure of Arms Act; 3 Misdemeanours Act; 4 Seditious Meetings Prevention Act; 5 The Blasphemous and Seditious Libels Act; 6 Newspaper Stamp Duties Act. Although the acts were highly controversial, they did succeed in contributing to the demise of the radical movement in 1820.
56 A poem, entitled 'Song' authored by 'T.H.' was published in the *Morning Post* on 14 January 1820 (15285).
57 Act One, scene three, l. 52. The poem is a parody of the following soliloquy from *Macbeth* Act Two, scene 1:

> Is this a dagger which I see before me,
> The handle toward my hand? Come, let me clutch thee.
> I have thee not, and yet I see thee still.
> Art thou not, fatal vision, sensible
> To feeling as to sight? Or art thou but
> A dagger of the mind, a false creation,
> Proceeding from the heat-oppressed brain?
> I see thee yet, in form as palpable
> As this which now I draw.
> Thou marshall'st me the way that I was going;
> And such an instrument I was to use.
> Mine eyes are made the fools o' the other senses,
> Or else worth all the rest; I see thee still,
> And on thy blade and dudgeon gouts of blood,
> Which was not so before. There's no such thing:
> It is the bloody business which informs
> Thus to mine eyes. Now o'er the one halfworld
> Nature seems dead, and wicked dreams abuse
> The curtain'd sleep; witchcraft celebrates
> Pale Hecate's offerings, and wither'd murder,
> Alarum'd by his sentinel, the wolf,
> Whose howl's his watch, thus with his stealthy pace.
> With Tarquin's ravishing strides, towards his design
> Moves like a ghost. Thou sure and firm-set earth,

> Hear not my steps, which way they walk, for fear
> Thy very stones prate of my whereabout,
> And take the present horror from the time,
> Which now suits with it. Whiles I threat, he lives:
> Words to the heat of deeds too cold breath gives.
> I go, and it is done; the bell invites me.
> Hear it not, Duncan, for it is a knell
> That summons thee to heaven or to hell (ll. 33–64)

58 *Black Dwarf*, 4:4 (1820), p. 143.
59 *Medusa*, 1:47 (1820), p. 371.
60 See note 55.
61 The Fifteenth Hussars.
62 The Holy Alliance was established in 1815 following the defeat of Napoleon. It comprised Russia, Prussia and Austria, who united to promote Christian values and the power of monarchy. Even though Britain did not sign, the alliance was supported by the Prince Regent.
63 Horsleydown was a small parish in Southwark situated opposite the Tower of London.
64 *Medusa*, 1:32 (1819), p. 355.
65 J. Tyas, 'Express from Manchester', *The Times* (19 August 1819), p. 2.
66 This probably refers to the rights enshrined in Magna Carta, such as the famous clause which states that 'No free man shall be seized or imprisoned, or stripped of his rights or possessions, or outlawed or exiled, or deprived of his standing in any other way, nor will we proceed with force against him, or send others to do so, except by the lawful judgement of his equals or by the law of the land. To no one will we sell, to no one deny or delay right or justice' (https://www.bl.uk/treasures/magnacarta/translation/mc_trans.html [accessed 19 November 2017]).
67 Songs.
68 See pp. 3, 7, 10.
69 Quoted in Thompson, *The Making of the English Working Class*, p. 747.
70 The invitation to the audience to listen to the ensuing story is a balladic convention, dating back many hundreds of years. An early example can be found in the opening verse of *The Rising in the North*, an Elizabethan ballad narrating the downfall of Thomas Percy, Earl of Northumberland who, in 1569, conspired with Mary, Queen of Scots and against Elizabeth I: Listen, lively lordings all, / Lithe and listen unto mee, / And I will sing of a noble earle / The noblest earle in the north country (Percy, *Reliques*, vol. 1, p. 71).
71 'Peterloo' and 'National Songs – No. 1' are also written to the tune of 'See the Conquering Hero Comes'. See pp. 80–1. According to Epstein, 'See the Conquering Hero Comes' was played by bands at Peterloo to herald Hunt's arrival (*Radical Expression*, p. 83).
72 F. Kidson, *Traditional Tunes* (Oxford: Taphouse, 1891), p. 161. The version in Palmer's *Ballad History of England* also comprises a single verse and

chorus, 'but the fragment is so powerful that it is worth a place here', a sentiment I share (p. 97).

73 The song, *The Nutting Girl*, dating back to at least the eighteenth century, has a chorus which begins, 'So a-nutting we will go, my boys / And a-nutting we will go' (S. Roud and J. Bishop (eds), *The New Penguin Book of English Folk Songs* (London: Penguin, 2012), pp. 204–5, 450). Again, the similarity to *With Henry Hunt We'll Go* suggests a shared tune.

In *Ballads and Songs of Lancashire*, published in 1865, John Harland writes that the ballad, 'The Hand-Loom Weavers' Lament' 'was sung to the favourite air of "A Hunting We Will Go", but better known in and near Manchester by a song of the time'. Harland then quotes the chorus from *With Henry Hunt We'll Go* (London: Whittaker, pp. 261–2). It would appear to date back to 1641 and the song 'A Begging We Will Go' by Richard Brome in his play *The Jovial Crew* (R. Bell, *Ancient Poems, Ballads and Songs of the Peasantry of England* (London: Parker and son, 1857, p. 251). 'A Hunting We Will Go' remains a popular nursery rhyme.

74 Bennett identifies 'Hafiz' as Thomas Stott, friend of Thomas Percy, whose poems were also published in *The Gentleman's Magazine* and *The Anti-Gallican* (*British War Poetry*, p. 293).

75 The sleeve note to the album *Waterloo: Peterloo*, recorded by The Critics in 1968, states that only one verse and the chorus are extant; however, the version of the song recorded by Harry Boardman and Dave Hillery on their 1971 album, *Songs of Lancashire and Yorkshire* contains three additional verses.

76 Joseph Nadin (1765–1848) was the Deputy Constable of Manchester in 1819. According to Read, Nadin was notorious for his methods of catching criminals and hated by the radicals in Manchester. On 16 August, Nadin was charged by the Manchester magistrates with the arrest of Hunt, and called for help from the military in order to do this. He then accompanied the MYC and arrested Hunt and Joseph Johnson (D. Read, *Peterloo: The Massacre and its Background* (Manchester: Manchester University Press, 1958), pp. 79, 136).

77 The MYC who led the charge against the crowd. As with several poems in this collection, the poet uses the image of dogs for those who attacked the protestors.

78 See Chapter 4, number 3 for further details.

Appendix
The Masque of Anarchy[1]

'Written on the Occasion of the Massacre at Manchester'

Described by Richard Holmes as 'the greatest poem of political protest ever written in English' and by Kelvin Everest as 'perhaps the greatest English poem of radical political thinking', *The Masque of Anarchy* is central to the poems written by Shelley in the aftermath of Peterloo.[2] Comprising ninety-one fast-paced verses, fuelled by fury yet clear in its rationality, *Masque* is remarkably similar to the poems being written and published at that time in the radical press. It was the first poem to be written by Shelley following his receipt of news in Italy regarding Peterloo from his friend, Thomas Love Peacock, in early September.[3] On receiving news of the massacre, Shelley wrote to the publisher, Charles Ollier:

> The torrent of [m]y indignation has not yet done boiling in my veins. I wait anxiously [to] hear how the country will express its sense of this bloody murderous oppression of its destroyers. 'Something must be done … What yet I know not.[4]

Written swiftly, the finished poem was sent to Leigh Hunt for publication on 23 September 1819, although it remained unpublished until Edward Moxon's single-volume edition in 1832 with a preface by Leigh Hunt.[5]

The poem begins languidly with its slow, dream-like rhythm beguiling the reader into the expectation of a more conventional, lyrical poem.[6] The resulting vision continues for the rest of the poem moving from the destructive 'masquerade' led by Anarchy[7] to his death at the hands of the shadowy 'Shape' and the speech to 'Men of England' by the figure of Hope. Following a consideration of slavery and freedom, Hope re-imagines Peterloo where the might of collective passive resistance results in the triumph of the people over the might of the state.

Shelley turned to the ballad in 1819 in order to give a bardic voice to his outrage at events in his native country.⁸ What he achieved in *Masque*, therefore, is both a traditional ballad in its presentation of England and a yearning for liberty, together with a contemporary satire that evokes the iconography of the day. Although he was not to return to the ballad again, *Masque* demonstrates the possibilities of the genre and its appropriateness as a method of engaging a diverse readership. Had it been published at the time of writing, it could have contributed invaluably to the ballad tradition, fuelling generic experimentation with ideological daring. Despite the failure of publication in 1820, *Masque* has enjoyed and continues to enjoy success over the ensuing two centuries and has been used by politicians ranging from Ghandi to Thabo Mbeki, as well as the student protestors in Tiananmen Square.⁹ It was performed superbly by Maxine Peake at the Manchester International Festival in 2013 and continues to be read at events commemorating the massacre.

> As I lay asleep in Italy
> There came a voice from over the Sea,
> And with great power it forth led me
> To walk in the visions of Poesy.¹⁰
>
> I met Murder on the way-
> He had a mask¹¹ like Castlereagh –¹²
> Very smooth he looked, yet grim;
> Seven blood-hounds¹³ followed him:
>
> All were fat; and well they might
> Be in admirable plight,
> For one by one, and two by two,
> He tossed them human hearts to chew
> Which from his wide cloak he drew.
>
> Next came Fraud, and he had on,
> Like Eldon,¹⁴ an ermined gown;
> His big tears, for he wept well,
> Turned to mill-stones as they fell.¹⁵
>
> And the little children, who
> Round his feet played to and fro,
> Thinking every tear a gem,
> Had their brains knocked out by them.
>
> Clothed with the Bible, as with light,
> And the shadows of the night,
> Like Sidmouth,¹⁶ next, Hypocrisy
> On a crocodile¹⁷ rode by.

And many more Destructions played
In this ghastly masquerade,
All disguised, even to the eyes,
Like Bishops, lawyers, peers, or spies.[18]

Last came Anarchy: he rode
On a white horse, splashed with blood;
He was pale even to the lips,
Like Death in the Apocalypse.[19]

And he wore a kingly crown;
And in his grasp a sceptre shone;
And on his brow this mark I saw –
'I AM GOD, AND KING, AND LAW.'

With a pace stately and fast,
Over English[20] land he passed,
Trampling to a mire of blood
The adoring multitude.

And a mighty troop around,
With their trampling shook the ground,
Waving each a bloody sword,
For the service of the Lord.

And with glorious triumph[21] they
Rose through England proud and gay,
Drunk as with intoxication
Of the wine of desolation.[22]

O'er the fields and towns, from sea to sea,
Passed the Pageant swift and free,
Tearing up, and trampling down,
Till they came to London town.

And each dweller, panic-stricken,
Felt his heart with terror sicken
Hearing the tempestuous cry
Of the triumph of Anarchy.

For with pomp to meet him came,
Clothed in arms like blood and flame,
The hired murderers, who did sing
'Thou art God, and Law, and King.

'We have waited, weak and lone
For thy coming, Mighty One!
Our purses are empty, our swords are cold,
Give us glory, and blood, and gold.

Lawyers and priests, a motley crowd,
To the earth their pale brows bowed;
Like a bad prayer not over loud,
Whispering – 'Thou art Law and God. –

Then all cried with one accord,
'Thou art King, and God, and Lord;
Anarchy, to thee we bow,
Be thy name made holy now!'

And Anarchy, the Skeleton,
Bowed and grinned to every one,
As well as if his education
Had cost ten millions to the nation.

For he knew the Palaces
Of our Kings were rightly his;
His the sceptre, crown, and globe,[23]
And the gold-inwoven robe.

So he sent his slaves before
To seize upon the Bank and Tower,[24]
And was proceeding with intent
To meet his pensioned Parliament[25]

When one fled past, a maniac maid,
And her name was Hope,[26] she said:
But she looked more like Despair,
And she cried out in the air:

'My father Time is weak and gray
With waiting for a better day;
See how idiot-like he stands,
Fumbling with his palsied hands!

'He has had child after child,
And the dust of death is piled
Over every one but me-
Misery, oh, Misery!'

Then she lay down in the street,
Right before the horses' feet,
Expecting, with a patient eye,
Murder, Fraud, and Anarchy.

When between her and her foes
A mist, a light, an image rose,
Small at first, and weak, and frail
Like the vapour of a vale:

Till as clouds grow on the blast,
Like tower-crowned giants striding fast,
And glare with lightnings as they fly,
And speak in thunder to the sky,

It grew-a Shape arrayed in mail[27]
Brighter than the viper's scale,
And upborne on wings whose grain
Was as the light of sunny rain.

On its helm, seen far away,
A planet, like the Morning's, lay;
And those plumes its light rained through
Like a shower of crimson dew.

With step as soft as wind it passed
O'er the heads of men-so fast
That they knew the presence there,
And looked, – but all was empty air.

As flowers beneath May's footstep waken,
As stars from Night's loose hair are shaken,
As waves arise when loud winds call,
Thoughts sprung where'er that step did fall.

And the prostrate multitude
Looked – and ankle-deep in blood,
Hope, that maiden most serene,
Was walking with a quiet mien:

And Anarchy, the ghastly birth,
Lay dead earth upon the earth;
The Horse of Death tameless as wind
Fled, and with his hoofs did grind
To dust the murderers thronged behind.

A rushing light of clouds and splendour,
A sense awakening and yet tender
Was heard and felt – and at its close
These words of joy and fear arose

As if their own indignant Earth
Which gave the sons of England birth
Had felt their blood upon her brow,
And shuddering with a mother's throe

Had turnèd every drop of blood
By which her face had been bedewed
To an accent unwithstood,-
As if her heart had cried aloud:

'Men of England, heirs of Glory,[28]
Heroes of unwritten story,
Nurslings of one mighty Mother,
Hopes of her, and one another;

'Rise like Lions after slumber
In unvanquishable number,[29]
Shake your chains to earth like dew
Which in sleep had fallen on you-
Ye are many – they are few.[30]

'What is Freedom? – ye can tell
That which slavery is, too well –
For its very name has grown
To an echo of your own.

'Tis to work and have such pay
As just keeps life from day to day
In your limbs, as in a cell
For the tyrants' use to dwell,

'So that ye for them are made
Loom, and plough, and sword, and spade,
With or without your own will bent
To their defence and nourishment.

''Tis to see your children weak
With their mothers pine and peak,
When the winter winds are bleak, –
They are dying whilst I speak.

''Tis to hunger for such diet
As the rich man in his riot
Casts to the fat dogs that lie
Surfeiting beneath his eye;

''Tis to let the Ghost of Gold
Take from Toil a thousandfold
More than e'er its substance could
In the tyrannies of old.

'Paper coin-that forgery[31]
Of the title-deeds, which ye

Hold to something of the worth
Of the inheritance of Earth.

''Tis to be a slave in soul
And to hold no strong control
Over your own wills, but be
All that others make of ye.

'And at length when ye complain
With a murmur weak and vain
'Tis to see the Tyrant's crew
Ride over your wives and you –
Blood is on the grass like dew.

'Then it is to feel revenge
Fiercely thirsting to exchange
Blood for blood – and wrong for wrong –
Do not thus when ye are strong.

'Birds find rest, in narrow nest
When weary of their wingèd quest;
Beasts find fare, in woody lair
When storm and snow are in the air.

'Asses, swine, have litter spread
And with fitting food are fed;
All things have a home but one –
Thou, Oh, Englishman, hast none!

'This is Slavery – savage men,
Or wild beasts within a den
Would endure not as ye do –
But such ills they never knew.

'What art thou Freedom? O! could slaves
Answer from their living graves
This demand – tyrants would flee
Like a dream's dim imagery:

'Thou art not, as impostors say,
A shadow soon to pass away,
A superstition, and a name
Echoing from the cave of Fame.

'For the labourer thou art bread,
And a comely table spread
From his daily labour come
In a neat and happy home.

'Thou art clothes, and fire, and food
For the trampled multitude
No – in countries that are free
Such starvation cannot be
As in England now we see.

'To the rich thou art a check,
When his foot is on the neck
Of his victim, thou dost make
That he treads upon a snake.

'Thou art Justice – ne'er for gold
May thy righteous laws be sold
As laws are in England – thou
Shield'st alike the high and low.

'Thou art Wisdom – Freemen never
Dream that God will damn for ever
All who think those things untrue
Of which Priests make such ado.

'Thou art Peace – never by thee
Would blood and treasure wasted be
As tyrants wasted them, when all
Leagued to quench thy flame in Gaul.[32]

'What if English toil and blood
Was poured forth, even as a flood?
It availed, Oh, Liberty,
To dim, but not extinguish thee.

'Thou art Love – the rich have kissed
Thy feet, and like him following Christ,
Give their substance to the free
And through the rough world follow thee,

'Or turn their wealth to arms, and make
War for thy belovèd sake
On wealth, and war, and fraud-whence they
Drew the power which is their prey.

'Science, Poetry, and Thought
Are thy lamps; they make the lot
Of the dwellers in a cot
So serene, they curse it not.

'Spirit, Patience, Gentleness,
All that can adorn and bless

Art thou – let deeds, not words, express
Thine exceeding loveliness.

'Let a great Assembly be
Of the fearless and the free
On some spot of English ground
Where the plains stretch wide around.

'Let the blue sky overhead,
The green earth on which ye tread,
All that must eternal be
Witness the solemnity.

'From the corners uttermost
Of the bounds of English coast;
From every hut, village, and town
Where those who live and suffer moan
For others' misery or their own,

'From the workhouse and the prison
Where pale as corpses newly risen,
Women, children, young and old
Groan for pain, and weep for cold –

'From the haunts of daily life
Where is waged the daily strife
With common wants and common cares
Which sows the human heart with tares –[33]

'Lastly from the palaces
Where the murmur of distress
Echoes, like the distant sound
Of a wind alive around

'Those prison halls of wealth and fashion,
Where some few feel such compassion
For those who groan, and toil, and wail
As must make their brethren pale-

'Ye who suffer woes untold,
Or to feel, or to behold
Your lost country bought and sold
With a price of blood and gold –

'Let a vast assembly be,
And with great solemnity
Declare with measured words that ye
Are, as God has made ye, free –

'Be your strong and simple words
Keen to wound as sharpened swords,
And wide as targes[34] let them be,
With their shade to cover ye.

'Let the tyrants pour around
With a quick and startling sound,
Like the loosening of a sea,
Troops of armed emblazonry.

'Let the charged artillery drive
Till the dead air seems alive
With the clash of clanging wheels,
And the tramp of horses' heels.

'Let the fixèd bayonet
Gleam with sharp desire to wet
Its bright point in English blood
Looking keen as one for food.

'Let the horsemen's scimitars[35]
Wheel and flash, like sphereless stars[36]
Thirsting to eclipse their burning
In a sea of death and mourning.

'Stand ye calm and resolute,
Like a forest close and mute,
With folded arms and looks which are
Weapons of unvanquished war,

'And let Panic, who outspeeds
The career of armèd steeds
Pass, a disregarded shade
Through your phalanx undismayed.

'Let the laws of your own land,
Good or ill, between ye stand
Hand to hand, and foot to foot,
Arbiters of the dispute,

'The old laws of England – they
Whose reverend heads with age are gray,
Children of a wiser day;
And whose solemn voice must be
Thine own echo – Liberty!

'On those who first should violate
Such sacred heralds in their state

Rest the blood that must ensue,
And it will not rest on you.

'And if then the tyrants dare
Let them ride among you there,
Slash, and stab, and maim, and hew, –
What they like, that let them do.

'With folded arms and steady eyes,
And little fear, and less surprise,
Look upon them as they slay
Till their rage has died away.[37]

'Then they will return with shame
To the place from which they came,
And the blood thus shed will speak
In hot blushes on their cheek.

'Every woman in the land
Will point at them as they stand –
They will hardly dare to greet
Their acquaintance in the street.

'And the bold, true warriors
Who have hugged Danger in wars
Will turn to those who would be free,
Ashamed of such base company.[38]

'And that slaughter to the Nation
Shall steam up like inspiration,
Eloquent, oracular;
A volcano heard afar.

'And these words shall then become
Like Oppression's thundered doom
Ringing through each heart and brain,
Heard again – again – again –

'Rise like Lions after slumber
In unvanquishable number –
Shake your chains to earth like dew
Which in sleep had fallen on you –
Ye are many –they are few.'

Notes

1 The title of the poem varies between 'masque' and 'mask'. Jack Donovan notes that Shelley used 'Mask' in the press-copy of the poem (P.B. Shelley,

The Poems of Shelley, ed. Jack Donovan, Cian Duffy, Kelvin Everest and Michael Rossington (London: Longman, 2011), vol. 3, p. 29). However in a letter to Hunt in November 1819, Shelley used 'masque' (P.B. Shelley, *The Letters of Percy Bysshe Shelley*, ed. F.L. Jones (Oxford: Clarendon Press, 1964), vol. 2, p. 152). When first published in 1832, the title *The Masque of Anarchy* was used, although *The Mask of Anarchy* is used in modern editions (Shelley, *The Masque of Anarchy* (London: Moxon, 1832); Shelley, *Poems*, vol. 3, pp. 35, 27).

2 R. Holmes, *Shelley: The Pursuit* (New York: New York Review Book, 1994), p. 532; K. Everest, *English Romantic Poetry* (Milton Keynes: Open University Press, 1990), p. 45. I have written elsewhere on *The Masque of Anarchy* and Shelley's other Peterloo poems. For a more detailed examination of this text, see A. Morgan, 'Shelley and Peterloo: Radical, Nationalist and Balladeer', PhD Thesis, University of Salford, 2012.

3 Shelley, *Letters*, vol. 2, p. 117. Peacock regularly sent copies of the *Examiner* to Shelley in Italy. John Tyas' eye-witness account of Peterloo was reprinted in the *Examiner* on 22 August. Post from England would routinely take two weeks to arrive in Italy. There is no evidence to suggest that Shelley had access to any of the other radical periodicals of the time.

4 The letter is dated 6 September and the quotation is from Shelley's play, *The Cenci* (Shelley, *Letters*, vol. 2, p. 117).

5 Hunt's imprisonment for libelling the Prince Regent in 1813 had understandably made him cautious with regard to the content of the *Examiner*. According to Nicholas Roe, Hunt had a real fear of being transported if he was prosecuted for libel a second time (*Fiery Heart: The First Life of Leigh Hunt* (London: Pimlico, 2005), p. 323).

6 The concept of the vision, a dream-like state in which the imagination flourishes, is a staple feature of Romantic poetry from Blake's prophetic verse in poems such as *The Four Zoas*, through Coleridge's hallucinatory 'Kubla Khan' to Keats' longing for oblivion in 'Ode to a Nightingale'.

7 For Shelley, anarchy represents the result of tyranny.

8 Shelley also used the ballad genre for his little-known poem, 'The Ballad of the Starving Mother', written in 1820. See Morgan, 'Shelley and Peterloo'.

9 T. Morton, 'Receptions', in T. Morton (ed.), *The Cambridge Companion to Shelley* (Cambridge: Cambridge University Press, 2006), pp. 35–41.

10 Shelley travelled to Italy in the spring of 1818 and was in Livorno when he heard news of Peterloo early in September 1819. The trope of awakening permeates the poem, beginning with Shelley being roused from sleep, and concluding with his invocation to the people to awaken. See the introduction to Chapter 1 for more information on the use of this trope in radical poetry.

11 See p. 127 for the motif of the mask.

12 Lord Castlereagh, the Foreign Secretary. In the 1832 version, 'Castlereagh' is printed in full whereas Eldon is printed as 'E—' and Sidmouth as '**' (Shelley, *Masque*, ll. 2, 3). I can only assume that these differing devices

were used because at the time of publication, Sidmouth and Eldon were still alive, whereas Castlereagh was dead.
13 Donovan notes that the 'seven bloodhounds' refers to the seven nations, including Britain, comprising the Holy Alliance which agreed to postpone the abolition of slavery in 1815 (*The Poems of Shelley*, p. 37). For more information on the image of bloodhounds, see pp. 12 and 63n.73.
14 Lord Eldon, the Lord Chancellor. Shelley's antipathy towards Eldon was in part due to Eldon presiding over the 1816 court case in which Shelley lost custody of his children by his first wife, Harriet (Holmes, *Shelley*, p. 356). Eldon also presided over the treason trials of Horne Tooke and John Thelwall in 1794, both of whom were acquitted.
15 In 'To the Lord Chancellor', written in 1819 or 1820, Shelley describes Eldon thus: And – (for thou canst outweep the crocodile) – / By thy false tears – those millstones braining men – (P.B. Shelley, *The Major Works*, ed. Z. Leader and M. O'Neill (Oxford: Oxford University Press, 2003), pp. 450, ll. 47–8).
16 Lord Sidmouth, the Home Secretary.
17 According to the *OED*, 'the crocodile was fabulously said to weep, either to allure a man for the purpose of devouring him, or while (or after) devouring him'. This allusion to the duplicitous behaviour of the crocodile may have influenced Shelley's selection of this image, although it was in fact Lord Eldon, rather than Sidmouth, who, when Attorney-General, was famous for weeping as he persuaded juries to hang men (Donovan, *The Poems of Shelley*, p. 38). In *Political Showman at Home*, Hone and Cruikshank also depict the crocodile as weeping in order to attract its prey: '[It] sheds tears, and, attracting the unwary, suddenly darts upon a man and gorges him with all he has' (W. Hone and G. Cruikshank, *The Political Showman at Home* (London: Hone, 1821), n. pag).
18 Shelley is attacking what he saw as weapons of the state: the judiciary, the church, the aristocracy and *agents provocateur*.
19 An allusion to *Revelation*: 'And I looked, and behold a pale horse; and his name that sat on him was Death, and hell followed with him. And power was given unto them over the fourth part of the earth, to kill with sword, and with hunger, and with death, and with the beasts of the earth' (Rev. 6.8). Shelley may also have been familiar with Benjamin West's 1796 painting *Death on a Pale Horse* and James Gillray's 1795 caricature, *Presages of the Millennium*, depicting a naked Pitt riding a Hanoverian horse over the people.
20 'England' and 'English' are used twelve times in this poem, more than any other poem by Shelley.
21 'Triumph' also means a procession, usually to celebrate a military victory.
22 Shelley could be alluding to the drunken state of the MYC.
23 Orb – another symbol of monarchy.
24 Bank of England and Tower of London – symbols of state power. The

capture of these buildings was one of the aims of the failed Spa Fields Uprising in 1816.
25 Ministers received a pension to ensure their loyalty to the government (Donovan, *The Poems of Shelley*, p. 44).
26 Haywood asserts that Hope is 'a hybrid symbol of self-sacrifice and resistance, and a figure who is clearly based on the trampled women who were at the visual and moral centre of the popular iconography of Peterloo' (I. Haywood, 'Shelley's *Mask of Anarchy* and the Visual Iconography of Female Distress', in P. Connell and N. Leask, eds, *Romanticism and Popular Culture in Britain and Ireland* (Cambridge: Cambridge University Press, 2009), p. 153). The introduction to Chapter 3 explores the presentation of women in Peterloo poems. Shelley often used females as political figures in his poems, such as *Queen Mab* and *Laon and Cythna*.
27 The identity of the chivalric Shape appears deliberately obscure, or, in the words of Haywood, 'allegorically unfixed' ('Shelley's *Mask*', p. 161). Donovan suggests it 'recalls the warrior Britannia of popular prints' *The Poems of Shelley*, p. 46).See the introduction to Chapter 5 for a discussion on the theme of chivalry in the Peterloo poems.
28 The identity of the speaker has been subject to critical debate: Holmes suggests Hope (*Shelley*, p. 535); Scrivener suggests Britannia (*Radical Shelley: The Philosophical Anarchism and Utopian Thought of Percy Bysshe Shelley* (Princeton: Princeton University Press, 1982), p. 205); Cross suggests Mother Earth (A. Cross, '"What a World We Make the Oppressor and the Oppressed": George Cruikshank, Percy Shelley and the Gendering of Revolution in 1819', *Journal of English Literary History*, 71 (2004), p. 14). Haywood cites the speaker as the Earth, 'a national female icon', who represents both Britannia and Liberty, part of the female iconography post-Waterloo ('Shelley's *Mask*, pp. 164–5). I share Haywood's view that the voice is the embodiment of English nationalism.
29 Webb notes that positive meanings underlie many of Shelley's negatives, as is the case here with 'unvanquishable' alluding to the strength and courage of the people (T. Webb, 'The Unascended Heaven: Negatives in *Prometheus Unbound*', in K. Everest (ed.), *Essays from the Gregnyog Conference* (Leicester: Leicester University Press, 1983), pp 37–62, at p. 57.
30 See the Introduction to Chapter 1 for an exploration of the exhortatory ballad.
31 Even though banknotes had been in circulation since the end of the seventeenth century, the Bank of England issued £1 and £2 notes during the Napoleonic Wars due to the drain on its gold reserves. Like many others, Shelley was deeply suspicious of paper money (P.B. Shelley, *The Major Works*, ed. Z. Leader and M. O'Neill (Oxford: Oxford University Press, 2003), p. 761).
32 The alliance of Prussia, Russia, Austria, Holland, Spain, Sardinia and Great Britain which defeated France and the values of the French Revolution.
33 Weeds.

34 Shields.
35 Scimitars are short, curved swords, associated with 'the military force of Oriental despotism' (*OED*). Comparisons between the MYC and Turkish soldiers can be found in Chapter 5, number 8.
36 Meteors.
37 Ghandi was influenced by Shelley's views on passive resistance (Leader and O'Neill (eds), *The Major Works* p. 762).
38 Shelley anticipates that regular troops, such as the Fifteenth Hussars, would reject the use of violence on the English people.

Select bibliography

Bamford, S. *Passages in the Life of a Radical*. 3 vols. (Manchester: Heywood, 1842).
Belchem, J. *Orator Hunt: Henry Hunt and English Working-Class Radicalism* (Oxford: Clarendon, 1985).
Bennett. B. *British War Poetry in the Age of Romanticism: 1793–1815* (New York: Garland, 1976).
Bush, M. *The Casualties of Peterloo* (Lancaster: Carnegie Publishing, 2005).
Bush, M. 'The Women at Peterloo: The Impact of Female Reform on the Manchester Meeting of 16 August 1819', *History* 89:294 (2004), pp. 209–32.
Chandler, J. *England in 1819: The Politics of Literary Culture and the Case of Romantic Historicism* (Chicago: Chicago University Press, 1998).
Chappell, W. *The Ballad Literature and Popular Music of the Olden Time* (New York: Dover Publications, 1965).
Chetham's Library, Manchester, *Hay Portfolio*, 1812–20.
Epstein, J.A. *Radical Expression: Political Language, Ritual, and Symbol in England, 1790–1850* (Oxford: Oxford University Press, 1994).
Hone, W. and G. Cruikshank. *The Political Showman at Home* (London: Hone, 1821).
Janowitz, A. *Lyric and Labour in the Romantic Tradition* (Cambridge: Cambridge University Press, 1998).
Keen, P. (ed.), *The Popular Radical Press in Britain 1817–21*. 6 vols. (London: Pickering and Chatto, 2003).
Kidd, A. and T. Wyke (eds), *Manchester: Making the Modern City* (Liverpool: Liverpool University Press, 2016).
Krantz, M. *'Rise Like Lions': The History and Lessons of the Peterloo Massacre of 1819* (London: Bookmark Publications, 2011).
Marlow, J. *The Peterloo Massacre* (London: Rapp and Whiting, 1969).
Mather, R. 'These Lancashire Women are Witches in Politics: Female Reform Societies and the Theatre of Radicalism, 1819–1820', in R. Poole (ed.), *Return to Peterloo. Manchester Region History Review*, 23 (2014), pp. 49–64.
McCalman, I. *Radical Underworld: Prophets, Revolutionaries and*

Pornographers in London, 1795–1840 (Cambridge: Cambridge University Press, 2004).

McKeiver, P. *Peterloo Massacre 1819* (Manchester: Advance Press, 2009).

McLane, M. *Balladeering, Minstrelsy and the Making of British Romantic Poetry* (Cambridge: Cambridge University Press, 2008).

Morgan, A. 'Shelley and Peterloo: Radical, Nationalist and Balladeer', PhD Thesis, University of Salford, 2012.

Palmer, R. (ed.), *A Ballad History of England from 1588 to the Present Day* (London: Batsford, 1979).

Palmer, R. *The Sound of History: Songs and Social Comment* (London: Pimlico, 1988).

——. *A Touch of the Times* (Middlesex: Penguin, 1974).

Peterloo Massacre, Manchester Region History Review (MRHR) 3: 1 (1989).

Pittock, M. *Poetry and Jacobite Politics in Eighteenth-Century Britain and Ireland* (Cambridge: Cambridge University Press, 1994).

Poole, R. 'By the Law and Sword: Peterloo Revisited', *History*, 91: 302 (2006), pp. 254–76.

Poole, R. 'The March to Peterloo: Politics and Festivity in Late Georgian England', *Past and Present*, 192 (2006), pp. 109–53.

Poole, R. (ed.), *Return to Peterloo. Manchester Region History Review*, 23 (2014).

Poole, R. 'What We Don't Know About Peterloo', in R. Poole (ed), *Return to Peterloo. Manchester Region History Review*, 23 (2014), pp. 1–17.

Read, D. *Peterloo: The Massacre and its Background* (Manchester: Manchester University Press, 1958).

Reid, R. *The Peterloo Massacre* (London: Heinemann, 1989).

Scrivener, M. (ed.), *Poetry and Reform: Periodical Verse from the English Democratic Press, 1792–1824* (Michigan: Wayne State University Press, 1992).

Spence, T. *Pigs' Meat; or Lessons for the Swinish Multitude*, vol. 1 (London: 1793).

——. *Pigs' Meat; or Lessons for the Swinish Multitude*, vol. 2 (London: 1794).

——. *Pigs' Meat; or Lessons for the Swinish Multitude*, vol. 3 (London: 1795).

Simpson, C.M. *The British Broadside Ballad and its Music* (New Jersey: Rutgers University Press, 1966).

Thompson, E.P. *The Making of the English Working Class* (Middlesex: Penguin, 1980).

Tyas, J. 'Dispersal of the Reform Meeting at Manchester by a Military Force', *Examiner*, 608 (22 August 1819), p. 529.

——. 'Express from Manchester', *The Times* (19 August 1819), p. 2.

Index of poem titles

Acrostic, an 211
'Acrostic to Liberty' (*Medusa*) 202
'Address to Britons' (*Medusa*) 55–6
'Address to Liberty' (*Medusa*) 200–1
'Address to the Prince Regent' (*Manchester Observer; Cap of Liberty*) 45–6
'Address to "The Rabble", an' (*Medusa*) 72–3
Another Song Concerning Peterloo 110–11
Answer to Peter-Loo, the 135–6
'Appeal of Blood, the' (*Briton*) 46–7
'Bloody Field of Peterloo! A New Song, the' (*Theological and Political Comet*) 160–1
'Britons Who Have Often Bled' (*Republican*) 71–2
'Butcher and Hog: In imitation of a scene on St. Peter's Field, Manchester, the' (*Manchester Observer*) 161
'Devils that Stirred up the Storm: A New Song by the R-G—T'S Ministers and the M——R MAG——TES, the' (*Manchester Observer; Cap of Liberty*) 169
'Downfall of Despotism' (*Medusa*) 203
'Elegiac Apostrophe to the Memory of the Unfortunate Persons Who Were Killed at Manchester, on 16th of August' (*Briton; Black Dwarf*) 126–7
Field of Peterloo: An Heroic Poem in Two Cantos to which is Added An Address to liberty, the 137–40
'Four Wise Heads Together' (*Black Dwarf*) 169–72

'From Mr Batty, Clerk to — Milne, Esq. Coroner, to his Friend in London' (*Black Dwarf*) 172–4
'Humble Address; 1.TO THE MAG-ST- – TES 2. TO THE M- – T- – Y; AND 3. TO THE SP-C- – L CONS- – BLES, an' (*Manchester Observer*) 177–9
'Hunt and Liberty' (*Medusa*) 208–9
'It is Lovely to Die for Our Country' (*White Hat*) 123
'Late Proceedings, the' (*Morning Post*) 142–3
'Lines Written During Confinement in Lancaster Castle By S. Bamford, author of the "Weaver Boy"' (*Manchester Observer; Examiner*) 203–4
'Manchester Heroes' (*Manchester Observer; Cap of Liberty*) 79–80
'Manchester Massacre, or Adieu to Slavery, the' (*The Radical Reformers' New Song Book*) 56–7
Manchester Meeting: A New Song 133–5
'Manchester Yeoman, the' (*Examiner*) 157
'Manchester Yeomanry Valour' (*Manchester Observer; Medusa*) 105
Masque of Anarchy, the 217–31
Measure of Ministers, the (*Cap of Liberty*) 77–8
Meeting at Peterloo, the 136–7
'National Songs. – No. 1' (*Manchester Observer*) 80–1
New Song, a 209–10
'New Song, a' (*Medusa*) 105–7
'New Song, a' (*Theological and Political Comet*) 50–1
New Song. On Peterloo Meeting, a 51–2

Index of poem titles

'Norwich Declaration, the' (*White Hat*) 167–8
'On a Bloody Massacre' (*Medusa*) 128
'Paddy Bull's Epistle to his Brother John' (*Medusa*) 174–7
'Patriotic Song' (*Medusa*) 48–9
'Patriot's Grave, the' (*Manchester Observer*) 123–4
'PETER LOO FIELD' (*Manchester Observer*) 158–9
'Peterloo' (*Manchester Observer*) 103–4
Peterloo (John Stafford) 108–10
Peterloo 199–200
Peterloo Man, the' (*Black Dwarf*) 102–3
Peterloo Massacre, the 141–2
'Peterloo Victim, the' (*Manchester Observer*) 128–9
'Plains of St Peter, the' (*Manchester Observer*) 132–3
'Prayer, a' (*Manchester Observer*) 164–5
'Reformer's Song of Liberty' (*Manchester Observer*) 82
Renowned Atchievements of Peter-Loo on the Glorious Sixteenth Day of August, 1819, the 155–6
'Saint Ethelstone's Day' (*Theological and Political Comet*) 180
'Soliloquy of Lord C——h, on beholding a Vision of the Goddess of Liberty as he rose from his dinner, to proceed to the H—e of C—s, with his new Bills against the remaining liberties of Englishmen, a' (*Black Dwarf*) 207–8
'Song of Liberty' (*Medusa*) 201–2
'Song of the Slaughter, To Commemorate the Horrid Deeds Performed at Manchester on the 16th of August, 1819, the' (*Manchester Observer*) 129–31
'Song to Liberty' (*Briton*) 47–8
'Song' (*Manchester Observer*) 75–7
'Song' (*Republican*) 52–3
'Sonnet' (*White Hat*) 77
'Stanzas Occasioned by the Manchester Massacre' (*Black Dwarf*) 127–8
'Sword King, the' (*Black Dwarf*) 107–8
'To Henry Hunt, Esquire' (*Manchester Observer*) 111–12
'To the Gentlemen Yeomanry of Manchester' (*Black Dwarf*) 161
'To the Livery'd Assassins' (*Manchester Observer*) 165–7
'To The Major of a Certain Regiment' (*Manchester Observer; Medusa*) 131–2
'TO THE YEO—N-Y, SP-C—L CON--BL-S, &c ON PETER'S FIELD' (*Manchester Observer*) 204–6
'Tribute to Certain Military Heroes Occasioned by the Recent Horrors of Manchester'(*Black Dwarf*) 162–4
Tribute to the Immortal Memory of the Reformers, Who Fell on the 16th of August, 1819 124–6
Untitled (*Briton*) 78–9
'Verses for the Boys of Manchester' (*Black Dwarf*) 157–8
'Voice of Britannia, the' (*Manchester Observer*) 83
'Watch Word of Britons, the' (*Medusa*) 53–5
'What is a Ruler' (*Briton*) 78–9
White Hat, the 73–5
With Henry Hunt We'll Go 210–11

Index

Literary works can be found under authors' names.

Addison, Joseph (1672–1719) 29–30, 114n.43
Spectator, the 14
Albion 43, 48, 55, 60n.35, 73, 77, 104, 195
Anglo-Saxon constitution *see* English Constitution
Anglo-Saxon rights 22, 60n.35, 67–8, 71, 91n.112, 194–5, 213n.47
apostrophe 44, 45, 47, 126

Bamford, Samuel (1788–1872) 2, 86n.56, 88n.68, 116–17n.65, 129–31, 148n.80, 184–5n.73, 203–4
bard 44, 138, 160, 177, 195
Battle of Waterloo (1815) 6, 13, 18, 101–2, 103–4, 107, 114n.35, 158, 164, 187n.115, 210
'Battle of Waterloo, the' 210
Bill of Rights, the (1689) 58n.18, 84n.10, 145n.35, 196, 213n.47
Birley, (Captain) Hugh (1788–1845) 131, 182n.32
Black Dwarf, the 12, 18, 23–4, 43, 97, 189n.155, 198
bloodhound 12, 55, 63n.73, 86n.47, 152, 158, 229n.13
Britannia 20, 47, 51, 54, 60n.33, 70, 82, 83, 92n.118, 121, 230n.28
British constitution *see* English Constitution
Briton, the 19, 20–2, 45
Burdett, (Sir) Francis (1770–1844) 4, 12–13, 24, 36n.54, 87n.64, 90n.102, 174
Burke, Edmund (1729–97) 16–17, 84n.19, 151, 153, 161

Byng, (Sir) John (1772–1860) 7, 52, 62n.58

Canning, George (1770–1827) 169, 189n.147
Cap of Liberty, the 19–20
caricature 60n.33, 93–5, 98–101, 151, 191n.176, 196
Carlile, Richard (1790–1843) 11–12, 24–5, 38n.85, 41, 71, 147–8n.78
Cartwright, (Major) John (1740–1824) 4, 15, 24, 62n.53, 68, 69, 90n.102, 204, 214n.52
Castlereagh, (Lord) Robert Stewart (1769–1822) 145n.43, 157, 169, 173, 175–6, 189n.145, 189n.153, 192n.189, 194, 207, 218, 228–9n.12
Charles I (1600–49) 41–4, 63n.64, 67–9, 74, 79, 85n.27, 87n.63, 88n.81
Cobbett, William (1763–1835) 4, 18–19, 23, 24
Constitution *see* English Constitution
Cromwell, Oliver (1599–1658) 23, 28, 31, 63n.64, 73–5, 87n.62, 88n.69, 88n.73, 88n.81
Cruikshank, George (1792–1878) 36n.37, 45, 59n.24, 60n.33, 63n.73, 93–6, 98–101, 150, 151, 191n.176, 196–7, 229n.17

Davenport, Allen (1775–1846) 22, 57, 180, 193n.210
Davison, Thomas (1794–1826) 19–20, 21, 22, 25, 37n.75
'Derry Down' 32–3, 168, 188n.138
Diggers, the 42, 67–8, 84n.19, 85n.22

Eaton, Daniel Isaac (1753–1814) 16–17, 37n.64, 151
English Civil War *see* English Revolution
English Constitution 11, 12, 22, 24, 67–8, 84n.19, 194, 205, 213n.47
English Revolution 41–3, 18, 67, 69–70, 73, 87n.60, 87n.61, 87n.62
Ethelstone, (Reverend) Charles Wicksted (1767–1830) 35n.18, 142, 180–1, 193n.216
Examiner, the 10–11, 25–6, 190n.156, 198, 228n.3

Fifteenth Hussars 2, 6, 186n.101
Fildes, Mary (1789–1876) 147–8n.78
French Revolution (1789–94) 13, 15, 29, 43, 66, 191n.173, 196

'Garland of Love, the' 158
'Gee-Up Dobbin' 141, 149n.93, 180
George, Prince Regent (1762–1830) 5, 25, 44, 45–6, 59n.24, 75, 91n.106, 93, 169, 192n.186, 215n.62, 228n.5
'God Save the King' 18, 53, 54, 138, 143, 148n.88, 158, 194, 200, 212n.26
'Green Upon the Cape' 108
Griffin, James (b. 1799) 20, 45, 46, 59n.24

Hampden, John (1595–1643) 60n.36, 64n.84, 69, 71, 73, 74, 85n.26, 87n.60
Hampden, John (1653–96) 63n.64, 69–70, 76, 77, 85n.26
Hay, (Reverend) William (1761–1839) 35n.18, 73, 86n.56, 145n.39, 182n.33
'Hearts of Oak' 48–50
Hone, William (1780–1842) 85n.22, 151, 188n.138
  Political House that Jack Built, the 150–1, 188n.138
  Political Showman at Home, the 63n.73, 229n.17
Hunt, Henry (1773–1835) 4–6, 8, 51–2, 55, 62n.55, 73–5, 76, 81, 87n.64, 88n.68, 111–12, 116n.63, 130, 135–43, 147–8n.78, 172–4, 199, 208–11
Hunt, Leigh (1784–1859) 217, 228n.5
  see also Examiner, the

'Jessie, the Flower o' Dunblane' 132–3, 147n.58
'Joan o' Greenfield' 110, 117n.68

Lees, John (d. 1819) 8, 117n.79, 172–3, 183n.44, 190n.159, 190n.166
Levellers 67, 68–9
Lilburne, John (1614–57) 68, 69, 85n.22
Liverpool government (1812–27) 2–5, 7–8, 10, 13–14, 17, 18–19, 41, 43, 45, 71, 77, 169, 189n.155, 196, 207

Magna Carta (1216) 55, 58n.18, 84n.10, 87n.65, 145n.35, 196, 213n.47, 215n.66
Manchester 33, 86n.46, 116n.59, 184–5n.73
  history 2–5
Manchester magistrates 6, 7–8, 45, 91n.106, 95, 135, 169, 177, 180, 183n.42, 189n.142, 216n.76
  see also Ethelstone, (Reverend) Charles Wicksted; Hay, (Reverend) William
Manchester Observer, the 1, 2, 26–7, 96
Manchester and Salford Yeomanry Cavalry (MYC)
  chivalry 103, 136, 139, 153, 154, 155, 158
  cowardice 101, 102, 105, 106–7, 112, 141–2, 253, 160
  drunkenness 111, 152, 187n.117, 229n.22
  satire 76, 104, 152, 159, 160
  support for 13, 135–6, 141–2
  violence 1–2, 8, 10, 12, 20, 23, 142, 161, 164, 165, 179, 180, 183n.44, 204–5, 211
  women 93–5, 97–8, 101, 102, 107–8, 124, 157
  see also Birley, (Captain) Hugh; Meagher, Edward; Trafford, (Major) Thomas
Meagher, Edward 117n.79, 148n.82
Medusa, the 19, 22, 43, 44
Milton, John (1608–74) 18, 41, 77, 89n.89, 120, 145n.41, 146n.50

Nadin, Joseph (1765–1848) 117n.66, 203, 210, 211, 216n.76
Napoleonic Wars (1793–1815) 3, 13, 31, 33, 59n.27, 65, 90n.101, 103, 116n.62, 122, 151, 183n.47, 190n.172, 230n.31
New Bailey Prison 51, 62n.55, 109, 111, 116n.63, 137, 148n.79, 159, 183n.46, 185n.76

Norman Yoke 63n.72, 67–8, 70–1, 84n.19

Paine, Thomas (1737–1809) 18, 68, 148n.86
   The Rights of Man 15, 32, 50, 84n.19, 116n.58, 175, 200, 213n.47
'Parker's Widow' 51, 62n.51
patriot 55, 65, 70, 73, 77, 82, 109–10, 123–4, 128–9, 170, 179, 195, 196, 199, 200, 202, 204, 208–9
patriotism 54, 60n.37, 66, 120–1
Pentridge Uprising (1817) 3, 26
Percy, Thomas (1729–1811) 29–31, 34
   Reliques of Ancient English Poetry (1765) 188n.138, 193n.212, 215n.70
Pigs' Meat 17–18, 19, 31, 32, 37n.68, 37n.70 43, 54, 84n.16, 151, 198
Pindar, Peter (John Wolcot) (1738–1819) 137, 184n.57
Politics for the People 16–17, 181n.11, 196
Prince Regent *see* George, Prince Regent

Republican, the 24–5
Ritson, Joseph (1752–1803) 30, 31, 34
'Rule Britannia' 53–4, 143, 194
Russell, (Lord) William (1639–83) 69, 70, 76, 89n.82

'Scots wha hae wi' Wallace Bled' 56–7, 75–6
'See the Conquering Hero Comes' 80–1, 199, 215n.71
Shakespeare, William (1564–1616) 30, 77
   Hamlet 77, 89n.83
   Henry IV 22, 187n.110
   Macbeth 187n.105, 207, 214n.57
   Romeo and Juliet 186n.104
Shelley, Percy Bysshe (1792–1822) 200, 212n.26, 217–18, 227–31
   Adonais 120
   'England in 1819' 25, 119, 126
   Masque of Anarchy, the viii, 25, 40, 43, 44, 146n.46, 217–31
Sherwin's Weekly Political Register 10–11, 24–5, 32, 193n.210
Shorter, Robert 22–3, 154
   'The Bloody Field of Peterloo' 160–1
Sidmouth, (Lord) Henry Addington (1757–1844) 3, 7, 10, 11, 12, 145n.43, 173, 175, 209, 218, 228–9n.12, 229n.17
Sidney (Sydney), Algernon (1623–83) 18, 69–70, 76, 88n.81
Six Acts (1819) 8, 14, 19, 77, 214n.55
slave trade 86n.51, 90n.102, 197–9
Spa Fields Uprising (1816) 20, 87n.64, 190n.162, 196, 229–30n.24
Spence, Thomas (1750–1814) 17–18, 30, 32–4, 37n.70, 43, 68, 84n.16, 151, 181n.10
   see also Pigs' Meat
Spenceans 21, 196
   see also Davenport, Allen; Spence, Thomas; Thistlewood, Arthur; Watson, ('Dr') James; Wedderburn Robert
Stafford, John 91n.109, 115n.53
   Another Song Concerning Peterloo 110–11
   Peterloo 108–10
'Sweet Lass of Richmond Hill, the' 201
'swinish multitude' 16, 151, 161
Sydney, Algernon *see* Sidney, Algernon

Theological and Political Comet, the 22–3
Thistlewood, Arthur (1774–1820) 4, 18, 20, 74, 87n.64, 88n.68
Trafford, (Major) Thomas (1778–1852) 131, 147n.57, 173
Tyas, John 10, 36n.38, 64n.84, 96, 208

Vansittart, Nicholas (1st Baron Bexley) (1766–1851) 189n.151, 190n.171

Wallace, William (1270–1305) 56–7, 64n.84
Watson, ('Dr') James (1766?–1838) 4, 18, 20, 74, 87n.64, 88n.68, 190n.162
Wedderburn, Robert (1762–1835) 20, 69–70, 198–9
White Hat, the 19, 23, 44
Wilson, Michael
   Answer to Peterloo, the 135–6
   Peterloo Massacre, the 141–2
Winstanley, Gerrard (1609–76) *see* Diggers, the
Wolseley, Sir Charles (1769–1846) 51–2, 62n.53, 134, 204
Wooler, Thomas Jonathan (1786?–1853) 12, 38n.94, 189n.155
   see also Black Dwarf, the
Wroe, James (1788–1844) 26, 96

EU authorised representative for GPSR:
Easy Access System Europe, Mustamäe tee 50,
10621 Tallinn, Estonia
gpsr.requests@easproject.com

www.ingramcontent.com/pod-product-compliance
Ingram Content Group UK Ltd.
Pitfield, Milton Keynes, MK11 3LW, UK
UKHW021835140426
5217IPUK00021B/1467